# Job Strategies for People with Disabilities

## Enable Yourself for Today's Job Market

### Melanie Astaire Witt

Peterson's Guides
Princeton, New Jersey

*With appreciation to*

my father, Anthony B. Ciston
my husband, Jim
my daughter, Rachel

*for inspiring, supporting, and helping.*

This book is dedicated to all Americans with disabilities, as personified by Hector Castaneda, the computer equipment technician who searched for a year before landing a job in California's Silicon Valley three years ago.

Castaneda, who walks with crutches because of childhood polio, found that interviewers were focusing not on what he can do but on a too familiar anxiety: "What happens if he falls?"

For people with disabilities, Castaneda's answer goes straight to the heart of being a success on the job:

**So, what if I fall? I get up.**

**Library of Congress Cataloging-in-Publication Data**
Witt, Melanie A. (Melanie Astaire), 1953–
    Job strategies for people with disabilities : enable yourself
for today's job market / Melanie A. Witt.
        p.    cm.
    Includes bibliographical references and index.
    ISBN 1-56079-143-8
    1. Vocational guidance for the handicapped—United
States. 2. Job hunting—United States. 3. Handicapped—
Employment—United States. I. Title.
HV1568.5.W58    1992
650.14'087—dc20                                  92-13864

Composition and design by Peterson's Guides

Printed in the United States of America

10  9  8  7  6  5  4  3  2  1

# Contents

# PART III JOB FINDING

# Foreword

This is the time and this is the book for which humans with disabilities have been waiting not decades, but centuries. For the first time in history people with characteristics setting them apart from the majority are protected against a spectrum of bias by the full force of the world's most powerful government.

Work is the focus of this book. Work is what makes the American dream happen, and work is what often has been denied to the one-fifth of American adults who have disabilities. With the safeguards supplied by the Americans with Disabilities Act of 1990, of which the employment title became effective in mid-1992, individuals who formerly warmed the bench can now look for a job on an equal footing with all other applicants.

Until there was an ADA, this groundbreaking guide could not have been written. Its savvy career advice rests on a clearly stated foundation of legally mandated safeguards. Earlier legislation battled the most flagrant prejudicial actions, but, in the employment arena, the ADA is the 800-pound legal bodyguard that seriously discourages purposeful bias and provides sanctions against employers who don't get the message. In a decade of fewer young people entering the job market, its timing couldn't be better for shoring up the nation's work force.

This is not the first useful book for those with career problems caused by a disability. A number of worthy volumes have lead the way to employment for those who wish to work despite inconveniences. But Melanie Astaire Witt's work is the first in my experience to combine state-of-art career decision making and employment search techniques with the special interests of the disability community. Many books do one or the other, but Witt's is the original contribution to a sophisticated synthesis for the 1990s job market.

With pleasure I will recommend this guide to readers of my column. Within the two decades that I have been writing for newspapers, thousands upon thousands of readers with disabilities have asked me for guidance along career pathways. For some, their generic or acquired physical limitations deny them freedom of career choice. Others find that the employment effects of a disease—cancer, heart, stroke—outlast the disease itself as employers fear high medical insurance expenses. Still others with invisible disabilities—diabetes and epilepsy—are screened out for a variety of reasons. Even people with psoriasis, a serious but noncontagious skin disorder that can cover the face and hands, tell me about being rejected in the job market.

Few career specialists are so naive as to think that ADA is a magical turning point. Job seekers who struggled to find work before will struggle still. But there appears to be a sea change in the way Americans feel about the last human frontier of workers. In a recent Louis Harris poll, a full 95 percent agreed with the prohibition on job discrimination based on disability.

Somewhat less celebratory is another finding of the same poll: "Large numbers of Americans now react to disabled persons with a mixture of admiration, pity, fear, embarrassment, and ignorance about how disabled people want to be treated."

As members of the disability community move more forcefully into the job market, they'll be able to help others to understand how they wish to be treated: not with pity, fear, or embarrassment, but as the able, potential-packed people they are.

Joyce Lain Kennedy
Nationally syndicated columnist,
*Careers*

# Acknowledgments

My Thanks Tree has many leaves. At the top, many thanks to the team at Peterson's. Personal thanks to editorial director *Jim Gish* for his belief in my vision, his staunch support of this work, and his continuous vote of confidence. Thanks beyond measure to president *Peter Hegener* and vice president *Casey Hegener* for taking a chance on this project—and for publishing this book. To publisher *Carole Cushmore* for taking an exceptional interest in the success of this work. To executive editor *Carol Hupping,* a great editor, for making this as pleasurable and painless a process as possible.

Heartfelt thanks to *Rachel A. Witt*—my number one assistant, my daughter, and *my always friend*—who was invaluable in every facet of this production and who made countless sacrifices to help me move this project from beginning to end.

My love and gratitude to my husband, *Jim Witt,* whose support and unbending belief has always gotten me through. His newly honed detective skills tracked down people who seemed to have fallen off the face of the earth.

Many, many thanks to my best friend, *Karen S. Schmitt,* for her relentless attention to detail and generous assistance in preparing Part IV: Appendixes. To *Muriel Turner* for her support, encouragement, advice, and assistance (not to mention the loan of her computer when mine wasn't accessible).

Untold gratitude to my friends and my family for their unceasing prayers and encouragement.

A million thanks to five brilliant minds who took precious time out of their already overbooked days and nights to review the manuscript and give me their expert opinions and advice. Their comments are reflected in the final product. It was a gargantuan task, and I am indebted to each of them:

*Jeffrey G. Allen, J.D., C.P.C.,* Director, National Placement Law Center, Los Angeles.

*Don Brandon,* Chairman, Alaska Governor's Committee on Employment of People with Disabilities, Anchorage, AK.

*Mary Jo Fisher, M.D.,* Family Health Care Associates, Springfield, MO.

*Betty J. Jackson, M.S.,* National Certified Counselor, Certified Rehabilitation Counselor, Certified Insurance Rehabilitation

Specialist, Vocational Consultant, and Career Consultant, San Diego.

**David L. Livers, Ph.D.,** Counselor Educator, Illinois State University, Normal, IL.

It would be impossible to thank by name all the people who either directly or indirectly contributed to this book, but I especially want to acknowledge the following people who gave freely of their time, advice, and professional expertise to make this book possible. At the risk of omitting someone who has made a significant contribution, my sincere thanks to: **Bob Ashby,** Deputy Assistant General Counsel, U.S. Department of Transportation, Washington, DC; **Gregory Best,** Program Analyst, The President's Committee on Employment of People with Disabilities, Washington, DC; **Donn Brolin, Ph.D.,** Professor, Life-Center Career Education, University of Missouri, Columbia; **Susan Brown,** Information Specialist, World Institute on Disability, Oakland, CA; **Robert Calvert Jr.,** Publisher, *Career Opportunities News,* Garrett Park, MD; **Chris Chapman,** Head of Library, University of California, San Diego Medical Center; **Diane L. Croft,** Director of Marketing, National Braille Press, Boston; **Ellen Daly,** Employment Advisor/Legislative Liaison, Office of Public Affairs/Legislative Services, The President's Committee on Employment of People with Disabilities, Washington, DC; **Carolyn Demaray,** History Supervisor, San Diego Public Library; **V. Paul Donnelly, Esq.,** Donnelly, Huizenga, Wahl, Hagan & Hergt, P.C., Detroit; **Sheila Duston,** Senior Attorney Advisor, Office of Legal Counsel, U.S. Equal Employment Opportunity Commission, Washington, DC; **Melvin Fountain,** Editor, *Occupational Outlook Quarterly,* U.S. Department of Labor, Washington, DC; **Richard Gulley,** Chief Executive Officer, Robert F. Driver [Insurance] Co., San Diego; **Admiral Thor Hanson,** President & CEO, National Multiple Sclerosis Society, New York; **Steven Haugen,** Economist, Bureau of Labor Statistics, U.S. Department of Labor, Washington, DC; **Anne Hirsh,** Human Factors Consultant, Job Accommodation Network, Washington, DC; **Kenneth B. Hoyt, Ph.D.,** University Distinguished Professor, Kansas State University, Manhattan, KS; **Kathleen A. Jennings,** President, ET Search Inc., La Jolla, CA; **Erica C. Jones,** Director, Pacific Disability and Business Technical Assistance Center (Region IX), Berkeley Planning Associates, Oakland, CA; **Lauralyn Jones,** Senior Employment Administrator, SmithKline Beecham Pharmaceuticals, Philadelphia; **Barbara Judy,** Project Manager, Job Accommodation Network, Morgantown, WV; **Eva June,** Executive Recruiter, Walling and June, Alexandria, VA; **Ronald L. Krannich, Ph.D.**, President, Impact Publications, Woodbridge, VA; **Darryl Laramore, Ph.D.**, Career Counselor, Santa Rosa, CA; **Nancy Law,** Program Development Manager, National Multiple Sclerosis Society, Westerville, OH; **Lee Lawrence,** Information Resource Specialist, National Organization on Disability, Washington, DC; **John Leslie Jr., Ph.D.**, Executive Vice President, Cerebral Palsy Research Foundation of Kansas, Wichita, KS; **Phyllis Martin,** Careers Columnist, *Cincinnati Post;* **Carl McDaniels, Ph.D.**, Professor and Program Area Leader for Counselor Education, Virginia Polytechnic Institute and State University, Blacksburg, VA; **Thomas Mehnert,** Survey Director, International Center for the Disabled, New York; **Mike Pilot,** Editor, *Occupational Outlook Handbook,* U.S. Department of Labor, Washington, DC; **Jack W. Plunkett,** Publisher, *Corporate Jobs Outlooks!,* Boerne, TX; **Thomas Potraza,** Management Employment Manager, JC Penney Company, Dallas; **Mary Kaye Rubin,** Acting Director of Public Affairs, Office of Public Affairs/Legislative Services, The President's Committee on Employment of People with Disabilities, Washington, DC; **James P. Sampson Jr., Ph.D.**, Professor, Human Services and Studies Department, Florida State University, Tallahassee, FL; **Milton Savage,** Grant Specialist, Community Service Center for the Disabled, San Diego; **Robert Silverstein,** Staff Director/Chief Counsel, Senate Subcommittee on Disability Policy, Washington, DC; **Boyd Stelle,** Branch Manager, Office of Federal Contract Compliance Programs, U.S. Department of Labor, Washington, DC; **Louis Stewart,** Attorney for the Coordination and Review Section, Civil Rights Division, U.S. Department of Justice, Washington, DC; **Robert Tate,** Special Assistant to the Chairman, U.S. Equal Employment Opportunity Commission, Washington, DC; **Lucy U. Trivelli,** Project Associate, RESNA Technical Assistance Project, Washington, DC; **Denise Valentine,** Rehabilitation Counselor, California Department of Rehabilitation, San Diego; **Diane Ward,** Director of Public Affairs, Council of Better Business Bureaus, Arlington, VA; and **Gerald Weisman,** Director of Rehabilitation Engineering, Rehabilitation Technology Services, Burlington, VT.

*Very special* thanks to my career godparent, who with the true modesty of a godparent wishes to remain nameless, for believing in me, encouraging me, and supporting me.

And to all of you—employees and job seekers alike—who let me into your lives and allowed me to share your inspiring stories with the readers, I thank you for making this book your book.

May God bless you all.

# Introduction

The time is here. The hour is now. Generation after generation of people with disabilities have been excluded from the mainstream of the job market. Today, we have the power to change that.

We must once and forever identify and accept members of the disability community as valuable individuals who happen to have disabilities, not disabilities who happen to be named John or Sue or Michael.

So why a career book specifically for people with disabilities? As long as the world in which we live and work attempts to isolate and exclude individuals with disabilities, it's crucial to learn effective, state-of-the-art job strategies to help you level the playing field—to enable yourself for today's job market.

After reading this book you'll know more about how to choose a career and find a job than the vast majority of Americans. You'll learn:

- How the Americans with Disabilities Act can change your life
- How to understand the working world and identify the brightest careers
- How to uncover your marketable skills
- How to make the job you want fit you
- How to find a topflight alternative occupation when your first choice of occupations just isn't in the cards
- How to match yourself with the world of work
- How to determine whether disclosing or not disclosing your disability supports your objective of getting hired
- How to create standout resumes and cover letters
- How to find job leads
- How to research employers
- How to make interviewers appreciate the valuable person you are

This book is the first to present collectively these points, all of which are essential to the employment success of Americans with disabilities. Extensive research and hundreds of interviews—with rehabilitation and service providers, advocacy organizations, business leaders, citizen advocates, and individuals and families of individuals with disabilities—confirm the need for the comprehensive guide you hold in your hands.

My fervent and sincere hope is that within these pages you will find the information that enables you to compete for and win good jobs.

—Melanie Astaire Witt

# 1

# Now you can

Tuberculosis, emphysema, pulmonary fibrosis, and cancer didn't keep my father from putting in a good day's work—but the doctors nearly did. They kept telling him he was going to die. For twenty-six years they kept telling Tony Ciston he was going to die. Being on a medical death row for more than two decades isn't the best motivation for picking up a lunch box and whistling your way to work each day.

Of course that was a long time ago. Today the medical community is leading the charge for rehabilitation and encouraging the employment of people with physical disabilities and mental impairments. But the forties, fifties, and sixties were a different age.

When my father's disability ground him down to the point where he could no longer carry mail, he changed careers and sold real estate, which allowed him to pace his activities and level of exertion to his breathing limitation. His powerfully positive attitude boosted his career success, repeatedly gaining him top salesperson awards in his office.

Where did my father find his positive attitude in spite of his suffering and adversity? He found it in his faith. His prayer of acceptance and strength are etched in my memory: "Lord, this is Your body—do with it what You will."

Obviously my father was not unique in finding motivation through spiritual belief. I hear confirmations of faith again and again from people with whom I've spoken in gathering information for this book. Others say they find their motivation from a variety of wellsprings apart from religion, including supportive family influence and an inborn determination to triumph.

Regardless of what turns it on, it's the motivation itself that is important. With strong motivation you've got a great chance of equipping yourself to find satisfying and rewarding employment. Without it, you'll become discouraged too soon and too often.

From where you sit, successful people may appear to be moving right along down one continuous freeway of success. What you can't see are their detours of defeats, failures, disappointments, and frustrations. Once detoured, individuals without strong motivation never seem to get back on track. But those who do have the will to keep on going find ways to return to the chosen freeway. Almost none of us rack up success after success after success without disappointments now and then. Learning to overcome them is a big part of arriving at the destination of our choice.

Observe the motivation to succeed in the following stories of two more winners who dared.

## READY TO GET ON WITH LIFE

On a rain-slickened South Carolina freeway, college student Susan Aude Fisher's world screeched to a standstill the instant a truck smashed into her automobile and severed her spine. Life could have turned dark gray for twenty-year-old Fisher had she not had a supportive home life. "I come from a great, close-knit family, a background that fortunately gave me a healthy sense of myself and my abilities," she says.

The encouragement from her family speared the clouds of despair and helped Fisher remember: "I'm young and I want to get on with life." The zest for life became a guiding force in Fisher's determination to wheel onto a fast career track.

"Immediately after the accident, my spinal cord was the least of my problems," she says. "I had massive internal injuries that could have ended my days. I was so sick and in so much pain and so miserable." How did Fisher cope? She told herself, "Hey, I've got the battle of my life to fight now. This is a question of survival."

"I think the key for me was when I finally started feeling good again—it was like being let out of prison," Fisher says. "I could actually go somewhere without throwing up or feeling pitifully weak." After eight months of surgery and six months of "learning what people in wheelchairs do," the student returned to college and finished her senior year.

Did Fisher enable herself and get on with her life? Yes—and how! Today, she is the award-winning co-anchor of the evening news on WIS-Channel 10 in Columbia, South Carolina.

# A WILL TO TRIUMPH

Don't ever tell Ken Metz of San Francisco that he can't do something. Anything. He'll do it and make a believer of you. That's because Metz doesn't back off a battle until he wins fair treatment.

Metz's persevering style began as a toddler. Like most younger brothers, Metz begged to tag along and do everything his older sibling did. Like most tagalongs, Metz somehow managed to keep pace with his big brother. Unlike most, Metz bumped into things more often than his brother because Metz is blind.

Whether as a youngster in a Chicago neighborhood giving it everything he had to fit in with the other kids, or as a college graduate tracking 450 job leads in the Bay Area, Metz is the ultimate role model of the persistent goal seeker.

"I went on about 150 job interviews where I was told many things. Many things except 'you're hired,'" Metz says. "I even overheard one employer tell his secretary to tell me that he couldn't meet with me. He said if he'd known I was blind, he wouldn't have agreed to the interview."

What motivated Metz to keep picking up a hostile telephone to bull-dog a job after hundreds of heart-breaking rejections? A strong sense of self-esteem. Metz seems to have an innate will to triumph. As he explains, "I faced each interview as if it were my first and no matter what, I tried hard to keep positive thoughts."

Metz's efforts eventually produced a job. Initially told by representatives at what is now Pacific Bell that an interview would be a waste of time because he couldn't pass the physical, Metz refused to take no for an answer. He relentlessly pursued a job at the company—especially after he learned it already had a few employees who were blind. Once decision makers realized Metz wasn't going to go away, they hired him as an operator.

Metz's employment crusade was worth it. Almost twenty-one years and many promotions later, Metz has accepted an early retirement offer from Pacific Bell and is seeking a new career opportunity.

Is Metz still fighting to "fit in with the other kids"? You be the judge. Recently, Metz was seen riding a mechanical bull in Billy Bob's, a Fort Worth, Texas, nightspot popular with convention-eers. When he wasn't trying to hang on for dear life, Metz was busy lining up jump partners for the next day's skydive.

## SEASON YOUR DREAMS WITH A DOSE OF REALITY

After seeing how motivation grows winners, you may be tempted to erase the word "can't" from your vocabulary. Don't.

Many successful people truly believe that if you can think it, you can do it. Unfortunately, that's not always so—for individuals without disabilities as well as for those with disabilities.

Realistic people know that if you can't visualize furniture in an empty room, you can't be an interior designer. If you can't speak, you can't be an air traffic controller. If you can't hold a basketball, you can't out-slam-dunk Michael Jordan.

Why the wet blanket of realism after such inspiring stories of winners who beat the odds? Because promising unattainable results carries a high risk of causing a psychological crash. Someone who inspires you is on your team. Someone who sets you up for a huge disappointment isn't. View "I can" as a battle cry to be tempered with realistic thought.

What else can you do to enable yourself?

## CHOOSE A PRODUCTIVE ATTITUDE

Have you chosen your attitude today? This isn't a flippant question. Your answer will determine how you position yourself to the world. One of the most important things I learned in talking with individuals with disabilities—starting with my father—is that:

> Attitude is perhaps the one thing that no one and no circumstance in your life has control over but you. Only you can choose your attitude.

Many people with disabilities understandably say they feel powerless in situations over which they have no control. When you feel frustrated because you think you are controlled by your circumstances, how do you manage your emotions?

The easy way is to color your day with a sullen or angry attitude to go with your raw feelings. Certainly, upon considering your pain or personal struggle, no one would argue that you don't have the undeniable right to adopt any attitude you like.

But, in the world of work, there's a price to pay for selecting indifference over enthusiasm, gloominess over cheerfulness, fear over courage. The price is rejection. Employers want workers who are enthusiastic, cheerful, and confident, not people who refuse to make the effort to fit in. It's impossible to overstate the importance of a productive attitude.

To better understand how our choice of attitudes can influence our futures, let's look at an extreme example of other individuals who are controlled by their circumstances—prisoners of war.

Prisoners of war cannot choose where they live, what they wear, what they eat, when they attend to bodily functions, where they go, or who they see. They sometimes are beaten and tortured and forced to say things they don't want to say. Some live on the edge of life and death for months or years. They are stripped of the right to make all external choices.

What choices are left for POWs? As they hope for release, their words reveal the power of *productive attitudes.*

> *I whispered prayers a lot, and it seemed like everything I prayed for I got, like praying for the guy to come take me to the bathroom—and sure enough, he would.*
>
> — **Robert Sweet**
> **(Air Force 1st Lt.,**
> **Persian Gulf POW,**
> **imprisoned twenty days)**

> *The Vietnamese would purge groups when they discovered our resistance organizations. Americans were killed. When I wouldn't submit to them, I was beaten and tortured. But I had to go on. I wasn't going to be used. . . . It's really a kind of willpower that says, "Over my dead body will I be used. Over my dead body will I let my fellow prisoners down."*
>
> — **James Bond Stockdale**
> **(Navy commander, Vietnam POW,**
> **imprisoned more than seven years)**

> *My biggest fear in prison camp was not the fear of dying, but the fear of dying in vain. See, I wanted to die for a purpose, and that's how I kept myself alive. I kept reminding myself that there was no more useless death in the world than to die in a rotten prison camp.*
>
> — **Wilburn Snyder**
> **(Army Pfc., World War II POW,**
> **imprisoned more than three years)**

Each POW took control of the one thing only he could—his attitude. In seizing control, each found freedom and won a personal victory over his captors.

You, too, can choose your attitude. You can join with many other Americans with disabilities who believe that failure is not an option.

"It's not what I've lost that's important, it's what I have left and how I use it," says Harold Russell, who lost both hands during World War II. Russell became a role model and source of inspiration for people with disabilities all over the world when he portrayed a veteran amputee in *The Best Years of Our Lives.* He won two Oscars for his performance in one of the first major motion pictures to cast a person with a disability in a starring role. Russell went on to become a member of what is now the President's Committee on Employment of People with Disabilities. He retired in 1989 after serving twenty-five years as the chairman of the executive agency.

Here are a few more inspiring examples of productive attitudes. The disabilities of the following people are presented not as definitions of who they are, but to clarify why their employment-ready attitudes hold true meaning.

*When I say "I can't," what I really mean is "I prefer not to." Be determined to find a way and you will find it. Stop saying "I can't" and ask instead "How can I?"*

**— Michael Conway**
**(editor, blindness)**

*What motivates me is trying to do something for the people, for the children (who have muscular dystrophy). As long as I have some wheels under me to get around, I'll keep doing the things I do.*

**— Virgie Sorrick**
**(fund raiser, muscular dystrophy)**

*When I see myself reflected in a storefront window or a mirror, I'm reminded of the fact that I am in a wheelchair, but even then I don't feel disabled. The feeling is one of limited mobility more than anything else.*

**—John Russell**
**(construction specialist, paraplegia)**

*You've just got to handle your disability. If you can't accept it, why should you expect anyone else to?*

> — **Deborah McFadden**
> **(U.S. Commissioner for the**
> **Administration on Developmental**
> **Disabilities, Health and Human**
> **Services, epilepsy/mobility**
> **impairment)**

*I'm not a great believer that failure makes you stronger. I think success makes you strong. . . . I want to win, and that carries over into everything I do.*

> — **Kirk Kilgour**
> **(television sports commentator/**
> **actor/writer, quadriplegia)**

## ADJUSTMENT IMPROVES YOUR FUTURE

Along with attitude, think adjustment. Adjustment means coming to terms with a disability and, despite its limitations, leading a satisfying life.

Adjustment is everything: that's what experts on employment and disabilities repeatedly say. It makes a lot of sense. Almost all we do in life requires us to make some type of an adjustment. When we enter a new classroom, we adjust to the teacher's methods of instruction. When we begin a new job, we adjust to the company's policies. When we marry, we adjust to another person's living habits.

You can see why adjustment is a crucial part of readying yourself to travel the employment circuit. When you've adjusted, you're comfortable with yourself. When you're comfortable with yourself, your odds of making an employer comfortable with you go up dramatically.

Your focus in a job interview should be on showing the employer how you and the job are a match. This is difficult when you're fractured with unresolved inner concerns.

What role does timing play in resolving concerns? It would appear that those who have always known a disability have the jump on adjustment over those who experience disabilities later in life. Although they've had longer to work on it, this may or may not be true. New or old to the challenge, to succeed in the job market you have to have adjusted to your own personal situation. Only you know if adjustment can be achieved on your own or if professional counseling is a better choice. However you do it, it is vital, experts say, to work past the incapacitating shock of feeling trapped and overwhelmed.

When a disability strikes later in life, recovery time from the initial blow varies enormously from person to person. One of the first processes you go through, say psychologists, is denial. "They mixed my tests up with someone else's—it happens all the time." "The doctors screwed up. They're not God—they make mistakes." After denial comes acceptance of your disability. After acceptance comes grieving for your personal loss. Grieving coupled with coping with new physical or mental challenges requires your full-time attention, leaving little heart for job hunting.

Individuals who already hold jobs when they are injured or develop a disabling disease are particularly hard hit by the need to cope with their changes. Not only have they sustained a loss physically or mentally but, in many cases, they have lost the livelihood they relied upon and now must find new careers.

Adjustment is everything. It's apparent the following people well understand the need for adjustment.

- One-handed pitcher Jim Abbott won twelve baseball games in his rookie season with the California Angels.

- Janni Smith, a nurse paralyzed from the chest down, helps youngsters at the Petrofsky Center, a California rehabilitation program, overcome disabilities like her own. She gained mobility with a walker and electrode stimulation.

- Marine scientist Dr. Richard Radtke continues underwater exploration for the Hawaii Institute of Marine Biology using special equipment to compensate for the functional limitations of his multiple sclerosis.

- Tom Clancy worked as a shop steward of a large industrial bakery by day and attended law school at night. Poliomyelitis, sixteen years of hospitalization, and postpolio quadriparesis changed Clancy's career path. Today he is a senior programmer analyst at New York University's administrative computer center.

- Actress and comedienne Kathy Buckley doesn't let deafness stop her from bringing laughter to audiences across the country.

## THE REAL RISK IS DOING NOTHING

Even if your attitude and adjustment are on target, do your career dreams need a call to action? A whimsical story motivational speakers use makes the point.

A frog we'll call Freddie is put in a pan of water, and the water is slowly heated to the boiling point. Instead of leaping out of the pan, Freddie adapts to the gradual increase in temperature. He never becomes uncomfortable enough to jump out. Freddie stays put and soon becomes frog soup.

What peril would Freddie have faced in attempting to escape? He may have burned a frog toe or two on the side of the hot pan. But, as you can see, his real risk was in doing nothing. Had he taken action, he may have lived to croak another day.

What is *your* real risk in taking action steps toward the job market? Rejection. Chances are you'll be rejected and depressed a few dozen times—or possibly hundreds of times, like Ken Metz, the brave San Franciscan who endured 150 interviews before receiving an offer.

Certainly you must be prepared to deal with repeated rejection, but look at it this way: Behind one of those many doors you're pounding on may be your new employer.

## THE REWARDS ARE RICH

We work for many reasons, starting with basic requirements for food and shelter and to accumulate savings for future goals. We also work to gain self-esteem and the satisfaction of a job well done. We use work to direct the course of our lives as well as to benefit society. "We work to discover both *who* we are and *why* we are," explains Dr. Kenneth B. Hoyt, university distinguished professor at Kansas State University. In the ideal employment scenario we work from a sense of mission, doing what we do not because we must but because we want to.

Whether you seek money to become economically independent or you wish to define yourself or feel more powerful, the joy of work can change your life.

Are you ready to commit yourself unreservedly to achieving your career goals? If your answer is yes, then remember:

- Find your internal motivator
- Temper your dreams with realism
- Choose a productive attitude
- Make adjustments
- Risk action

# 2

## ADA at work for you— with an assist from the Rehabilitation Act of 1973

Have you ever been a victim of job discrimination based on your disability? Do you sometimes feel as though no one but you faces difficulty in finding employment? Not true. You're in good company.

Greg Parsons of Dallas, is a bright, handsome, articulate young man with a bachelor's degree in engineering science from the U.S. Naval Academy. He dreamed of being a pilot. His dreams were grounded during flight training when he was incorrectly diagnosed as having severe depression. Six years later, his diagnosis was corrected to partial-complex epilepsy.

Today Parsons has a new career goal. Equipped with engineering, science, and math skills and sales and teaching experience, he is looking for a job in sales with a pharmaceutical company. "I've mailed about 250 resumes," says Parsons, "interviewed with more than a dozen companies, and have had as many as four follow-up interviews for several positions."

He does not disclose his epilepsy in his resume, but does when he interviews to explain the gaps in employment during the years he was undergoing unsuccessful treatment for depression. In interviews Parsons always stresses the positive, telling prospective employers that his epilepsy is completely managed by medication and that his job abilities are 100 percent.

But Parsons hasn't been able to get a job since 1989. Is he a disability discrimination victim? Yes. Sometimes when Parsons tells employers he has epilepsy and explains his misdiagnosis of major depression, the discrimination is blatant. The interviewer's interest switches off and the meeting virtually ends. Other times, the interviewer is more subtle and Parsons is told later that the job was given to someone else.

"All disabled people share one common experience—discrimination," says Patrisha Wright, Washington D.C. director of governmental affairs at the Disability Rights Education and Defense Fund, a nonprofit organization that protects civil rights for the disability community. Soon that will be changing.

On July 26, 1990, President George Bush signed the *Americans with Disabilities Act (ADA)* and set the clock ticking toward enforcement dates. "With ADA," Bush says, "every man, woman, and child with a disability can now pass through once-closed doors into a bright new era of equality, independence, and freedom."

As you read through this explanation of how ADA and the earlier *Rehabilitation Act of 1973* can change your life, remember that employment is the key to full equality.

| **Federal Job Rights When ADA Employment Protection Is Fully Implemented** | |
|---|---|
| *Title I* | Protects applicants and employees in private sector and state and local government agencies with 15 or more employees. By far, the most important and most encompassing of employment rights legislation for the disability community. |
| *Title II* | Protects applicants and employees in small state and local government agencies employing fewer than 15 workers. |
| Note: Americans with Disabilities Act of 1990 employment protection will be fully implemented by July 26, 1994. | |

| Federal Job Rights Under the Rehabilitation Act of 1973 | |
| --- | --- |
| *Section 501* | Protects applicants and employees in federal government agencies. |
| *Section 503* | Protects applicants and employees in private sector and state and local government agencies receiving federal contracts in excess of $2,500. |
| *Section 504* | Protects applicants and employees in private sector and state and local government agencies receiving any federal financial assistance. |

## ADA TITLE I—EMPLOYMENT

The shameful walls of employment discrimination are shattering. Some employers have educated themselves about the law. Others have reviewed hiring practices. Still others have made physical changes in the workplace. But the employers who will come out top winners in hiring and keeping qualified workers with disabilities will be those who make and foster attitudinal changes—and that takes time.

Where can disability discrimination be found in the job market? Everywhere.

Perhaps you have encountered application forms and preemployment interviews you suspect were meant to focus on your disability rather than your on-job capabilities. Before receiving an offer, were you ever asked to take a medical exam that other applicants for the same position were not? Have you been steered into a dead-end job that lacked opportunities for promotion merely because you have a disability? If so, that's discrimination.

For a larger sampling of what is discrimination in the workplace, review the table on employment discrimination.

---

Take Time Now
to Read
**Employment Discrimination Prohibited by ADA**

---

The law says employers must begin by updating application forms and rethinking preemployment inquiries. Questions are to be structured to determine an applicant's ability to perform essential job-related functions—with or without reasonable accommodation (explained later in this chapter)—*not* to determine if the applicant has a disability.

ADA's purpose is to level the playing field. It forces employers to concentrate on abilities, not disabilities, and to match workers to jobs on the basis of qualifications. The law's employment provisions are effective in two steps.

**Step One.** July 26, 1992: Employers with twenty-five or more employees are prohibited from discriminating against job applicants or employees with disabilities when making employment decisions. Private employers, state and local governments, employment agencies, labor organizations, and joint labor-management committees all must comply with ADA.

**Step Two.** July 26, 1994: Employers with fifteen to twenty-four employees are added to the above compliance list.

## ARE YOU COVERED BY ADA?

The law pinpoints three categories of individuals with disabilities. If you answer "yes" to any of the following questions, ADA protects you:

1) Do you have a physical or mental impairment that substantially limits one or more major life activities?
2) Do you have a record of such an impairment?
3) Are you regarded as having such an impairment?

## Category 1: Having a Substantially Limiting Physical or Mental Impairment

A disability may be a **physical or mental impairment that substantially limits at least one major life activity.** This category covers an individual who *currently has a substantially limiting impairment.*

Questions? Before going further, review the definitions of ADA disability terms.

# Employment Discrimination Prohibited by ADA

Under the Americans with Disabilities Act of 1990, it is unlawful for employers to discriminate on the basis of disability against qualified individuals with disabilities in regard to:

- recruitment, advertising, and job application procedures

- hiring, upgrading, promotion, award of tenure, demotion, transfer, layoff, termination, right of return from layoff, and rehiring

- rates of pay or any other form of compensation and changes in compensation

- job assignments, job classifications, organizational structures, position descriptions, lines of progressions, and seniority lists

- leaves of absence, sick leave, or any other leave

- fringe benefits available by virtue of employment, whether or not administered by the organization

- selection and financial support for training, including: apprenticeships, professional meetings, conferences and other related activities, and selection for leaves of absence to pursue training

- activities sponsored by an employer, including social and recreational programs

- any other term, condition, or privilege of employment

Based on U.S. Equal Employment Opportunity Commission's 29 CFR Part 1630, Equal Employment Opportunities for Individuals with Disabilities Final Rule, July 26, 1991.

```
┌─────────────────────────────────┐
│          Take Time Now          │
│            to Read              │
│     ADA Disability Definitions  │
└─────────────────────────────────┘
```

## Category 2: Having a Record of Such an Impairment

This category uses the same definition of disability as the first, but identifies a disability as **having a record of a physical or mental impairment that substantially limits at least one major life activity.** ADA establishes "having a record of" in two ways.

First, a person who *has a history of a substantially limiting impairment* is protected under the "having a record of" category. It may be an impairment—such as cancer, emotional illness, or illegal drug use—from which a person has recovered.

Cristine Sarno of Port Orange, Florida, developed dermatomyositis, a severe neuromuscular disease, at age five. For months she was expected to die, and for several years she couldn't walk. Following experimental treatment funded by the Muscular Dystrophy Association, Sarno began to play and skip again and says that "by tenth grade, you couldn't tell there was anything wrong."

Today Sarno is a full-time college student with a part-time job. Her disease has not recurred, and she no longer takes medication. "They say I've outgrown it," she says. Sarno is covered under ADA's second category of a disability because she has a record of a physical impairment that substantially limits a major life activity.

Second, a person who *has been misclassified as having a substantially limiting impairment* is protected under the "having a record of" category. An example of a misclassification may be mental retardation. Remember Greg Parsons? He's protected under this category because he was misclassified as having severe depression.

## Category 3: Being Regarded as Having Such an Impairment

This category uses the same definition of disability as the first two, but says that a disability may be **being regarded as having a physical or mental impairment that substantially limits at least one major life activity.** ADA classifies "being regarded as having" in three ways.

# ADA Disability Definitions

A *physical or mental impairment* is any physiological disorder or condition, cosmetic disfigurement, or anatomical loss affecting one or more of a variety of body systems. It is also any mental or psychological disorder.

It may be orthopedic, visual, hearing, or speech. It may be cerebral palsy, epilepsy, muscular dystrophy, multiple sclerosis, HIV infection, cancer, heart disease, or diabetes. It may be mental retardation, emotional illness, or specific learning disabilities.

Past illegal use of drugs is protected as a disability, but current illegal use of drugs or use of prescription drugs in an illegal manner is not. The same rules apply for alcoholism. Individuals who are currently in supervised drug or alcohol rehabilitation programs are also protected.

A *major life activity* affected by a disability means a basic function such as walking, seeing, hearing, speaking, breathing, caring for oneself, learning, performing manual tasks, and working. Sitting, standing, lifting, and reaching are also considered major life activities.

*Substantially limited* in a major life activity is determined by the type of and severity of a disability. Also taken into consideration is how long the disability is expected to last. If it isn't a permanent disability, the long-term result must be evaluated. A person who had polio, for example, may have a postpolio disability that substantially limits walking.

Temporary or nonchronic impairments—such as broken bones, concussions, and appendicitis—are not considered to be substantial limitations on major life activities and are not protected.

First, a person who *has an impairment that is wrongly regarded as being substantially limiting* is protected under the "being regarded as having" category. It may be a physical or mental impairment—such as diabetes that is under control or a hearing impairment corrected by a hearing aid—that does not substantially limit a major life activity but is treated by people as if it does. Greg Parsons, who is protected by the previous disability category, is also protected under this category because he is treated by people as if his epilepsy is substantially limiting when, in fact, it is not.

Second, a person who *has an impairment that is substantially limiting only as a result of the attitudes of others toward the impairment* is protected under the "being regarded as having" category. Such a disability may be a prominent facial burn or disfigurement. It may also be a nonlimiting condition that periodically causes an involuntary jerk of the head.

Third, a person who *has no impairment at all, but is treated by the employer as having a substantially limiting impairment* is protected under the "being regarded as having" category. A person falsely assumed, possibly by rumor, to have an emotional disorder or to be infected with human immunodeficiency virus (HIV) may fall under this coverage.

## Protection for Family and Friends

ADA provides some job protection for individuals who provide care for relatives and friends with disabilities. The law says employers can't exclude or deny an equal job or benefits to qualified individuals because of a relationship or association—family, business, social, or other—with an individual who has a known disability.

Suppose you are a qualified job applicant without a disability and you have a spouse who has lupus. You disclose this during your interview. You cannot be refused employment merely because the employer believes health insurance costs will increase or you will miss work frequently because of your spouse.

But ADA does not require the employer to provide an accommodation to you—the duty only applies to the person with the disability. You are not entitled to a modified work schedule, for example, and you must follow the employer's policy on time and attendance. If you don't, you may be terminated or disciplined consistent with the employer's policy for all employees.

## ARE YOU A QUALIFIED INDIVIDUAL WITH A DISABILITY?

ADA does not require employers to hire all applicants with disabilities or promote all employees with disabilities. Rather, ADA says employers are not to screen out qualified individuals when making employment decisions merely because they have disabilities.

**Qualified individuals with disabilities** *are applicants or employees who satisfy job-related requirements of the position sought or held.* These requirements may include education, skills, licenses, and work experience. Individuals must also be able—with or without reasonable accommodation—to perform the essential functions of the position.

## What Are Essential Functions?

**Essential functions** *are the fundamental job duties of the position.* In a professional office, essential functions for a receptionist may include greeting clients and answering telephones. Other functions, such as getting coffee for clients and escorting them to meeting rooms, may be marginal functions if the employer has sufficient staff to reassign the duties to other employees. If not, they, too, are essential functions.

Who determines what constitutes the essential functions of a job? The employer does, unless a discrimination claim is filed. Then the enforcing government agency steps in and investigates.

What can you do to thwart attempts to disqualify you by employers who use "essential functions" as a dodge? The surest way is to work from a job description prepared specifically for the position you seek. But that may not be possible, as is discussed in Chapter 11 on researching employers. In general, companies large enough to have a director or manager of personnel or human resources will have prepared a job description before interviewing for a position. It helps interviewers focus on the credentials needed to meet the specifications of the position. Further, job descriptions are ammunition for employers when they must defend their actions in discrimination cases.

If you're lucky enough to get the job description, review it, making sure it's a job description and not an employer "wish list." Is it really essential, for example, for you to have a car available on a daily basis? Does this position involve driving, or does the boss want every employee to have a car available to run an occasional errand?

If you spot an essential function that you sense the employer is afraid to ask you how you would accomplish because of your disability, bring it up. The employer may think you can't do the task, knowing only one way to do it—in which case you won't get the offer, even though you may know one or two other ways to get the job done.

## What Is Reasonable Accommodation?

A **reasonable accommodation** *is a modification or adjustment to a job or work environment.* ***If you have a disability that requires a job accommodation, you must make employers aware of it before they have any obligation under ADA to provide it.*** Job accommodations fall into three types.

*Type One.* Preemployment reasonable accommodations are required to ensure equal opportunity in the application process. A prospective employer may make a reader available, for example, to read employment forms to an applicant who has low vision.

When Don Brandon received a call for an interview with an Anchorage, Alaska, company that is located in a third floor office, he inquired about the building's accessibility. "No problem, the building has an elevator," the prospective employer assured him. But the day of the interview Brandon arrived to be faced with an out-of-order sign on the building's only elevator, making the third floor not so accessible to the job candidate and his wheelchair. The employer made a reasonable accommodation in the application process by moving Brandon's interview location to the first floor. (Brandon received a job offer but, deciding he and the position were not a good match, turned it down.)

*Type Two.* On-job reasonable accommodations are required to enable employees with disabilities to perform the essential functions of the job. An employer may modify a work schedule, provide an amplified telephone handset, or reassign nonessential tasks to other workers.

*Type Three.* On-job reasonable accommodations are required to enable employees with disabilities to enjoy benefits and privileges of employment that are equal to those that are enjoyed by employees without disabilities. An employer may have to make the employee lounge physically accessible. If that's not possible, a comparable lounge that is accessible may have to be provided.

## What Does *Reasonable* Mean?

The test of reasonable accommodation is made on an individual basis. *What may be reasonable for one employer in one situation may be classified as* **undue hardship** *for another in a similar situation.*

It would be considered reasonable in most circumstances for an employer to raise a desk on wooden blocks for an employee who uses a wheelchair or to allow an employee who is blind to bring a guide dog to work. Why? Because these accommodations require little cost and little effort.

Would it be considered reasonable for an employer to be asked to purchase a voice-synthesized computer for an employee who is without speech? Install an elevator in an old office building for an employee who has a mobility impairment? Or provide an interpreter for an employee who is deaf? It may or may not be reasonable, depending on the employer's size and financial strength.

In calculating undue hardship under ADA, employers must include in their figures any funds available from outside sources—such as state vocational rehabilitation agencies and tax deductions or credits—to offset the cost of the accommodation.

If the first choice of accommodation proves to be an undue hardship, alternative accommodations must be considered. Perhaps an applicant for a small mom-and-pop business needs a telephone device to accommodate a limited grasping ability. Either a telephone headset or a speaker phone will do the job. Mom and pop are not in a financial position to purchase new telephone equipment at this time, but their receptionist has a telephone headset they are willing to transfer to the new employee's office. Even though the applicant prefers a speaker phone, the employer has met ADA's requirement for reasonable accommodation.

Finally, you—the applicant or employee—must be given the opportunity to pay the portion of the accommodation that constitutes undue hardship to the operation of the employer's business. Many employers do not know this.

Since you'll be discussing job accommodations for your disability anyway, use this opportunity to calm the unspoken anxieties many employers will have about the cost of hiring a person with a disability and providing accommodations. If you're willing and able to help with the provision or cost of the accommodation, tell the employer. Communicate that you understand the employer's financial situation and are willing to do what must be done to make you and the job a reality.

How might you bring up the topic with an interviewer? As an example, if you have a hearing impairment you can say: *Although text telephones can be purchased today for a fairly reasonable price, I want you to know I stand ready to help in any way I can if your company isn't able to buy one right now. I'd be happy to locate the best price on the equipment and help with the cost, if needed.* An alternative offer may be to say: *I can disconnect the equipment from my home phone and bring it to work every day.*

Whether or not you are actually called on to open your wallet or assist with the accommodation, offering up front may greatly enhance your chances of landing the job. You'll turn a potential negative into a plus by showing the employer that you're a team player.

## Posing a Direct Threat

Another standard by which individuals are judged to be qualified is whether or not they pose a **direct threat**—*a significant risk of substantial harm*—*to the health or safety of themselves or others in the workplace.* Employers may include this qualification standard if they apply it neutrally to all employees.

ADA says the employer may not simply assume a threat exists but must examine factual evidence—such as input from the individual with the disability and objective opinions of professional health care workers and rehabilitation counselors. If a direct threat does exist, the employer must determine if a reasonable accommodation would eliminate it or reduce it to an acceptable level.

The risk must be highly probable—a slightly increased risk does not meet the test. An individual who has narcolepsy, for instance, which causes frequent and unexpected losses of consciousness, is unlikely to be considered qualified for a power line worker position where contact with electric voltages can cause death.

ADA outlines four factors employers must consider when making a determination of direct threat on a case-by-case basis:

1) The duration of the risk
2) The nature and severity of the potential harm
3) The likelihood that the potential harm will occur
4) The imminence of the potential harm

Employers legally may refuse to hire and may terminate individuals who pose a direct threat.

## PERMISSIBLE INQUIRIES, TESTS, AND EXAMS

ADA identifies inquiries, tests, and examinations that are allowable before a job offer is made, after an offer is made, and after an employee is on the job. The law's intent is to keep employers from using tests and exams as tools to screen out qualified job candidates with disabilities.

## Preemployment Inquiries

Prior to an employer making an offer of employment, inquiries must be kept to essential job-related functions to determine whether an applicant is qualified to perform them. The interviewer is not allowed to ask if the applicant has a disability but may ask the applicant specific questions about essential functions of the job. An employer may ask, for example, "Can you lift fifty pounds?" but not "Do you have a bad back?"

If the applicant has a visible disability or has chosen to disclose a disability, the interviewer is not legally allowed to ask questions about its nature and severity. If the employer considers the task difficult or impossible to perform because of the disability, the employer may ask the applicant to explain or demonstrate how an essential job function can be accomplished. For instance, if Tony Melendez, a guitarist from Chicago who is armless, applied for a music gig, the employer may ask him how—with or without reasonable accommodation—he would perform. Melendez would demonstrate how he plays guitar with his feet, as he did for Pope John Paul II during his visit to San Antonio, Texas.

## Employment Tests

ADA says employment tests must be related to the position sought. They must be designed to reflect accurately the aptitude, skills, and other qualifying factors of job candidates, not to identify disabilities. A man has low vision, for instance, that will not affect his ability to perform in the position sought but may cause him to score poorly on a written test. For the results to accurately reflect job abilities and not merely identify his disability, the candidate may be given an oral test in place of the written one.

If the applicant informs the employer of a disability prior to the administration of a test, a reasonable accommodation must be made. In the above example, the reasonable accommodation was administering an oral test.

## Medical Examinations

Under ADA medical exams are not allowable before a job offer is made. After an offer is extended and before work commences, the employer may require a medical exam if it is job related and required of all new employees in the same job category. The employer may make the offer contingent on the successful outcome of the exam. If the offer is withdrawn, the employer must inform the candidate that the withdrawal is based on the preemployment medical exam, showing the individual will not be able to perform the essential functions of the job. The employer must explore reasonable accommodation before making that determination. Employers also are allowed to require medical exams of existing employees, consistent with the above information.

ADA says all information gathered must be kept confidential and only released on a need-to-know basis. A supervisor may need to know of accommodations and specific restrictions on duties. Safety and medical personnel usually need to know of a disability that may require emergency treatment.

Physical agility tests are not considered medical exams under ADA and may be given at any point in the application or employment process. Again, tests must be job related and essential to the business, they must be given to all applicants or employees in a job category, and consideration must be given to reasonable accommodation.

Drug testing is not considered a medical exam under ADA. Employers are allowed to screen applicants and employees for illegal drug use and make employment decisions based on the results.

## CHARGES, COMPLAINTS, AND LAWSUITS

The goal of ADA is to encourage employers to voluntarily comply with its provisions because it makes good business sense for them. It makes good sense for the entire nation, too.

"When you add together federal, state, local, and private funds," says President Bush, "it costs almost $200 billion annually to support Americans with disabilities, in effect, to keep them dependent." Some experts boost that number to $300 billion annually when lost taxes and productivity are included.

Regardless, some employers will fail to see the benefits of tapping this ready, willing, and able pool of workers. When employers lack this vision and the rights of individuals are blatantly infringed, the result will be lawsuits.

Before filing a charge of employment discrimination based on disability, Patrisha Wright of the Disability Rights Education and Defense Fund urges caution: "Make sure the person or entity you are going after is one that you need to go after."

Try these questions. Is it possible the employer has never heard of ADA? Is the employer willing to comply but is having trouble understanding the law? Or is the employer flagrantly disobeying the law?

If you do choose to file a charge, where do you turn? It depends on which portion of which law covers your employer.

Prior to ADA, disability discrimination was outlawed in some job markets by the Rehabilitation Act of 1973. Federal employers, federal contractors, and federal grant recipients were covered under various sections of the act. Many state and local laws existed that prohibited disability discrimination, but they varied greatly and some provided only minimal relief. *But no federal law prohibited private employers and state and local government agency employers—unless federal contractors or federal grant recipients—from discriminating against individuals with disabilities.*

Although ADA is far more sweeping than earlier laws, your protection may still be under the Rehabilitation Act or under a state or local law. ADA does not preempt any other law—federal, state, or local—if the earlier law provides greater protection. If you're discriminated against based on your disability, you may, in fact, be able to bring charges against the employer under multiple laws with multiple government agencies for enforcement. *If so, it's important to check for coordination agreements among government agencies.*

As a starting point, you must first know into which of three categories an employer or prospective employer falls:

1) Private employers, employment agencies, labor organizations, and joint labor-management committees

2) State and local agencies

3) Federal agencies

The following discussion is not meant to serve as legal advice but merely to help you understand the parameters of your **federal** protection. Enforcement procedures are complex, so read the next sections carefully—and perhaps several times. Admittedly, it's a tough read, but it will help you understand your rights. Every attempt has been made to use general language. However, ADA is the result of efforts by many attorneys, and legalese is used where necessary to prevent misinterpretation.

## Category 1: Private Employers and Others

If you're an applicant or employee of a private employer, employment agency, labor organization, or joint labor-management committee, you have three chances at federal equal employment protection. The law and provision that protects you from disability discrimination depends on the size of the employer and whether or not any federal funds are involved.

ADA says an employer's size is determined by the number of workers employed at all business locations. An employer who has a main office with twenty workers and a branch office with ten workers, for example, has a total of thirty employees. In making a calculation, applicants and employees must know whether the employer is a chain operation, as in this example, or a franchise. Franchises are independently owned businesses, and employer size is determined by the total number of employees at a location or locations owned by a single employer.

## *Title I—ADA*

If the employer has twenty-five or more employees—or if it's after July 26, 1994, and the employer has fifteen or more employees—the discrimination busters to turn to are enforcement personnel in the U.S. Equal Employment Opportunity Commission (EEOC). Start with your local EEOC office, found in the telephone directory under U.S. Government.

How quickly must you file a charge with the EEOC? Charges must be filed within 180 days of a discriminatory event (that occurred after the pertinent ADA section is in effect, whether 1992 or 1994). You may have up to 300 days to file where there is a *comparable* state or local law. The key word is comparable. Check the laws in your local area and state. *Legal experts strongly recommend, however, that you file within 180 days to guarantee federal protection.*

The EEOC will investigate and attempt to resolve your charge through conciliation. If attempts fail, the agency may file suit against the employer. If it decides not to litigate the case, you will be given a "notice of right-to-sue." You will have ninety days to file a lawsuit yourself, if you choose to do so.

Timing is everything in the legal system. To best protect your rights, noted employment attorney V. Paul Donnelly of Donnelly, Huizenga, Wahl, Hagan, & Hergt in Detroit, says, "See an employment discrimination lawyer before you file a charge and get advice on what to say to the government agency. You can go straight to the agency and file, but sometimes a charge that isn't backed up by a lawyer is shoved aside—it's not as strong."

Donnelly says you can find an attorney who, for an affordable fee, will advise you before and during the period the government agency is investigating your charge. If the agency is successful, great. If not, the attorney will switch your case over to a contingency fee basis—meaning you owe nothing except court costs and expenses if you lose—and you're set to move on the private lawsuit.

Whether you or the EEOC seeks enforcement of ADA, you may expect one or more of the following results if you win: a job offer, reasonable accommodation, promotion, retroactive seniority, restored benefits, reinstatement, back pay for lost wages, or whatever is necessary to put you where you would have been had the employer not discriminated against you. You are also entitled to attorney's fees and more—as the next paragraph explains.

Although your protection is under Title I of ADA, you may want to keep an eye on changes in *Title VII of the Civil Rights Act of 1964.* Title I of ADA incorporates the procedures and remedies of that law, and because it does, any changes made in Title VII will automatically change ADA. The recent civil rights legislation signed, for example, providing for jury trials and punitive and compensatory damages under Title VII, has upped your remedies to the same limit under ADA. Now you have the right to a jury trial, and if your case is won, you may be awarded punitive and compensatory damages.

Are any employers exempt under Title I? Yes, federal government agency employers, Indian tribes, and tax-exempt private membership clubs are not covered. Religious organizations are not prohibited from giving preference in employment decisions to individuals of their religion.

### Section 503—Rehabilitation Act of 1973

Working for—or applying for employment with—U.S. government contractors presents a challenge in understanding where your protection lies. *The determining factors are size of the establishment and date of the action.*

If the employer is a U.S. government contractor or subcontractor receiving federal funds in excess of $2,500, your protection is under Section 503 of the Rehabilitation Act. (You also may be protected under ADA if the contractor has a sufficient number of employees.)

The U.S. Department of Labor, Office of Federal Contract Compliance Programs is the discrimination cop to call. A claim must be filed within 180 days, and under Section 503 you do not have the right to sue privately.

### Section 504—Rehabilitation Act of 1973

Very similar to federal contractors, employers who are federal grant recipients—such as hospitals, elementary and secondary schools, universities, and social service agencies—present a protection quandary to applicants and employees because they may be regulated by more than one piece of legislation.

If the employer receives federal financial assistance, you are protected under Section 504 of the Rehabilitation Act. (You also may be protected under ADA if the federal grant recipient has a sufficient number of employees.)

You must file a charge with the funding agency within 180 days. Although the right to sue privately is not stated explicitly in the law, according to the U.S. Department of Justice, the vast majority of courts allow private lawsuits under Section 504.

The following are examples of how each law or a combination of laws may apply in a variety of situations where the employer is a federal contractor or receives federal financial assistance:

- The employer holds a federal contract for $3,000 (or has a federally funded program) but has only ten employees. Your protection is under Section 503 (or Section 504) of the Rehabilitation Act.

- On September 5, 1993, the employer holds a federal contract for $3,000 (or has a federally funded program) and has twenty employees. You are protected under Section 503 (or Section 504) of the Rehabilitation Act. On July 26, 1994, you will also be protected under Title I of ADA, gaining the right to sue privately.

- The employer has a federal contract for $1,500 and has twenty-five employees. Your protection is under Title I of ADA.

# Category 2: State and Local Government Agency Employers

Thanks to ADA, if you're an applicant to or employee of a state or local government agency employer, you now have federal employment rights protection against disability discrimination. Your protection may be under Title I or Title II of ADA, or it may be under Section 503 or Section 504 of the Rehabilitation Act.

## Title I—ADA

The EEOC is also the discrimination cop for state and local government agency employers under Title I of ADA. By 1994 all state and local agency employers with fifteen or more employees will be covered. The same rules apply as to the private employers category above.

## Title II—ADA

State and local agency employers are also covered under Title II of ADA, which provides for a private right to sue. A charge must be filed with one of eight agencies designated in this section of the law within 180 days of a discriminatory act. The U.S. Department of Justice, Office of the Americans with Disabilities Act is the coordinating agency. Questions may be directed to a special ADA hotline at the Justice Department (see Appendix A2).

Title II coverage is especially meaningful. If the state or local government agency employer is not covered by Title I—or until it is covered by Title I—Title II provides protection. The number of employees and enactment dates are key. In the long haul, applicants and employees of small agency employers may find their only federal employment protection here.

### Section 503—Rehabilitation Act of 1973

If the state or local government agency employer is a U.S. government contractor or subcontractor receiving federal funds in excess of $2,500, the same rules apply as to the private employers category above.

### Section 504—Rehabilitation Act of 1973

If the state or local government agency employer receives federal financial assistance, you have protection under Section 504 of the Rehabilitation Act. The same rules would apply as to the private employers category above. This coverage may prove unimportant since you are also protected under Title II of ADA, which incorporates the procedures and remedies of Section 504.

## Category 3: Federal Government Agency Employers

Generally, if the employer is a federal government agency, Section 501 of the Rehabilitation Act provides protection. You must file a complaint with the equal employment opportunity counselor at the federal agency where the violation occurred within thirty days.

If you're an applicant or employee of the executive or legislative branch of the federal government, check with the EEOC to determine where your protection lies and how anti-discrimination in employment on the basis of disability is enforced there.

Does mastering the Rubik's Cube seem easy in comparison with understanding which employment discrimination law or laws cover which employers—and which employers in which circum-

# Federal Employment Rights Protection at a Glance

| Employer Category | Law | Effective Date | Government Agency for Enforcement | Filing Deadline | Private Right-to-Sue |
|---|---|---|---|---|---|
| Private employer | Title I-ADA | 7/26/92 if 25+ employees; 7/26/94 if 15+ employees | EEOC | 180 days, 300 if comp state or local law | Yes |
| | Section 503-RA | Existing for federal contractors (in excess of $2,500) | OFCCP | 180 days | No |
| | Section 504-RA | Existing for federal grant recipients | Funding agency | 180 days | Often |
| State/local agency employer | Title I-ADA | 7/26/92 if 25+ employees; 7/26/94 if 15+ employees | EEOC | 180 days, 300 if comp state or local law | Yes |
| | Title II-ADA | 1/26/92 | DOJ is coordinating agency | 180 days | Yes |
| | Section 503-RA | Existing for federal contractors (in excess of $2,500) | OFCCP | 180 days | No |
| | Section 504-RA | Existing for federal grant recipients | Funding agency | 180 days | Often |
| Federal agency employer | Section 501-RA | Existing | EEO counselor at agency | 30 days | Yes |

KEY: **ADA** = **Americans with Disabilities Act of 1990**
RA = Rehabilitation Act of 1973
DOJ = U.S. Department of Justice, Office of the Americans with Disabilities Act
EEOC = U.S. Equal Employment Opportunity Commission
OFCCP = U.S. Department of Labor, Office of Federal Contract Compliance Programs

stances? The chart on employment rights may help solve the federal employment rights protection puzzle.

*Caution:* A complaint alleging employment discrimination must be filed within a relatively short period of time. If you feel you've been discriminated against on the basis of your disability, don't rely on any printed materials—which can easily become outdated—regardless of the source. Even the government inadvertently circulates outdated materials. *Check with the agency assigned enforcement responsibility for **current** law and filing requirements.*

## WHAT ELSE DOES ADA SAY?

ADA strikes a blow at disability discrimination in more arenas than just employment. It tackles state and local government services, public accommodations, transportation, and telecommunications as well. Significantly, many of the items it regulates can directly or indirectly enhance equal employment opportunities for individuals with disabilities.

A recent Louis Harris survey conducted for the International Center for the Disabled in New York reports that 28 percent of people with disabilities say that a lack of accessible or affordable transportation is an important barrier to work for them. ADA's Title II and III address public transportation issues.

## ADA Title II—Public Services

In addition to the employment provisions discussed earlier, ADA targets state and local governments, outlawing discrimination against qualified individuals with disabilities in the provision of public services, programs, and activities. All government facilities, services, and communications must be accessible.

Another benefit of the public services provision is that public buses and intercity Amtrak coaches as well as bus and rail stations must be accessible to individuals with disabilities.

How does Title II translate into an employment benefit? If city buses and commuter trains are accessible to job applicants and employees who have mobility impairments, for instance, affordable transportation is available to interviews and workplaces. Generally speaking, transportation access will be available by the mid-1990s and in some cases sooner.

# Americans with Disabilities Act of 1990
# Employment Opportunity Enhancers

| | | |
|---|---|---|
| **Title I** | **Employment** | Protects applicants and employees in private sector and state and local government agencies with 15 or more employees. By far, the most important and most encompassing of employment rights legislation for the disability community. |
| **Title II** | **Public Services** | Protects applicants and employees in small state and local government agencies employing fewer than 15 workers.<br>Requires that all state and local government services, programs, and activities be accessible.<br>Targets accessibility in public transportation, such as city buses and commuter trains, operated by state and local government agencies. |
| **Title III** | **Public Accommodations and Services Operated by Private Entities** | Targets accessibility in public transportation, such as buses and vans, operated by private entities.<br>Prohibits private business and service providers, such as restaurants and banks, from discriminating against, refusing to serve, or excluding individuals with disabilities.<br>Addresses accessibility in existing and newly constructed/altered public accommodations and commercial facilities. |
| **Title IV** | **Telecommunications** | Requires telephone companies to offer 24-hour telecommunications relay services to customers who have hearing and speech impairments.<br>Addresses closed captioning of public service announcements. |
| **Title V** | **Miscellaneous** | Prohibits retaliation against individuals who exercise their rights under ADA. |

Note: Most aspects of the Americans with Disabilities Act of 1990 will be implemented by 1994; some extensions on public transportation allowed until 2020.

## ADA Title III—Public Accommodations and Services Operated by Private Entities

ADA's Title II addresses public transportation operated by the government. Title III goes on to require public transportation operated by private entities—such as bus and van companies—to meet accessibility standards. Bus station facilities and other private transportation operations fall under this provision. You may be able to catch a ride to work with private companies, too, but it may take them longer to become fully accessible than it will government transportation.

In addition, the public accommodations section prohibits all private business and service providers from discriminating against, refusing to serve, or excluding individuals with disabilities. ADA bars discrimination in the use of places such as restaurants, hotels, clothing stores, theaters, and doctors' and lawyers' offices. No longer will private schools, groceries, convention centers, pharmacies, and bakeries be allowed to discriminate against you on the basis of your disability, nor will libraries, retail stores, museums, banks, parks, laundromats, and daycare centers.

Are any private entities exempt? Yes, private clubs and religious organizations are not covered by Title III.

*Rules of reasonableness similar to those in the employment provision of ADA are applied to determine if a public enterprise must provide* **auxiliary aids or services** *to individuals with disabilities. If it is determined that doing so will impose an* **undue burden** *on the establishment or if it will* **fundamentally alter** *the goods, services, or operations, no requirement exists.* Practicality and effectiveness are key here. Restaurants are not required to have brailled menus, for instance, nor retail stores brailled price tags as long as waiters and sales personnel are available to read upon request.

New construction of places of public accommodation and commercial facilities, such as office buildings, must be physically accessible. But elevators are generally not required in buildings under three stories, for example, unless they are shopping centers, malls, or health care offices.

**Readily achievable** *is the test for removing physical barriers from existing buildings.* If removal of a barrier can be accomplished easily and carried out without significant difficulty or expense, it must be done. For example, an existing hardware store may be required to ramp a few steps or to lay out racks and shelves to permit wheelchair access. But the store may not be required to reduce the height of shelves if employees are available to assist with out-of-reach items.

In most cases, it would be unlikely that a store would be required to rework its facilities to install elevators, unless such installation is readily achievable.

What is Title III's tie-in to employment? If computer stores, theaters, and other such places of business are accessible to patrons who use wheelchairs, for example, employees who use wheelchairs can now work there.

## ADA Title IV—Telecommunications

The Harris poll cited earlier also finds that 23 percent of people with disabilities who are not working, or are working part-time, say that they don't have needed equipment or devices to help them work easier or communicate with other workers. ADA's Title IV addresses telecommunications.

Telephone companies must offer telecommunications relay services (TRS) to customers who have hearing impairments and speech impairments. Third-party communications assistants enable conversations between users of nonvoice terminal devices and users of voice equipment. Nonvoice terminals may be text telephones (TTs), or they may be other nonvoice devices—such as a computer equipped with a modem.

How does TRS work? An individual with a hearing or speech impairment—or both—places a call to or receives a call from TRS using nonvoice equipment. A communications assistant at TRS translates conversation from text to voice and from voice to text, as needed, between the person with a disability and the person without a disability.

TRS must be provided by July 26, 1993, at rates no greater than rates for similar voice communication services. If, for instance, both a TRS call and a voice call are made from San Diego to Washington, D.C., the TRS call must cost no more than the voice call. ADA requires TRS facilities to operate twenty-four hours a day, 365 days a year.

Also, closed captioning must be included in all federally funded public service announcements for television.

What part can Title IV play in employment? If TRS are available to employees who have speech disorders, for example, they can have telephone conversations with business associates who are not TT users.

## ADA Title V—Miscellaneous

Title V is a catch-all section for miscellaneous provisions. One item bears special mention. If you act in a way endorsed by ADA and as a result are threatened, intimidated, or retaliated against, you are legally protected under Title V. Employers are forbidden to "get you" because you insist on your ADA rights.

"Let's say there's a threat to you—you may be worried that you're going to be demoted or terminated," says attorney V. Paul Donnelly. "I can't stress enough that you should do something while on the job rather than waiting until you're shown the door." Donnelly says that filing a discrimination charge with the proper government agency while still on the job ensures that "from that point on they can't retaliate against you with demotion or termination."

(For a list of agencies offering specific information on requirements and effective dates of the various provisions of ADA, see Appendix A.)

## UNPRECEDENTED WINDOW OF OPPORTUNITY

ADA is building power just as an unprecedented window of opportunity bursts open. In addition to advancing technology, three major factors contribute to the greatest chance ever for people with disabilities to become permanently entrenched in the work force.

First, the shrinking labor pool of employment-ready personnel may create worker shortages during this decade. Employers will compete to effectively recruit and retain qualified employees. Since Americans with disabilities represent the largest single bloc of potential employees, wise businesses will court this underemployed community.

Second, a new wave of young Americans educated under the *Education for All Handicapped Children Act of 1975* (commonly known as *Public Law 94-142*) is graduating now. This new generation will have comparatively better educations and expectations for themselves after graduating from high school and college and will be more adaptable to competitive jobs than previous generations of individuals with disabilities. They've been taught to fit in with the general population. "There is no question they expect to work," says Patrisha Wright, "and it does not dawn on them that society has a mindset to think of them as different or as dependents."

Third, many students of this graduating generation who do not have disabilities have gone through school studying math, eating lunch, and running laps with classmates who have disabilities. Much of the discrimination in the work force will naturally dissolve as these young people, with and without disabilities, enter the workplace side by side. Many of the myths and fears about disabilities that exist in today's older work force will gradually be replaced with facts and with the growing acceptance of employees with disabilities.

## YOUR BALL—RUN WITH IT!

ADA is not merely the responsibility of legislators, government agencies, the courts, lawyers, or employers. All of us are partners in a heroic new effort to break the barriers of bias. We must read the law, know the law, and (tactfully) help educate employers about their obligations to be fair. This is how ADA's promise of equality will be fulfilled.

"The Americans with Disabilities Act is law—a landmark in the evolution of human beings, the world's first comprehensive civil rights law for the people with disabilities by any nation," says Justin Dart, chairman of the President's Committee on Employment of People with Disabilities. "ADA holds the potential for the emancipation and productive independence of every person with a disability on earth," Dart says. "America is watching. The world is watching."

# 3

# The real world of work

The 1990s offer everyone less job security but expand and enrich job possibilities for the disability community. You may be a first-time worker or a career changer—either one who simply wants to move to greener pastures or one whose disability necessitates a change of scenery. In any case, in this decade you face a new kind of job market, as economic, political, and demographic pressures close down old opportunities and open up new ones.

As we prepare to turn the calendar to the next millennium, startling changes are taking place. Changes that can affect your career. Soviet-American pen pals have displaced the cold war, "baby busters" (born 1960 to 1978) are competing with graying "baby boomers" in the workplace, and the United States is sharing the global marketplace with Japan, other members of the Pacific Rim, and the European Community.

In this chapter, we glance at an overview of the job market in the United States between now and the year 2005 as projected by the U.S. Department of Labor's Bureau of Labor Statistics. Here are highlights based on the Labor Department's "Outlook: 1990-2005," as reported in the *Occupational Outlook Quarterly* and the *Monthly Labor Review.*

## JOB TRENDS THROUGH 2005

- Economic growth will be slower through 2005 than during the 1970s and mid-1980s when the baby-boom generation entered the work force. But there will be fewer people in the labor force.
- Women's share of the labor force will continue to increase.
- We're still moving toward a service-producing economy and

away from a manufacturing economy. The services and retail trade industries will account for three-fourths of the growth in employment. Health, education, business services, and eating and drinking places will make up a very large part of growth.

- Manufacturing is expected to lose 600,000 jobs by 2005. Of jobs making products, many of the best will be in industries that export a part of their products overseas—such as medical instruments, aircraft, computers, and pharmaceuticals.

- Employment will grow faster for occupations that require higher levels of education or training and slower for those with minimal formal requirements. This does not necessarily mean four years of college. A community college or vocational-technical education will be ideal for the bulk of jobs requiring education beyond high school. For other top jobs, you will need a bachelor's or advanced degree.

- Technology is changing the structure of employment and how work is done. Computer technology is being used more and more. As a result, systems analyst and programmer will be among the fastest-growing occupations, and more workers in other occupations will need to become computer literate. (This is a boon for workers with mobility problems because there's a better than ever chance the work can be done at home.) The downside is that improved office technology is limiting the growth of administrative support occupations.

- The manner in which businesses operate is changing so that greater interpersonal skills and greater analytical skills are needed.

The Department of Labor maintains a mountain of detail on the job and labor markets. Ask a reference librarian to help you locate the precise data you need, which may be found in the Department's *Occupational Outlook Handbook*, the *Occupational Outlook Quarterly*, or the *Monthly Labor Review*.

## BRIGHT CAREER SPOTS THROUGH 2005

Which occupations are the fastest growing and which offer the greatest number of jobs? According to the Bureau of Labor Statistics, the two categories sometimes overlap.

The bureau's projections are shown in a series of charts that are grouped within this chapter. As a yardstick when analyzing an occupation's employment growth or decline, use the average employment figure for all occupations—a 20 percent increase, or more than 147,000 jobs, in the period from 1990 to 2005.

# Fastest-Growing vs. Largest Job-Growth Occupations

The fastest-growing occupations are those expected to have the *highest rate of growth* between now and 2005.

The largest job-growth occupations in the same time frame are those expected to have the greatest *number of job openings* because they already employ huge numbers of people. An often overlooked fact is that more job openings result from the need to replace workers who leave or die than to fill newly created jobs.

Even though an occupation is expected to grow rapidly, it may produce fewer openings than a slower-growing, larger occupation.

*Super-growth occupations are the ideal combination—fairly large occupations that enjoy galloping growth.*

## Super-Growth Career Fields

Here are selected key trends for the two career fields—health, and business and office—that include several chart-topping occupations both for rapid growth and large numbers of jobs.

### Health

The health care industry is still the nation's hottest ticket in employment after more than a decade in that position. This career field has more than ten million workers and is second in size only to local government at eleven million.

Four health occupations are super-growth occupations—fairly large occupations showing rapid growth: registered nurse, licensed practical nurse, nursing aide/orderly/attendant, and home health aide.

Why has the health care industry continued to hire while other industries have been laying off? Some key reasons are new technologies that require newly trained people to use them, an older America needing recurrent health care, and the AIDS epidemic.

### Business and Office

Like health careers, the business and office field is a top job award winner. Three business and office occupations have achieved super-growth status: systems analyst/computer scientist, computer programmer, and receptionist/information clerk.

## SHRINKING OCCUPATIONS THROUGH 2005

Some occupations will be parched by the year 2005, as demand dries up for their services. The three career fields that will lose the

# Fastest-Growing Occupations

The fastest-growing occupations are those expected to have the *highest rate of growth*. These occupations may have the biggest growth spurts, but that doesn't mean there'll be tons of job openings.

### 1990–2005
### Percent Growth

1990–2005
Numerical Growth

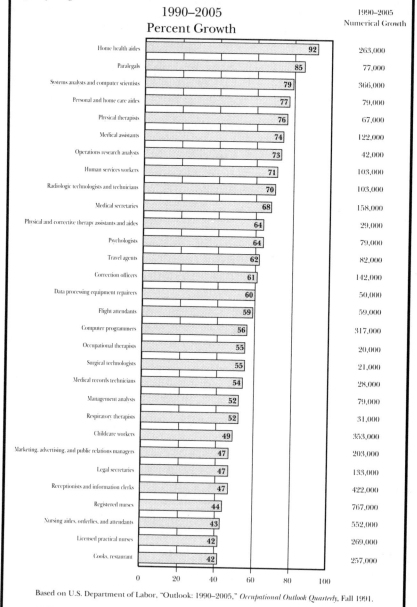

| Occupation | Percent Growth | Numerical Growth |
|---|---|---|
| Home health aides | 92 | 263,000 |
| Paralegals | 85 | 77,000 |
| Systems analysts and computer scientists | 79 | 366,000 |
| Personal and home care aides | 77 | 79,000 |
| Physical therapists | 76 | 67,000 |
| Medical assistants | 74 | 122,000 |
| Operations research analysts | 73 | 42,000 |
| Human services workers | 71 | 103,000 |
| Radiologic technologists and technicians | 70 | 103,000 |
| Medical secretaries | 68 | 158,000 |
| Physical and corrective therapy assistants and aides | 64 | 29,000 |
| Psychologists | 64 | 79,000 |
| Travel agents | 62 | 82,000 |
| Correction officers | 61 | 142,000 |
| Data processing equipment repairers | 60 | 50,000 |
| Flight attendants | 59 | 59,000 |
| Computer programmers | 56 | 317,000 |
| Occupational therapists | 55 | 20,000 |
| Surgical technologists | 55 | 21,000 |
| Medical records technicians | 54 | 28,000 |
| Management analysts | 52 | 79,000 |
| Respiratory therapists | 52 | 31,000 |
| Childcare workers | 49 | 353,000 |
| Marketing, advertising, and public relations managers | 47 | 203,000 |
| Legal secretaries | 47 | 133,000 |
| Receptionists and information clerks | 47 | 422,000 |
| Registered nurses | 44 | 767,000 |
| Nursing aides, orderlies, and attendants | 43 | 552,000 |
| Licensed practical nurses | 42 | 269,000 |
| Cooks, restaurant | 42 | 257,000 |

Based on U.S. Department of Labor, "Outlook: 1990–2005," *Occupational Outlook Quarterly*, Fall 1991.

# Largest Job-Growth Occupations

The largest job-growth occupations are those expected to have the greatest *number of job openings* because they already employ huge numbers of people. These will be the occupations that will have job openings year after year.

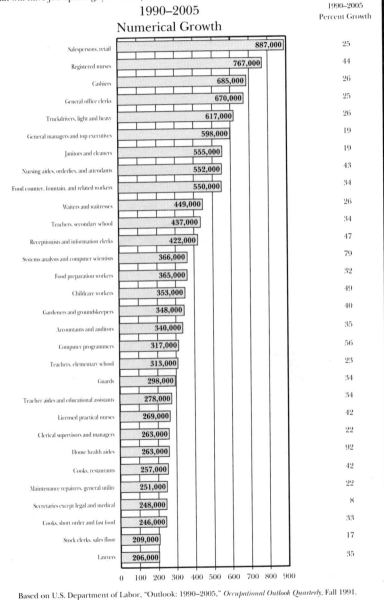

## 1990–2005
### Numerical Growth

1990–2005
Percent Growth

| Occupation | Numerical Growth | Percent Growth |
|---|---|---|
| Salespersons, retail | 887,000 | 25 |
| Registered nurses | 767,000 | 44 |
| Cashiers | 685,000 | 26 |
| General office clerks | 670,000 | 25 |
| Truckdrivers, light and heavy | 617,000 | 26 |
| General managers and top executives | 598,000 | 19 |
| Janitors and cleaners | 555,000 | 19 |
| Nursing aides, orderlies, and attendants | 552,000 | 43 |
| Food counter, fountain, and related workers | 550,000 | 34 |
| Waiters and waitresses | 449,000 | 26 |
| Teachers, secondary school | 437,000 | 34 |
| Receptionists and information clerks | 422,000 | 47 |
| Systems analysts and computer scientists | 366,000 | 79 |
| Food preparation workers | 365,000 | 32 |
| Childcare workers | 353,000 | 49 |
| Gardeners and groundskeepers | 348,000 | 40 |
| Accountants and auditors | 340,000 | 35 |
| Computer programmers | 317,000 | 56 |
| Teachers, elementary school | 313,000 | 23 |
| Guards | 298,000 | 34 |
| Teacher aides and educational assistants | 278,000 | 34 |
| Licensed practical nurses | 269,000 | 42 |
| Clerical supervisors and managers | 263,000 | 22 |
| Home health aides | 263,000 | 92 |
| Cooks, restaurants | 257,000 | 42 |
| Maintenance repairers, general utility | 251,000 | 22 |
| Secretaries except legal and medical | 248,000 | 8 |
| Cooks, short order and fast food | 246,000 | 33 |
| Stock clerks, sales floor | 209,000 | 17 |
| Lawyers | 206,000 | 35 |

0  100  200  300  400  500  600  700  800  900

Based on U.S. Department of Labor, "Outlook: 1990–2005," *Occupational Outlook Quarterly,* Fall 1991.

# On Balance

Even though an occupation is projected to grow rapidly, it may produce fewer openings than a slower-growing, larger occupation. Super-growth occupations are the ideal combination—fairly large occupations showing rapid growth from 1990 to 2005.

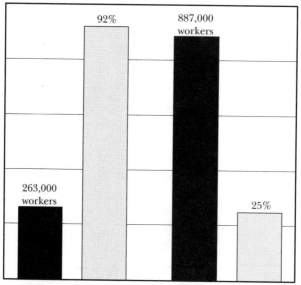

*Fastest-growing occupation*
**Home health aides**

*Largest job-growth occupation*
**Retail salespersons**

 Numerical Growth

 Percent Growth

# Fastest-Growing Occupations Requiring Degree

Of the twenty fastest-growing occupations requiring a bachelor's degree or more education, the top seven are tied to the health services industry or computer technology.

## 1990–2005
### Percent Growth

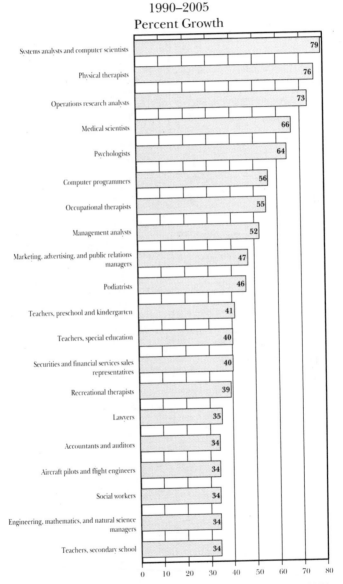

| Occupation | Percent Growth |
|---|---|
| Systems analysts and computer scientists | 79 |
| Physical therapists | 76 |
| Operations research analysts | 73 |
| Medical scientists | 66 |
| Psychologists | 64 |
| Computer programmers | 56 |
| Occupational therapists | 55 |
| Management analysts | 52 |
| Marketing, advertising, and public relations managers | 47 |
| Podiatrists | 46 |
| Teachers, preschool and kindergarten | 41 |
| Teachers, special education | 40 |
| Securities and financial services sales representatives | 40 |
| Recreational therapists | 39 |
| Lawyers | 35 |
| Accountants and auditors | 34 |
| Aircraft pilots and flight engineers | 34 |
| Social workers | 34 |
| Engineering, mathematics, and natural science managers | 34 |
| Teachers, secondary school | 34 |

Based on U.S. Department of Labor, "Outlook: 1990–2005," *Occupational Outlook Quarterly*, Fall 1991.

# Fastest-Growing Occupations Requiring Training

Health services occupations are a sizable proportion of the fastest-growing occupations requiring some postsecondary training or extensive employer training.

## 1990–2005
### Percent Growth

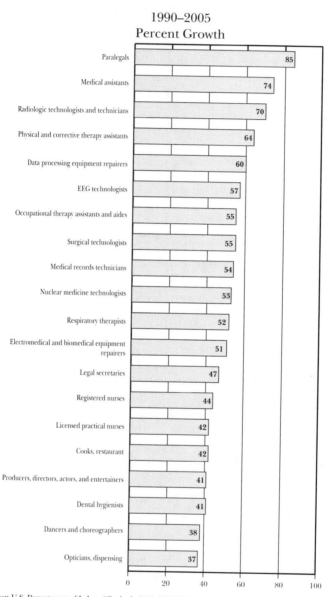

| Occupation | Percent Growth |
|---|---|
| Paralegals | 85 |
| Medical assistants | 74 |
| Radiologic technologists and technicians | 70 |
| Physical and corrective therapy assistants | 64 |
| Data processing equipment repairers | 60 |
| EEG technologists | 57 |
| Occupational therapy assistants and aides | 55 |
| Surgical technologists | 55 |
| Medical records technicians | 54 |
| Nuclear medicine technologists | 53 |
| Respiratory therapists | 52 |
| Electromedical and biomedical equipment repairers | 51 |
| Legal secretaries | 47 |
| Registered nurses | 44 |
| Licensed practical nurses | 42 |
| Cooks, restaurant | 42 |
| Producers, directors, actors, and entertainers | 41 |
| Dental hygienists | 41 |
| Dancers and choreographers | 38 |
| Opticians, dispensing | 37 |

Based on U.S. Department of Labor, "Outlook: 1990–2005," *Occupational Outlook Quarterly*, Fall 1991.

# Fastest-Growing Occupations Requiring HS Diploma or Less

Service occupations account for nearly half of the fastest-growing occupations requiring a high school graduation or less education. These jobs often require some on-job training.

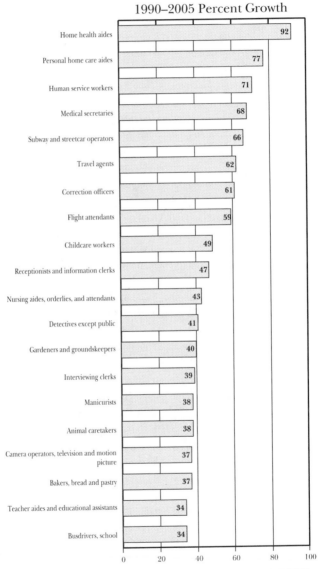

## 1990–2005 Percent Growth

| Occupation | Percent Growth |
|---|---|
| Home health aides | 92 |
| Personal home care aides | 77 |
| Human service workers | 71 |
| Medical secretaries | 68 |
| Subway and streetcar operators | 66 |
| Travel agents | 62 |
| Correction officers | 61 |
| Flight attendants | 59 |
| Childcare workers | 49 |
| Receptionists and information clerks | 47 |
| Nursing aides, orderlies, and attendants | 43 |
| Detectives except public | 41 |
| Gardeners and groundskeepers | 40 |
| Interviewing clerks | 39 |
| Manicurists | 38 |
| Animal caretakers | 38 |
| Camera operators, television and motion picture | 37 |
| Bakers, bread and pastry | 37 |
| Teacher aides and educational assistants | 34 |
| Busdrivers, school | 34 |

Based on U.S. Department of Labor, "Outlook: 1990–2005," *Occupational Outlook Quarterly*, Fall 1991.

# Occupations Losing Workers

Shrinking occupations are projected by the *number of job openings*, rather than by the rate of decline. Many occupations with the fastest rates of decline are small in size, resulting in employment declines that aren't very significant.

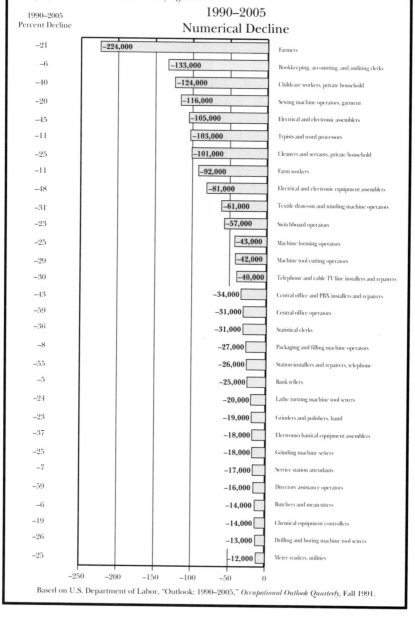

| 1990–2005 Percent Decline | 1990–2005 Numerical Decline | |
|---|---|---|
| –21 | –224,000 | Farmers |
| –6 | –133,000 | Bookkeeping, accounting, and auditing clerks |
| –40 | –124,000 | Childcare workers, private household |
| –20 | –116,000 | Sewing machine operators, garment |
| –45 | –105,000 | Electrical and electronic assemblers |
| –11 | –103,000 | Typists and word processors |
| –25 | –101,000 | Cleaners and servants, private household |
| –11 | –92,000 | Farm workers |
| –48 | –81,000 | Electrical and electronic equipment assemblers |
| –31 | –61,000 | Textile draw-out and winding machine operators |
| –23 | –57,000 | Switchboard operators |
| –25 | –43,000 | Machine forming operators |
| –29 | –42,000 | Machine tool cutting operators |
| –30 | –40,000 | Telephone and cable TV line installers and repairers |
| –43 | –34,000 | Central office and PBX installers and repairers |
| –59 | –31,000 | Central office operators |
| –36 | –31,000 | Statistical clerks |
| –8 | –27,000 | Packaging and filling machine operators |
| –55 | –26,000 | Station installers and repairers, telephone |
| –5 | –25,000 | Bank tellers |
| –24 | –20,000 | Lathe turning machine tool setters |
| –23 | –19,000 | Grinders and polishers, hand |
| –37 | –18,000 | Electromechanical equipment assemblers |
| –25 | –18,000 | Grinding machine setters |
| –7 | –17,000 | Service station attendants |
| –59 | –16,000 | Directory assistance operators |
| –6 | –14,000 | Butchers and meatcutters |
| –19 | –14,000 | Chemical equipment controllers |
| –26 | –13,000 | Drilling and boring machine tool setters |
| –25 | –12,000 | Meter readers, utilities |

Based on U.S. Department of Labor, "Outlook: 1990–2005," *Occupational Outlook Quarterly*, Fall 1991.

largest number of jobs are manufacture and repair, business and office, and agriculture.

### Manufacture and Repair

More than half of the thirty occupations on the bureau's list of declining occupations are in manufacturing. Job losses will result from projections of reduced defense expenditures, increased imports, jobs moving overseas, and higher levels of productivity resulting from advances in technology.

### Business and Office

The business and office career field landed on both the list of super-growth occupations and the list of shrinking occupations. As technology advances, corporate America is reorganizing, and business and office occupations are being restructured.

Some white-collar workers may find office automation grinding their occupation growth to a halt. Bookkeeping, accounting, and auditing clerks are among the most heavily hit. Typists and word processors also are on the down curve.

### Agriculture

Some agriculture occupations continue to slip into history. Advanced technology and larger machinery used in crops and livestock production will mean jobs lost for farmers and farm workers.

## FORWARD TO THE FUTURE

It's important to keep abreast of world events and read the signs of the U.S. and global economies because the same events that cause change in national and international affairs eventually affect jobs. What's the best way to stay current? Follow the media. Television, radio, newspapers, and magazines churn out up-to-the-minute employment and economy trends. Another good source is books.

An award-winning and comprehensive guide containing timely career information from A to Z is *Joyce Lain Kennedy's Career Book*, co-authored by Dr. Darryl Laramore.

For a glimpse into the future that may directly or indirectly influence your career, check out such predictive works as *Megatrends 2000* by John Naisbitt and Patricia Aburdene, *Crystal Globe: The Haves and Have-Nots of the New World Order* by Marvin Cetron and Owen Davies, and *The Popcorn Report* by Faith Popcorn.

Sometimes information can be misleading, so read with the eyes of a critic. Avoid blind acceptance of forecasts and suggestions.

Consider what is said and who says it. Is the information too general? Is it biased? Is it recent? Is it complete? Is it fair to all people? Keep in mind that even the best projections are imperfect. Remember the "unsinkable" Titanic? Once you've made a value judgment on the validity of the information, you can apply the trends to your personal situation as you make career decisions.

# 4

# Self-assessment: able to do the job

Fashion model Ivy Gunter has many skills and talents. In addition she has a self-assurance and a presence that makes everyone in the room turn when she enters. When Gunter lost a leg to bone cancer, she refused to give up her modeling career. Gunter keeps on showing the world that she and her beautiful legs — one real, one sculptured — can be successful.

Another who has enviable abilities, including the skills to persuade and to lead, is a pioneer activist in the disability community: Eunice Fiorito. As the political leader says, "I'm a human being who happens to be blind, not a blind being who happens to be human."

Both Gunter and Fiorito are *able to do the job*. That's the point. They—like hundreds of thousands of other people with disabilities—are blessed with skills and talents that see them through the rough times. If you've never considered going into the job market before or feel you're in the wrong job, perhaps you haven't spent much time assessing your interests and your skills—your gifts as they might apply to work.

That's the mission of this chapter. You will focus as objectively as possible on *you*—your current work values, personal values, interests, personality traits, and skills. By the end of the chapter, you'll be better able to answer these questions:

- What do I want most from work?
- What is important to me?
- What do I like to do best?
- What are my personality traits?

- What are my skills and aptitudes?
- What is my true ability?
- What am I willing to trade to get what I want most?

After doing the exercises that follow, you will have a much clearer understanding of what makes you desirably unique in the workplace. But please note that this chapter is not meant to take the place of more extensive and excellent books and computer programs on aptitude and interest testing. Nor is it meant to replace the myriad of test batteries provided by various public and private counselors.

Instead, this chapter encourages you to open the special package that is you and see what treasures lie within. It is meant to cut the ribbon that opens your road to self-discovery.

Don't worry about trick questions or right vs. wrong answers. There aren't any. Focus on stating what you know about yourself— and what you discover as you work through the exercises here. The goal is to prove to yourself that you are equal to the task.

Each facet of getting to know yourself asks you to fill out an **Equal-to-the-Task Snapshot**. At the end of the chapter, you'll compile your five snapshots into your personalized **Equal-to-the-Task Composite**.

Let's begin.


## ANALYZE YOUR WORK VALUES

Your first snapshot helps you decide how you really feel about work. Choose one of the items in each group of work values on the following list that you prefer. Only opposite extremes are given for each preference. You actually may prefer something in the middle, but choose the extreme that is closer to your feelings. When thinking about where you want to work, for instance, you see the choices are *working in the city* and *working in the country*. Suppose you prefer to work in a suburb with lots of services nearby. That's more like the city than the country, so mark *working in the city*.

An important work value to Joseph Hogg is the ability to work at home. Born with cerebral palsy, Hogg cannot speak, walk, or move his arms. With the aid of a specially designed pointer attached to a cap, Hogg works on a computer, communicating by a word board to his employer. Hogg is a software specialist at Bull Worldwide Information Systems in Phoenix, Arizona. If Hogg were filling out the **Work Values Survey**, he might check *bringing work home* rather than *leaving work at work*.

# Work Values Survey

I prefer these work factors
(check one box from each group that comes closest to your preference)

| | |
|---|---|
| ❑ Working for an organization<br>❑ Self-employment | ❑ Working on a salaried or hourly basis<br>❑ Working on a commission or free-lance basis |
| ❑ Full-time work<br>❑ Part-time work | ❑ Working indoors<br>❑ Working outdoors |
| ❑ Flexible hours<br>❑ Structured hours | ❑ High responsibility<br>❑ Minimal responsibility |
| ❑ Working alone<br>❑ Working with other people | ❑ Motivated by money<br>❑ Motivated by personal satisfaction |
| ❑ Fast pace<br>❑ Slow pace | ❑ Close work with machines<br>❑ Little work with machines |
| ❑ Working within a half-hour of home<br>❑ A long commute is okay | ❑ Formal business environment<br>❑ Informal business environment |
| ❑ Well-defined duties and responsibilities<br>❑ Room for creativity and initiative | ❑ Work opportunities available after 65<br>❑ Early retirement |
| ❑ Close or moderate supervision<br>❑ Little or no supervision | ❑ Many opportunities for advancement<br>❑ Advancement isn't important |
| ❑ Working in a large, open space<br>❑ Working in a small, restricted area | ❑ Guaranteed regular hours<br>❑ Possibility of overtime |
| ❑ Work that offers security<br>❑ Work that is interesting, but may offer little security | ❑ Working with people with disabilities<br>❑ Working with people without disabilities |
| ❑ High prestige and status<br>❑ Prestige and status aren't important | ❑ Working in a specific geographic area<br>❑ Willing to relocate |
| ❑ Working in the city<br>❑ Working in the country | ❑ Working with children or senior adults<br>❑ Working with adults |
| ❑ Working with things<br>❑ Working with information | ❑ Outside social activities available through job<br>❑ Social activities aren't important |
| ❑ Need benefits package<br>❑ Benefits aren't important | ❑ Working at a desk<br>❑ Being mobile in work |
| ❑ Frequent travel<br>❑ Little or no travel | ❑ Seeing tangible end products<br>❑ Dealing in long-range goals |
| ❑ Being the boss<br>❑ Being supervised by others | ❑ Working with the less fortunate<br>❑ Working with the mainstream population |
| ❑ Working for a large company<br>❑ Working for a small company | ❑ Bringing work home<br>❑ Leaving work at work |
| ❑ Routine assignments<br>❑ Variety in work | ❑ Working in the private sector<br>❑ Working for the government or a nonprofit agency |
| ❑ Need to be on a public transportation line<br>❑ Public transportation isn't important | ❑ _____<br>❑ _____ |

You may have to wrestle with your innermost feelings to make some of these choices. Think it through—don't take shortcuts.

> Take Time Now
> to Complete Your
> **Work Values Survey**

Review your choices. Select the ten work values that are the most important to you. Write them down on your **Equal-to-the-Task Snapshot No. 1**. If you think of values that fit you better than those on the sample list, use them. For example, is it important for you to *work with teenagers?* It isn't on the list? Put it on the list. Remember, this is *your* snapshot.

*Tip:* Throughout this chapter, always include items that specifically fit you even if they are not on the sample list.

---

## MY TOP 10 WORK VALUES
### Equal-to-the-Task Snapshot No. 1

1. _____   6. _____

2. _____   7. _____

3. _____   8. _____

4. _____   9. _____

5. _____   10. _____

---

## RANK YOUR PERSONAL VALUES

Now that you have a better idea of what you want most from work, shift gears and ask yourself what's important in your personal life. For example, *loyalty* in yourself or in others may be important to you. Although you may not want to be a dancer, you may consider *dance* important if you love the ballet.

In filling out your **Personal Values Survey** on the following chart

# Personal Values Survey

I think these things are important
(check boxes that apply)

| | |
|---|---|
| ❏ Ability to influence | ❏ Material possessions |
| ❏ Achievement | ❏ Mental challenge |
| ❏ Adventure | ❏ Music |
| ❏ Art | ❏ Neatness and orderliness |
| ❏ Availability to my children | ❏ Patriotism |
| ❏ Beautiful surroundings | ❏ Peace of mind |
| ❏ Church participation | ❏ Personal appearance |
| ❏ Community participation | ❏ Pets |
| ❏ Companionship | ❏ Physical challenge |
| ❏ Competitiveness | ❏ Pioneering |
| ❏ Creativity | ❏ Power |
| ❏ Dance | ❏ Recognition |
| ❏ Education | ❏ Reputation |
| ❏ Ethics | ❏ Respect |
| ❏ Excitement | ❏ Satisfying love relationship |
| ❏ Exercise | ❏ Security |
| ❏ Fame | ❏ Self-esteem |
| ❏ Family time | ❏ Self-improvement |
| ❏ Financial comfort | ❏ Self-knowledge |
| ❏ Flexibility | ❏ Sense of accomplishment |
| ❏ Generosity | ❏ Sense of control |
| ❏ Good family relationships | ❏ Social status |
| ❏ Happiness | ❏ Spiritual development |
| ❏ Health | ❏ Sports |
| ❏ Helping others | ❏ Theater |
| ❏ Hobby | ❏ Time to yourself |
| ❏ Honesty | ❏ Tolerant attitudes |
| ❏ Humility | ❏ Travel |
| ❏ Independence | ❏ Truth |
| ❏ Integrity | ❏ Volunteering |
| ❏ Intellectual stimulation | ❏ Wealth |
| ❏ Justice | ❏ World in which humans and nature are in balance |
| ❏ Leisure time | ❏ World without discrimination |
| ❏ Loving and understanding friends | ❏ _____ |
| ❏ Loyalty | ❏ _____ |
| ❏ Making the "team" | ❏ _____ |

you may say, "All these things are important to me!" They may be, but this snapshot should reflect only your heart-of-heart desires.

Margy Spezia has known she has Charcot-Marie-Tooth, a disease of the peripheral nerves, since she was three years old. She says, "I'm hoping I can project an example that will make people see those who are disabled in a different light—not their dependent side, but their independent side." This young mother works full-time as a management intern with the Defense Mapping Agency in St. Louis. She also goes to night school, enters 10K runs, is an aspiring author, and is president of the executive committee of Muscular Dystrophy Association's Mississippi Valley chapter. Spezia says she'd check *independence* and *self-respect* if she filled out the **Personal Values Survey**.

> Take Time Now
> to Complete Your
> **Personal Values Survey**

Personal values are an important consideration in your career choice. It's a good idea to discuss your ranking with friends and family who know you well.

Did you come up with important personal values not on the list? Good, you're getting the hang of it. From the sample list and your own ideas, narrow your personal values to ten. Fill in your **Equal-to-the-Task Snapshot No. 2.**

---

## MY TOP 10 PERSONAL VALUES
### Equal-to-the-Task Snapshot No. 2

| | |
|---|---|
| 1._____ | 6._____ |
| 2._____ | 7._____ |
| 3._____ | 8._____ |
| 4._____ | 9._____ |
| 5._____ | 10._____ |

# INVENTORY YOUR INTERESTS

"Too often people—young people and adults—are only asked 'What do you want to do?'" says Dr. Carl McDaniels, a prominent counselor educator at Virginia Polytechnic Institute and State University. "They also should be asked 'What do you spend your leisure time on?'"

It's a fact that we are most likely to succeed at what we like to do. Think of a situation where you've succeeded. Were you the *volunteer*, for example, who raised the most money for your local senior adult center? To make top fundraiser you probably enjoyed the work. Maybe you enjoyed the *challenge* of *influencing* people. Maybe you felt a warm glow of satisfaction knowing your efforts will *make life better for others.*

It's also a fact that just because we're interested in something doesn't mean we automatically are good at it, much less successful. To see the point, think of something in your past that you've been interested in but just couldn't master. Maybe you loved science in school, but no matter how hard you tried you never scored higher than a "C." Did that suggest to you that you'd probably never make a living in gene engineering?

Unfortunately, the advice we often hear to "do what you love and the money will follow" is more wishful thinking than reality. But your career planning should *begin* with what you like best.

What *do* you like best? Your everyday actions provide clues. What are the things you say you like to do that you actually spend time doing? Which activities genuinely excite you and make you feel special while you're doing them? Which make the time fly?

Suppose one day you opened a newspaper and found this recruitment ad:

---

**WORKERS WANTED**
Get paid for doing
anything you like

---

Your reaction? It would be like winning the lottery. You'd zip right out and take the employer up on the offer. Remember, you can be paid for doing things that you would do for fun—if those skills are in demand in the world of work.

Here's a sample list of activities, functions, and career fields to pique your interest. Check the boxes next to those you're interested in or that are things you like to do. Select only the most compelling—the ones to which you're most drawn.

If Tim Venetis filled out the **Interests Survey**, he probably would mark *assembling, building things, mechanical design, precision work, repairing,* and *working with objects*. Since childhood, Venetis has had an insatiable interest in taking things apart and putting them back together. Venetis, a skilled auto mechanic in the Automotive Lubrication Section at Texaco's Research Center in Beacon, New York, has been blind since birth.

```
+---------------------------+
|      Take Time Now        |
|      to Complete Your     |
|  Interests Survey: Part A |
+---------------------------+
```

Now use the boxes you checked in Part A of your **Interests Survey** to fill in Part B. You'll definitely want to pick subjects, activities, and career fields that are not just included on the list in Part A because that list is only a small sampling of the possibilities available. If your favorite hobby is stamp collecting, for example, use it.

Part B of your **Interests Survey** asks you to list what you like and dislike about the subjects, activities, and career fields that you include. When you're thinking about what you dislike about them, write down the activities that make you feel uncomfortable and anxious to move on to something else when you're doing them. You can use items you checked in Part A of your **Interests Survey** to get you going.

```
+---------------------------+
|      Take Time Now        |
|      to Complete Your     |
|  Interests Survey: Part B |
+---------------------------+
```

Although many of our interests change as we mature, some stay with us for a lifetime. Interests are difficult to limit, so carefully review Parts A and B when choosing your top ten. *The ten you list in your* **Equal-to-the-Task Snapshot No. 3** *should be interests you would like to pursue in your career.*

## STUDY YOUR PERSONALITY TRAITS

One of the best ways to see yourself is through other people's eyes. How do you do that? Pay attention to how others relate to you.

# Interests Survey: Part A

I am interested in or like these activities, functions, and career fields
(check boxes that apply)

| | | | |
|---|---|---|---|
| ❏ Accounting | ❏ Designing | ❏ Law enforcement | ❏ Raising funds |
| ❏ Acting | ❏ Developing | ❏ Libraries | ❏ Reading |
| ❏ Administering | ❏ Editing | ❏ Listening | ❏ Recruiting |
| ❏ Advising | ❏ Engineering | ❏ Machine operation | ❏ Religious activities |
| ❏ Agriculture | ❏ Entertaining | ❏ Maintaining information | ❏ Repairing |
| ❏ Analyzing | ❏ Entrepreneurship | ❏ Making decisions | ❏ Researching |
| ❏ Animals | ❏ Evaluating | ❏ Making policy | ❏ Resolving conflict |
| ❏ Appraising | ❏ Exchanging information | ❏ Managing people | ❏ Risk |
| ❏ Architecture | ❏ Film watching | ❏ Mechanical design | ❏ Running |
| ❏ Art | ❏ Finance | ❏ Medical science | ❏ Selling |
| ❏ Assembling | ❏ Fine manual work | ❏ Military | ❏ Service |
| ❏ Assisting | ❏ Forestry | ❏ Ministry | ❏ Singing |
| ❏ Biological sciences | ❏ Freedom | ❏ Moderating | ❏ Social sciences |
| ❏ Brainstorming | ❏ Gardening | ❏ Money | ❏ Solving problems |
| ❏ Building morale | ❏ Golf | ❏ Motivating | ❏ Strategy |
| ❏ Building things | ❏ Government | ❏ Mountain climbing | ❏ Supervising |
| ❏ Business management | ❏ Graphic arts | ❏ Music | ❏ Supporting |
| ❏ Challenge | ❏ Guiding | ❏ Negotiating | ❏ Swimming |
| ❏ Chess playing | ❏ Handling detail | ❏ Office management | ❏ Systems and procedures |
| ❏ Civic activities | ❏ Health services | ❏ Organizing | ❏ Teaching |
| ❏ Clerical work | ❏ Helping people | ❏ Participating | ❏ Teamwork |
| ❏ Clothes | ❏ History | ❏ Performing | ❏ Thinking |
| ❏ Coaching | ❏ Horseback riding | ❏ Philosophy | ❏ Translating |
| ❏ Communication | ❏ Identifying needs | ❏ Photography | ❏ Transportation |
| ❏ Conceiving ideas | ❏ Implementing | ❏ Physical sciences | ❏ Traveling |
| ❏ Consulting | ❏ Improving | ❏ Physical work | ❏ Unifying |
| ❏ Cooking | ❏ Influencing | ❏ Planning | ❏ Volunteering |
| ❏ Coordinating | ❏ Initiating | ❏ Politics | ❏ Winning |
| ❏ Counseling | ❏ Installing | ❏ Precision work | ❏ Woodworking |
| ❏ Crafts | ❏ Integrating | ❏ Procuring | ❏ Working outdoors |
| ❏ Creating | ❏ Interpreting | ❏ Production | ❏ Working with children |
| ❏ Cutting costs | ❏ Inventing | ❏ Programming | ❏ Working with objects |
| ❏ Data | ❏ Investigating | ❏ Promoting | ❏ Writing instructions |
| ❏ Decorating | ❏ Laboratory sciences | ❏ Public service | ❏ _____ |
| ❏ Delegating | ❏ Languages | ❏ Public speaking | ❏ _____ |
| ❏ Demonstrating | ❏ Law | ❏ Publishing and printing | ❏ _____ |

# Interests Survey: Part B

| Activity | What I Like About It | What I Dislike About It |
|---|---|---|

**School Subjects**

*Example:* Geography — learning about world — reading

1. _____
2. _____
3. _____
4. _____
5. _____

**Extracurricular Activities**

*Example:* Acting — performing, entertaining — memorizing

1. _____
2. _____
3. _____
4. _____
5. _____

**Recreational Activities**

*Example:* Wheelchair tennis — exercise, winning — losing

1. _____
2. _____
3. _____
4. _____
5. _____

**Civic Activities**

*Example:* Hospital volunteer — peer counseling — clerical work

1. _____
2. _____
3. _____
4. _____
5. _____

**Work Experience**

*Example:* Word processor — keyboarding — rush work

1. _____
2. _____
3. _____
4. _____
5. _____

What kinds of tasks or favors do friends and family ask you to do for them? Organize a closet? Maybe you're *neat*. Transport a traveler to the airport on time? Maybe you're *punctual*. Perhaps you're sought for your advice. Could it be because you're *resourceful* or because you're a *good listener?*

---

## MY TOP 10 INTERESTS
### Equal-to-the-Task Snapshot No. 3

1. _____    6. _____

2. _____    7. _____

3. _____    8. _____

4. _____    9. _____

5. _____    10. _____

---

Dr. I. King Jordan, president of Gallaudet University in Washington, D.C., might check these personality traits if he filled out the **Personality Traits Survey:** *businesslike, charming, cheerful, competent, confident, considerate, dedicated, determined, funny, intelligent, professional, realistic, tactful, well adjusted.* Jordan is the first president of the venerable institution who is deaf.

Now look in the following survey mirror and check the personality traits that apply to you. Your object is to find traits that surface again and again. Don't forget to include the pesky traits you wish you *didn't* own.

> Take Time Now
> to Complete Your
> **Personality Traits Survey**

A word used to describe a personality trait sometimes can be interpreted as positive—and sometimes as negative. It's a mistake to get hung up on a word itself.

Suppose being *critical* is one of your traits. This may be a plus if

# Personality Traits Survey

I think these traits best describe me
(check boxes that apply)

| | | | |
|---|---|---|---|
| ❑ Accepting | ❑ Diligent | ❑ Inventive | ❑ Reserved |
| ❑ Accurate | ❑ Direct | ❑ Investigative | ❑ Resourceful |
| ❑ Adventurous | ❑ Dishonest | ❑ Irritable | ❑ Risk-taking |
| ❑ Affectionate | ❑ Dreamer | ❑ Judgmental | ❑ Rude |
| ❑ Agreeable | ❑ Easily bored | ❑ Lazy | ❑ Scientific |
| ❑ Aggressive | ❑ Easygoing | ❑ Logical | ❑ Secretive |
| ❑ Alert | ❑ Economical | ❑ Loner | ❑ Self-directed |
| ❑ Ambitious | ❑ Efficient | ❑ Loyal | ❑ Sensitive |
| ❑ Angry | ❑ Elegant | ❑ Lucky | ❑ Serious |
| ❑ Artistic | ❑ Empathetic | ❑ Mature | ❑ Shy |
| ❑ Assertive | ❑ Emotional | ❑ Mean | ❑ Sincere |
| ❑ Authoritative | ❑ Energetic | ❑ Messy | ❑ Slow to forgive |
| ❑ Awkward | ❑ Enterprising | ❑ Methodical | ❑ Spontaneous |
| ❑ Bossy | ❑ Enthusiastic | ❑ Neat | ❑ Steady |
| ❑ Businesslike | ❑ Fair | ❑ Open minded | ❑ Stingy |
| ❑ Calm | ❑ Flexible | ❑ Optimistic | ❑ Stubborn |
| ❑ Cautious | ❑ Flighty | ❑ Organized | ❑ Suspicious |
| ❑ Charming | ❑ Flippant | ❑ Outgoing | ❑ Sympathetic |
| ❑ Cheerful | ❑ Foresighted | ❑ Patient | ❑ Tactful |
| ❑ Childish | ❑ Forgiving | ❑ Perfectionist | ❑ Thick skinned |
| ❑ Compatible | ❑ Friendly | ❑ Persevering | ❑ Think for myself |
| ❑ Competent | ❑ Funny | ❑ Persuasive | ❑ Thorough |
| ❑ Competitive | ❑ Generous | ❑ Pessimistic | ❑ Thoughtful |
| ❑ Conceptual | ❑ Gentle | ❑ Polite | ❑ Thoughtless |
| ❑ Confident | ❑ Goof-off | ❑ Practical | ❑ Tolerant |
| ❑ Conscientious | ❑ Gracious | ❑ Professional | ❑ Trusting |
| ❑ Considerate | ❑ Gutsy | ❑ Progressive | ❑ Understanding |
| ❑ Cooperative | ❑ Hard-working | ❑ Prompt | ❑ Unpretentious |
| ❑ Courageous | ❑ Honest | ❑ Proud | ❑ Unshakable |
| ❑ Creative | ❑ Impatient | ❑ Punctual | ❑ Unsure of myself |
| ❑ Critical | ❑ Impulsive | ❑ Quality conscious | ❑ Vivacious |
| ❑ Decisive | ❑ Independent | ❑ Quick to anger | ❑ Warm hearted |
| ❑ Dedicated | ❑ Individualistic | ❑ Quitter | ❑ Well adjusted |
| ❑ Dependable | ❑ Innovative | ❑ Realistic | ❑ _____ |
| ❑ Dependent | ❑ Intelligent | ❑ Rebellious | ❑ _____ |
| ❑ Determined | ❑ Intense | ❑ Receptive | ❑ _____ |

you're a movie reviewer or a meat inspector. It may be a negative if you are trying to establish rapport with a client in a counseling situation. Inclined toward *risk taking* may help an entrepreneur but create a problem for an airline pilot. Similarly, being *realistic* may be invaluable for a financial planner but a real drawback for a science fiction writer.

It's time to record your personality traits on your **Equal-to-the-Task Snapshot No. 4.** If you feel you possess other qualities not on the sample list, add them now.

---

## MY TOP 10 PERSONALITY TRAITS
### Equal-to-the-Task Snapshot No. 4

1. _____   6. _____

2. _____   7. _____

3. _____   8. _____

4. _____   9. _____

5. _____   10. _____

---

## TAKE STOCK OF YOUR SKILLS

So far you've surveyed your work values and your personal values. You've also surveyed your interests and your personality traits. Which snapshot is left to make up the composite that is YOU? It is the one that reveals what you can do—your skills snapshot.

Don't panic. Unclench your teeth and relax your shoulders. You *do* have skills.

### Everyone Has Skills

Even young children have skills. Some can throw a ball, jump rope, or make mud pies. Others can color in the lines, add 2 + 2, or memorize the words of "Twinkle, Twinkle, Little Star." Still others can dance to the beat or lead their friends in a song. Everyone has skills!

If you have lingering doubts, read the enlightening story of how forty-six-year-old Daryl Smith of Moulton, Alabama, uses marketable abilities despite a devastating illness. "I want to show folks what the most severely disabled can do—all forty-one pounds of me," says Smith. For twenty years a rare disease called dermatomyositis turned his life into a living hell.

In 1973 the ravaging disease finally played out and Smith's life began to get brighter. Smith began his higher education at Calhoun Community College, later transferring to the University of Alabama. In 1982 he became the first person in the United States—perhaps in the world—to earn a college degree by telephone. Since then he's topped that with a master's degree.

Apart from becoming educated, given his physical limitations, what can Smith actually do? Using an environmental-control unit, he operates a speaker phone, tape recorder, TV, or anything that plugs in by slightly moving one finger. How far can one finger get you? The staff at Alabama's Huntsville Hospital can answer that one. They hired Smith to telephone the institution's former patients to measure satisfaction with the hospital's services.

Smith's skills don't end with those used in patient follow-up. Working with an engineer, he helped pair sip-and-puff with computer technology to permit individuals who can do little more than breathe to maintain a measure of control over their environments.

If you were analyzing Smith's skills, which abilities would you name? Might they include *asking questions, being methodical, cheerfulness, developing ideas, identifying problems, interpreting, listening, reporting?*

Everyone has skills.

## What Can You Do?

You may not be able to explain what you're good at because you've never taken the time to think seriously about it. If so, you're not alone. Experts say that 90 percent of the people employers interview cannot adequately describe the skills they have to do the job.

Break out of the crowd. Increase your chances of becoming employed. Join the 10 percent of the people who know what skills they have that make them able to do the job.

As you go through some of the several exercises that follow and begin to believe that you do have skills, remember this. Many people think the only question is, "What can I do?" The real question is "What can I do uncommonly well?" Most of us have a few things that we do much better than average. These are the skills you present to an employer.

How did you acquire your skills? You may have developed them formally by taking classes or reading books (for example, learning to *type* or to *build* a bookcase). You may have acquired them informally, trying and failing and trying again until you learned (perhaps *surfing* or *running a photocopy machine*). You may also be naturally skilled or born with a talent for something (such as *painting* or *working with numbers*).

In most cases it doesn't matter how you acquired your skills, it only matters that you did. The same skill may come to one person through formal training, to another informally, and to a third as a natural talent. Or it may be the result of a combination of these. The only time the method of acquiring your skill really matters is when it comes to credentials and professional licensure (for instance, earning a law degree before representing a defendant).

Experts take many approaches to looking at skills. Because skill identification is such an important tool in career planning, we'll tackle two methods of skill exploration. You may prefer one method over another, but completing both methods provides a more detailed snapshot.

These exercises alone will not give you a conclusive picture of your skills. Consider them a starting point, not a finish line in determining your skill assets.

## Method 1: Skills for Success

Job skills can be grouped in several ways. Although the category names are not identical, skills are separated here into three classifications, a system inspired by the career development concepts of Dr. Sidney A. Fine.

1) **Good worker skills** allow you to adapt to situations on *many jobs.*
   Examples:  Getting along with others
   Acting with honesty
   Meeting deadlines

2) **Functional skills** are general skills useful in a *variety of jobs.*
   Examples:  Managing money
   Supervising others
   Operating machinery

3) **Technical skills** apply to a *specific job or occupation.*
    Examples:  Drawing—cartoonist
                  Teeth cleaning—dental hygienist
                  Sewing—tailor

Good worker skills and functional skills frequently are transferable from one job to another. Technical skills may or may not be transferable.

As you fill out the **Skills Survey: Part A, Good Worker Skills,** you may notice similarities between these skills and the personality traits in your earlier survey. There are two reasons for this. First, the meanings of terms frequently are blurred in daily usage. And second, many positive personality traits and characteristics—although not skills in the traditional sense of the word—are seen by employers as basic to the workplace and are included as good worker skills.

---

Take Time Now
to Complete Your
**Skills Survey: Part A**

---

Functional skills are easier to look at by dividing them into three broad groupings.

- **Data**—information, statistics, facts, and ideas
- **People**—any and all kinds
- **Things**—tools, machines, equipment, and materials

All jobs involve data, people, and things, but most jobs emphasize one category over the others. Journalists work with data, childcare specialists work with people, and repairers work with things.

Part B of the **Skills Survey** lists a number of functional skills. As you check your skills on the survey, do you notice more marks in one column—data, people, or things—than in the other two? Do extra items that you add seem mainly to fall in one column? If so, you have new direction in mapping out your future.

---

Take Time Now
to Complete Your
**Skills Survey: Part B**

---

# Skills Survey: Part A

## Good Worker Skills

I possess these skills
(check boxes that apply)

| | | |
|---|---|---|
| ❑ Absorb stress | ❑ Honest | ❑ Relay accurate information |
| ❑ Accept supervision | ❑ Identify alternative action | ❑ Reliable |
| ❑ Alert | ❑ Identify needs | ❑ Remember facts |
| ❑ Ambitious | ❑ Identify problems | ❑ Resourceful |
| ❑ Ask questions | ❑ Imaginative | ❑ Responsible |
| ❑ Assertive | ❑ Independent | ❑ Responsive |
| ❑ Capable | ❑ Industrious | ❑ Results oriented |
| ❑ Cheerful | ❑ Ingenious | ❑ Self-confident |
| ❑ Competent | ❑ Intelligent | ❑ Self-esteem |
| ❑ Complete assignments | ❑ Intuitive | ❑ Self-motivated |
| ❑ Conscientious | ❑ Know how to learn | ❑ Sense of humor |
| ❑ Concerned for others | ❑ Leadership | ❑ Sensitive |
| ❑ Considerate | ❑ Learn quickly | ❑ Serious |
| ❑ Cooperative | ❑ Logical | ❑ Set goals |
| ❑ Coordinate | ❑ Loyal | ❑ Set priorities |
| ❑ Creative thinker | ❑ Manage time well | ❑ Sincere |
| ❑ Deal with ambiguity | ❑ Mature | ❑ Spontaneous |
| ❑ Delegate | ❑ Meet deadlines | ❑ Steady |
| ❑ Dependable | ❑ Methodical | ❑ Strong |
| ❑ Eager | ❑ Modest | ❑ Tactful |
| ❑ Enthusiastic | ❑ Motivated | ❑ Take responsibility |
| ❑ Expressive | ❑ Open minded | ❑ Teamwork |
| ❑ Flexible | ❑ Optimistic | ❑ Tenacious |
| ❑ Follow instructions | ❑ Organized | ❑ Thrifty |
| ❑ Follow through | ❑ Original | ❑ Trustworthy |
| ❑ Friendly | ❑ Patient | ❑ Unpretentious |
| ❑ Get along with others | ❑ Persistent | ❑ Use common sense |
| ❑ Get things done | ❑ Physical strength | ❑ Versatile |
| ❑ Good attendance | ❑ Practical | ❑ Well-informed |
| ❑ Good listener | ❑ Pride in doing a good job | ❑ Well-organized |
| ❑ Good natured | ❑ Problem solver | ❑ Willing to learn new things |
| ❑ Good sense of direction | ❑ Productive | ❑ _____ |
| ❑ Hard worker | ❑ Punctual | ❑ _____ |
| ❑ Helpful | ❑ Realistic | ❑ _____ |

# Skills Survey: Part B

## Functional Skills

I possess these skills
(check boxes that apply)

| Data | People | Things |
|------|--------|--------|
| ❏ Analyzing | ❏ Advising | ❏ Adjusting |
| ❏ Calculating | ❏ Caring for | ❏ Assembling |
| ❏ Classifying | ❏ Confronting others | ❏ Building |
| ❏ Collating | ❏ Consulting | ❏ Calibrating |
| ❏ Comparing | ❏ Coordinating | ❏ Carrying |
| ❏ Compiling | ❏ Counseling | ❏ Crafting |
| ❏ Composing | ❏ Directing | ❏ Cutting |
| ❏ Computing | ❏ Empathizing | ❏ Demonstrating |
| ❏ Coordinating | ❏ Entertaining | ❏ Designing |
| ❏ Copying | ❏ Guiding | ❏ Disassembling |
| ❏ Creating | ❏ Helping | ❏ Driving/Operating |
| ❏ Developing ideas | ❏ Influencing others | ❏ Emptying |
| ❏ Evaluating | ❏ Informing | ❏ Feeding/Offbearing |
| ❏ Examining | ❏ Instructing | ❏ Finishing/Refinishing |
| ❏ Filing | ❏ Interpreting procedures | ❏ Guiding |
| ❏ Gathering | ❏ Leading | ❏ Handling |
| ❏ Interpreting | ❏ Listening | ❏ Loading |
| ❏ Investigating | ❏ Managing | ❏ Manipulating |
| ❏ Managing money | ❏ Mentoring | ❏ Monitoring |
| ❏ Observing | ❏ Motivating | ❏ Moving |
| ❏ Organizing | ❏ Negotiating | ❏ Operating/Controlling |
| ❏ Presenting | ❏ Persuading | ❏ Precision working |
| ❏ Reading | ❏ Serving | ❏ Preparing |
| ❏ Recording | ❏ Speaking/signaling | ❏ Pushing |
| ❏ Reporting | ❏ Supervising | ❏ Regulating |
| ❏ Researching | ❏ Supporting | ❏ Remodeling |
| ❏ Sorting | ❏ Taking instructions | ❏ Repairing |
| ❏ Synthesizing | ❏ Teaching | ❏ Setting up |
| ❏ Transcribing | ❏ Training | ❏ Stacking |
| ❏ Writing | ❏ Treating | ❏ Tending |
| ❏ _____ | ❏ _____ | ❏ _____ |
| ❏ _____ | ❏ _____ | ❏ _____ |

Part C of the survey lists a sampling of technical skills—skills needed for a specific job or occupation. Try on some of these skills. Don't be discouraged if you can't check any of the sample items listed. Unless you're seeking a specific job or occupation requiring one of the sample technical skills, your list probably will be blank. But the samples may help you come up with technical skills you do own that you can add to the list.

> Take Time Now
> to Complete Your
> **Skills Survey: Part C**

## Method 2: Skill Clues from the Past

Method 2 takes a different approach to identifying skills. Here you zero in and write a sort of "This Is Your Life" script to spark memories of yesterday's accomplishments that may lead to future success.

What qualifies as an accomplishment? Previous accomplishments can be anything that you think you did well or you're proud of having done. They need not be monumental but they do have to have been satisfying moments or events in your life. You may want to recruit your family and friends to help you travel memory lane. A few examples are offered to get you started:

- Won ribbon at science fair
- Resisted peer pressure to smoke cigarettes
- Participated in Special Olympics
- Worked backstage in school play
- Graduated with service dog
- Earned money to buy car
- Hooked up VCR correctly on first try
- Organized neighborhood block party
- Learned to type with mouthstick
- Made top salesperson in office
- Operated ham radio station
- Designed more efficient conveyor belt
- Started own business

So far, so easy. Now here's the tricky part. To make valuable a backward glance at your life's accomplishments, analyze the skills used to make the accomplishments happen.

## Skills Survey: Part C

### Technical Skills

I possess these skills
(check boxes that apply)

❑ Acupuncture
❑ Acting
❑ Auto body repair
❑ Auto engine tune-up
❑ Basketball
❑ Blueprint reading
❑ Bookbinding
❑ Bricklaying
❑ Bridge designing
❑ Building inspection
❑ Cabinetmaking
❑ Cake decorating
❑ Carpet installation
❑ Chimney cleaning
❑ Choreography
❑ Clowning
❑ Color analyzing
❑ Computer programming
❑ Cooking
❑ Cost estimating
❑ Costume design
❑ Drawing
❑ EEG procedures
❑ Electrical skills
❑ Elevator repair
❑ Embalming
❑ Eyeglass fitting
❑ Farm equipment repair
❑ Firefighting
❑ First-aid skills
❑ Fishing gear operation
❑ Flower arranging
❑ Flying
❑ Food packing

❑ Framing
❑ Glazing
❑ Hairstyling
❑ Harvesting
❑ Horse breeding
❑ Housekeeping
❑ Hunting
❑ Intelligence gathering
❑ Jewelry making
❑ Landscaping
❑ Legal research
❑ Line installation
❑ Manicuring
❑ Meat inspection
❑ Medicine dispensing
❑ Metalworking skills
❑ Milk processing
❑ Millwright skills
❑ Mine cutting
❑ Motion picture directing
❑ Navigating
❑ Orthodontic appliance
   making
❑ Patternmaking
❑ Pet grooming
❑ Photography
❑ Plastering
❑ Plumbing
❑ Poultry cutting
❑ Precision assembling
❑ Printing press operation
❑ Proofreading
❑ Radar operation
❑ Radio announcing

❑ Real estate appraising
❑ Refereeing
❑ Roofing
❑ Runway modeling
❑ Sailing
❑ Sculpting
❑ Set design
❑ Sewing
❑ Sharpshooting
❑ Sheet-metal skills
❑ Shipfitting
❑ Shoe repair
❑ Solar heater installation
❑ Spacecraft designing
❑ Spinal column adjustments
❑ Surveying
❑ Tax preparation
❑ Teeth cleaning
❑ Telegraph operation
❑ Tilesetting
❑ Timber cutting
❑ Toolmaking
❑ Typesetting
❑ Upholstery
❑ Violin playing
❑ Warehousing
❑ Weaving
❑ Welding
❑ Window dressing
❑ Window washing
❑ Writing advertisements
❑ X-ray machine operation
❑ _____
❑ _____

If, for example, you won a ribbon at your school science fair, a variety of skills came into play. These most likely included: *researching* and *planning* experiment, *recording* data, *writing* report, *designing* and *building* display.

Suppose you graduated with your service dog; then you used another mix of skills. These might have included: *caring for, instructing, leading, listening, motivating, taking instructions, training.*

Maybe you organized a neighborhood block party. This would have called for skills such as: *coordinating, negotiating, instructing, supervising, persuading.*

Breaking down accomplishments into skills isn't something you do every day. If you get stuck, jump start your analysis by reviewing the examples given here and the previous parts of the **Skills Survey.**

Part D of the **Skills Survey** gives you space to list three accomplishments for each age range, but it doesn't matter if you have more than or fewer than three. If the format of the survey doesn't work for you, make your own on a separate sheet of paper. Customize the survey to give you the room to write what you want for age ranges that make sense to you.

Take Time Now
to Complete Your
**Skills Survey: Part D**

## Aptitudes Are Not Skills

When choosing what we can do well, it's important to differentiate between our aptitudes and our skills:

> **Aptitudes**—Things or activities we have the potential to do or perform well that seem to come easily and naturally. These natural talents can be polished and perfected into skills.

> **Skills**—Abilities we currently possess.

Recognizing your aptitudes gives direction to your career search. Remember, we are most likely to succeed at what we like to do. We also tend to enjoy things we do well. Following that line of thinking: If you have an aptitude for something, you probably enjoy doing it; and if you enjoy doing it, you have a greater chance of succeeding at it than if you don't.

To illustrate the relationship between aptitudes and skills, read

# Skills Survey: Part D

## Skill Clues from the Past

| My Life | Accomplishments | Skills Used |
|---|---|---|
| **Ages 6–9** | | |
| *Example:* Hearing loss | learned sign language | memorizing, concentrating |
| 1. _____ | _____ | _____ |
| 2. _____ | _____ | _____ |
| 3. _____ | _____ | _____ |
| **Ages 10–13** | | |
| 1. _____ | _____ | _____ |
| 2. _____ | _____ | _____ |
| 3. _____ | _____ | _____ |
| **Ages 14–17** | | |
| 1. _____ | _____ | _____ |
| 2. _____ | _____ | _____ |
| 3. _____ | _____ | _____ |
| **Ages 18–21** | | |
| 1. _____ | _____ | _____ |
| 2. _____ | _____ | _____ |
| 3. _____ | _____ | _____ |
| **Ages 22–25** | | |
| 1. _____ | _____ | _____ |
| 2. _____ | _____ | _____ |
| 3. _____ | _____ | _____ |
| **Ages 26–29** | | |
| 1. _____ | _____ | _____ |
| 2. _____ | _____ | _____ |
| 3. _____ | _____ | _____ |
| **Ages 30–33** | | |
| 1. _____ | _____ | _____ |
| 2. _____ | _____ | _____ |
| 3. _____ | _____ | _____ |
| **Ages 34–37** | | |
| 1. _____ | _____ | _____ |
| 2. _____ | _____ | _____ |
| 3. _____ | _____ | _____ |

the following anecdotes to see how Rachel's and Mike's aptitudes relate to their skills.

Rachel has an "ear" for music. She can hear a song on the radio, sit down at the piano, and figure out the melody. But she can't read music, doesn't know anything about music theory, and hasn't developed piano technique. To polish and perfect her musical aptitude into a musical skill, Rachel should study music.

Mike, a high school senior, has watched the movie *Top Gun* forty-three times and dreams of being Tom Cruise's wingman. Mike's career counselor asks if he likes math. "I hate it," he says. She asks him about his math grades. "They stink," he says, "but I don't want to be a mathematician—I just want to fly." Mike's counselor explains that mathematics is the key to flying and that pilots must have a higher-than-average aptitude for math. Mike may learn to fly, but he won't be going to Fightertown U.S.A. at Miramar Naval Air Station, San Diego. He lacks the aptitude for mathematics to perfect the high level of math skill needed to be an elite pilot.

Even when you lack an aptitude for a task, you may be able to acquire the necessary technical skills. But to do something exceptionally well, it helps to have both an aptitude for it and the skill to do it. Many people can learn the mechanics of acceptable writing; fewer people have an aptitude to write such terror-filled tales like those Stephen King creates.

For a quick search for your aptitudes, jot down on a piece of paper the school subjects that interested you most—no matter how long ago you left school. If you're still in school, you can use past or present subjects. In another column write the subjects you got the best grades in. Are any subjects in both columns? When you score doubles, it's a safe bet you have an aptitude for the subject.

Keep in mind the difference between aptitudes and skills when it's time to fill out your **Equal-to-the-Task Snapshot No. 5.**

## Sum Up Your Skills

Now count your skills on your **Skills Survey: Parts A, B, C, and D.** When adding up your skills, don't forget to include those you wrote in at the bottom of your four surveys. Do you have more than ten? If you do, it's time to reduce your list again.

Pick the top ten skills you possess *that will help your career.* Don't include skills you hate and don't want to use. Do include aptitudes—if they're important to you—that you think you may be able to develop in the future with training and experience. Put a star next to these items so you'll remember they're "future" skills.

List your skills on your **Equal-to-the-Task Snapshot No. 5.** It really doesn't matter how many you choose from each of the four surveys, as long as they're your top ten skills. If you're having trouble limiting yourself to ten, select the skills that you do much better than average—those most likely to impress a prospective employer.

## MY TOP 10 SKILLS
### Equal-to-the-Task Snapshot No. 5

1._____  6._____

2._____  7._____

3._____  8._____

4._____  9._____

5._____  10._____

## FOCUS ON JOB REQUIREMENT COMPETENCIES

Because individuals with disabilities often face challenges in meeting job requirements, here's a checklist of requirements frequently found in job descriptions. Each identifies an activity, either physical or mental.

The following **Job Requirement Competencies Survey** is an informal awareness exercise that can become ammunition for your job search. The survey asks you to check each job requirement competency you possess. After each competency marked, indicate the level of your ability: satisfactory, above average, or exceptional.

For example, if *balancing* is a competency you own, mark it and note how well you can do it. Check "satisfactory" if you can walk from one end of a room to another without falling. Check "above average" if you can walk along an icy sidewalk. Check "exceptional" if your balancing competency would allow you to walk a skyscraper beam.

Unless you have been professionally evaluated, your self-ratings are subjective. They aren't definitive because you may lack the frame of reference to compare properly your ability levels with those of others. Even so, the exercise adds another view to your self-assessment. Concentrate on the competencies you have—even if you have only a few—rather than on those you do not have.

> Take Time Now
> to Complete Your
> **Job Requirement Competencies Survey**

When you have finished the survey, you will not make an **Equal-to-the Task Snapshot** as you did with the earlier surveys. You will write down *all* of your job requirements on your **Equal-to-the-Task Composite**.

Here's why. The previous surveys on values, interests, personality traits, and skills are designed to help you zero in on what's important to you and to identify special strengths you can sell in the job market. You are making choices.

By contrast, the purpose of the survey on job requirement competencies is to make you more aware of how you are able to deal with physical or mental activities and to help prepare you to sell your competencies in the job market. You may be able to compensate for the lack of one competency with another. As a single illustration, remember how Daryl Smith's *fingering* ability compensates for his lack of *handling* ability at his patient follow-up job with Huntsville Hospital.

## Job Requirement Competencies Survey

| I possess these requirements (check boxes that apply) | | Of requirements I possess, my level of ability is *Satisfactory* *Above Average* *Exceptional* (check columns that apply) | | |
|---|---|---|---|---|
| | | "S" | "AA" | "E" |
| ☐ Balancing | Maintain body equilibrium to prevent falling when standing, crouching, walking, or running on narrow, slippery, or erratically moving surfaces. Or maintain body equilibrium when performing gymnastic feats. | | | |
| ☐ Clerical perception | Perceive pertinent detail in verbal or tabular material. Observe differences in copy, to proofread words and numbers and to avoid perceptual errors in arithmetic computation. | | | |
| ☐ Climbing | Ascend or descend stairs, ramps, ladders, scaffolding, poles, and ropes using feet and legs and often hands and arms. | | | |
| ☐ Color vision | Identify and distinguish colors and shades. | | | |
| ☐ Crawling | Move about on hands and knees or hands and feet. | | | |
| ☐ Crouching | Bend body downward and forward by bending legs and spine. | | | |
| | *(continued)* | | | |

# Job Requirement Competencies Survey *(cont'd.)*

| I possess these requirements<br>(check boxes that apply) | Of requirements I possess,<br>my level of ability is<br>*Satisfactory*<br>*Above Average*<br>*Exceptional*<br>(check columns that apply) | | |
|---|---|---|---|
| | "S" | "AA" | "E" |
| ❑ Depth perception — Three-dimensional vision. See objects or scenes in true relationship. | | | |
| ❑ Feeling — Perceive size, shape, temperature, or texture of objects and materials by touching or handling, particularly with fingertips. | | | |
| ❑ Field of vision — Area that can be seen up and down and to right and left while eyes are fixed on given point. | | | |
| ❑ Finger dexterity — Move fingers rapidly and accurately to work with small objects. | | | |
| ❑ Fingering — Picking, pinching, or otherwise working primarily with fingers (rather than with whole hand or arm as in handling). | | | |
| ❑ Form perception — Perceive detail in objects in pictorial or graphic material. Effectively make visual comparisons of shapes and shadings of figures and widths and lengths of lines. | | | |
| ❑ Handling — Hold, grasp, turn, or otherwise work with hand or hands (fingering involved). | | | |
| ❑ Hearing — Perceive sounds by ear. | | | |
| ❑ Intelligence — General learning ability. "Catch on" or understand instructions, facts, and underlying principles. Reason and make judgments. | | | |
| ❑ Kneeling — Bend legs and come to rest on knee or knees. | | | |
| ❑ Lifting — ❑ **Sedentary**—10 pounds maximum and occasional lifting/carrying such articles as ledgers and small tools. Although sedentary job is one that involves sitting, certain amount of walking and standing often necessary in carrying out job duties. Jobs are sedentary if walking and standing are required only occasionally and other sedentary criteria are met.<br><br>❑ **Light**—20 pounds maximum with frequent lifting/carrying of objects weighing up to 10 pounds. Even though weight lifted may be only negligible amount, job is in this category when it requires walking or standing to significant degree, or when it involves sitting most of time with degree of pushing and pulling of arm and/or leg controls.<br><br>❑ **Medium**—50 pounds maximum with frequent lifting/carrying of objects weighing up to 25 pounds.<br><br>❑ **Heavy**—100 pounds maximum with frequent lifting/carrying of objects weighing up to 50 pounds.<br><br>❑ **Very Heavy**—In excess of 100 pounds with frequent lifting/carrying of objects weighing 50 pounds or more. | | | |
| ❑ Manual dexterity — Move hands easily and skillfully, as in placing and turning motions. | | | |
| ❑ Motor coordination — Coordinate eyes and hands or fingers to perform tasks rapidly and accurately. | | | |
| ❑ Numerical aptitude — Perform arithmetic operations quickly and accurately. | | | |
| ❑ Reaching — Extend hands and arms in any direction. | | | |
| ❑ Spatial aptitude — Look at two-dimensional drawings and think visually of three-dimensional objects. *(continued)* | | | |

## Job Requirement Competencies Survey *(cont'd.)*

| I possess these requirements (check boxes that apply) | | Of requirements I possess, my level of ability is *Satisfactory* *Above Average* *Exceptional* (check columns that apply) | | |
|---|---|---|---|---|
| | | "S" | "AA" | "E" |
| ❏ Stooping | Bend body downward and forward by bending spine at waist. | | | |
| ❏ Talking | Express or exchange ideas by spoken words. | | | |
| ❏ Verbal aptitude | Understand meaning of words and ideas and present them effectively. | | | |
| ❏ Vision accommodation | Adjustment of lens of eye to bring object into sharp focus. Especially important when doing near-point work at varying distances. | | | |
| ❏ Vision acuity, far | Clarity of vision at 20 feet or more. | | | |
| ❏ Vision acuity, near | Clarity of vision at 20 inches or less. | | | |

## LAY OUT YOUR EQUAL-TO-THE-TASK COMPOSITE

Now is the time to bring together all the work you've done in this chapter. Turn back to the snapshots. Using one more round of elimination, cut in half your top ten picks for each snapshot. Within each category, rank each item in importance. The most important number is one, the least important number is five.

- Reduce your top ten work values to five. Rank them.
- Reduce your top ten personal values to five. Rank them.
- Reduce your top ten interests to five. Rank them.
- Reduce your top ten personality traits to five. Rank them.
- Reduce your top ten skills to five. Rank them.

In ranked order, record your five picks from each snapshot on your **Equal-to-the-Task Composite**. Next, as earlier mentioned, record all of your job requirement competencies on your **Equal-to-the-Task Composite**.

> Take Time Now
> to Complete Your
> **Equal-to-the-Task Composite**

# Equal-to-the-Task Composite

| Work Values | Job Requirement Competencies |
|---|---|
| **Work Values** | |
| 1. _____ | 1. _____ |
| 2. _____ | 2. _____ |
| 3. _____ | 3. _____ |
| 4. _____ | 4. _____ |
| 5. _____ | 5. _____ |
| **Personal Values** | 6. _____ |
| 1. _____ | 7. _____ |
| 2. _____ | 8. _____ |
| 3. _____ | 9. _____ |
| 4. _____ | 10. _____ |
| 5. _____ | 11. _____ |
| **Interests** | 12. _____ |
| 1. _____ | 13. _____ |
| 2. _____ | 14. _____ |
| 3. _____ | 15. _____ |
| 4. _____ | 16. _____ |
| 5. _____ | 17. _____ |
| **Personality Traits** | 18. _____ |
| 1. _____ | 19. _____ |
| 2. _____ | 20. _____ |
| 3. _____ | 21. _____ |
| 4. _____ | 22. _____ |
| 5. _____ | 23. _____ |
| **Skills** | 24. _____ |
| 1. _____ | 25. _____ |
| 2. _____ | 26. _____ |
| 3. _____ | 27. _____ |
| 4. _____ | 28. _____ |
| 5. _____ | |

The process of continually whittling down the most important items on your snapshots—and then for a final time on your composite—is valuable in fixing the information in your mind. The process of thinking through your job requirement competencies and transferring that information to the composite also helps cement the information in your mind. A look inside—self-discovery—puts your abilities into perspective, at least at this time in your life.

Now, with your snapshots and composite in hand, are you better able to answer these questions?

- What do I want most from work?
- What is important to me?
- What do I like to do best?
- What are my personality traits?
- What are my skills and aptitudes?
- What is my true ability?
- What am I willing to trade to get what I want most?

Do you feel you have a pretty good handle on your self-assessment? If not, what else can you do?

## FURTHER SELF-ASSESSMENT

If you would like to delve deeper into self-assessment, pick up one of the many good career workbooks on the market. *Creating Careers with Confidence* by Edward Colozzi is a self-paced exercise book that is also produced in braille. John Holland's *The Self-Directed Search* is another popular self-marking test. *Discover What You're Best At: The National Career Aptitude System and Career Directory* by Barry and Linda Gale is an easy-to-use-guide that measures what you can do now (skills) and what you will be able to do in the future if given the opportunity to learn (aptitudes).

If you prefer computers to books, you can use software at home or at high schools, community colleges, four-year colleges, universities, public libraries, and public employment services. Affordable software for personal computers include Crystal-Barclay's *Career Design* and John Holland's *The Self-Directed Search*. Among the most popular institutional offerings are *Discover, Choices, GIS (Guidance Information Systems), C-LECT (Chronicle Guidance), CIS (Career Information System)*, and *SIGI+ (System of Interactive Guidance and Information)*.

Which are the best institutional programs? "Go with the

recommendations of counselors or career technicians at institutions where you are using the service," advises Dr. James Sampson, a nationally renowned computer guidance expert at Florida State University.

Access to computer guidance systems is not readily available to individuals who are visually impaired. Still, the graphics-dependent systems can be valuable if a sighted friend or relative tags along as a reader. Users who are visually impaired can type the answers on the computer keyboard if they're familiar with its layout. If not, they can answer aloud and let their readers key for them.

If you feel you need human help, you may want to enlist the services of a private career counselor. As in any consumer market, beware of charlatans who charge a lot of money for their heavily promoted services. Many reputable colleges and universities offer career testing and counseling services to the general public as well as to their student bodies. Check around to be sure the fee you're quoted is average for your area.

Don't overlook the freebies either. When it comes to career information, the government has lots of it. One place is your state department of vocational rehabilitation. Agency names vary—you might find your state's department listed in the telephone directory under Department of Rehabilitation, Department of Rehabilitative Services, or Office of Vocational Rehabilitation. Most provide testing and counseling. They also provide other vocational assistance to people with disabilities based on each person's individual needs.

You may know that the public employment service offers job listings. But did you know it also may provide free aptitude testing, depending on the area in which you live? The test is called the General Aptitude Test Battery (GATB). Ask for it.

Uncle Sam offers another vocational test—the Armed Services Vocational Aptitude Battery (ASVAB). Although the test is intended for people without disabilities interested in joining the Armed Forces, it is possible for some individuals with disabilities to take the test. How? The Armed Forces makes the ASVAB available as a community service to aid students in career exploration. It is offered through many high schools and community colleges to *any* registered student. If you haven't graduated from high school yet or if you're enrolled at a community college, take the test. It is free.

# LIFE-LONG SELF-ASSESSMENT

The process of self-evaluation is never ending. That's why it's a good idea to open this book every now and then to the **Equal-to-the-Task Composite** and look over your top choices. Are they up to date? Your number one work value today may slip to number four next year. Or your skills may change substantially six months after starting a new job.

Expect some changes in your wants and abilities. Your physical condition may improve or deteriorate. Your values wish list may seem too modest or too demanding once you experience the realities of the marketplace. The change itself isn't as important as how you recognize it, articulate it, and deal with it.

The relative significance of how your abilities fit together as you approach most tasks is well explained by co-founder of the American Coalition of Citizens with Disabilities Dr. Frederick A. Fay, who faces each day with multiple disabilities, quadriplegia complicated by a neurologic disorder:

*It doesn't matter whether you walk on wheels, talk with your hands and hear with your eyes, see with your ears, or communicate with the world with a computer keyboard and modem as I do. What matters is that you consciously keep a contemporary self-portrait in your mind of what you want and what you can do in the world of work.*

This is a part of career management and of the preliminary work needed to keep your resume up to date, ready to market. In an era when job security is elusive, a state of readiness is a very good idea.

# 5

# Making the job fit you

Emmy-winning actress Suzanne Rogers is the beautiful Maggie Horton to millions of NBC-TV "Days of Our Lives" viewers. Eleven years into playing the soap opera character, Rogers awoke one morning unable to speak, smile, or swallow—one side of her face was paralyzed. Diagnosed with myasthenia gravis, a chronic muscle disease that produces weakness and abnormally rapid fatigue, Rogers' thymus gland was removed. As a result of medication, the star's face became bloated and her luxuriant red hair thinned.

What job accommodation did the show's producers provide when Rogers returned to work? A makeup artist? A hairdresser? Certainly, but the real job accommodation Rogers received was a story line of scripts that incorporated her illness into Maggie Horton's character. Her fictional portrayal mirrored her own day-to-day battles—voice weakness, eye drooping, hospitalization. And as Rogers' condition improved, so did Horton's.

"Days of Our Lives" producers made an appropriate and reasonable accommodation in a unique situation. Rogers' experience illustrates that all job accommodations are not prewritten in a master guidebook somewhere, but rather may be the result of the creative efforts of the employer and the individual with the disability.

## JOB ACCOMMODATIONS

"Reasonable accommodation" has become the new disability employment buzz word, but what does it really mean? It means that an employer may be required to modify a task or workplace to accommodate a job-related functional limitation you have as a result of your disability.

Job accommodations are made for:
- New employees
- Employees who are being promoted or transferred
- Employees who—as a result of a new or progressive disability—have acquired functional limitations

When you are a *qualified individual with a disability* and when the *employer is covered* by a statute prohibiting disability discrimination, here is what an employer must do for you.

- *Consider basic elements of the job:* The employer must analyze the job for *essential functions.* (Remember, your best chances may come when the employer has analyzed the job's requirements before you disclose your disability.)

- *Make worker/workplace assessment:* After informing the employer you require an accommodation, the employer must evaluate your job abilities/limitations and potential obstacles at the work site.

- *Engage in mutual consultation:* The employer must informally consult with you in selecting and implementing a *reasonable accommodation.*

- *Offer opportunity to share cost:* When an accommodation proves to be an *undue hardship* on the business, the employer must offer you the option of paying the portion of the accommodation that is judged to be an undue hardship.

(For a refresher on any unfamiliar terms mentioned above, see Chapter 2 on the Americans with Disabilities Act.)

## IDENTIFYING FUNCTIONAL LIMITATIONS

"Functional limitations of employees—including those without disabilities—are accommodated in the workplace everyday," says Gerald Weisman, director of rehabilitation engineering at Rehabilitation Technology Services in Burlington, Vermont.

Perhaps a writer needs an *air-conditioned environment* because her creativity sags when the room temperature hits 80 degrees. Perhaps a plant supervisor needs a *telephone that "remembers" numbers* because she can't. Perhaps a clerk needs a *numerical filing system* because he regularly misfiles documents in an alphabetical filing system. In each of these instances, an accommodation is made for a task not performed well because the person doing it has a functional limitation. Similar types of accommodations are needed for people with disabilities.

William Schwall is a telephone installer for Southwestern Bell in

Little Rock, Arkansas. His functional limitation is a partial loss of hearing. Schwall is able to do the job with the help of cards his clever supervisor had printed: "Please show me what you want me to do." When Schwall arrives at the installation site, he hands a card to the customer along with a message pad to communicate. For instant contact, Southwestern Bell purchased a text telephone (TT) for the main office and a pocket-size TT for Schwall to carry in the field. How does Schwall test a telephone after installing it? He uses a device that translates sounds into light signals.

What you say makes a difference in getting what you want. The starting point in determining a needed accommodation is to define a person's *job-related functional limitations*. Describing an individual as having cerebral palsy, for example, does little to define an appropriate accommodation because the limitations of cerebral palsy vary dramatically. Rather, identifying an individual as *unable to stand*—no matter the cause—is a concrete limitation that can be accommodated.

It really doesn't help much to tell employers in general terms that you have a particular impairment or disability — such as a spinal cord injury. For the purpose of seeking accommodations, it is important to learn to express yourself in words that describe specific functional limitations—such as a *difficulty handling* or the *inability to climb stairs*. The following list will help you use terms that make it easier for the employer to understand your needs. Perhaps there are others you can add.

### TERMS TO HELP IDENTIFY YOUR FUNCTIONAL LIMITATION

| | |
|---|---|
| • attention span | • head, moving |
| • balancing | • hearing, partial loss |
| • bending | • hearing, total loss |
| • carrying | • interpreting data |
| • climbing | • judgment |
| • communication | • kneeling |
| • concentration | • learning |
| • coordination | • lifting |
| • crawling | • lower extremities |
| • crouching | • memory, long-term |
| • fainting | • memory, short-term |
| • feeling | • operating foot pedal |
| • fingering | • perception |
| • grasping | • planning |
| • handling | • pulling |

- pushing
- reaching
- reading
- seizures
- sequencing
- sight, partial loss
- sight, total loss
- sitting
- speech, partial loss
- speech, total loss
- squatting
- stair climbing
- stamina
- standing
- stooping
- task sequencing
- thinking
- upper extremities
- walking
- writing

To make an accommodation really useful, it's valuable to identify the degree of your functional limitation—such as a man *without speech* as opposed to a man with a speech disorder. It is also important to identify whether the limitation is a right-, left-, or both-sided body limitation—for example, a woman with the *inability to grasp with her right hand.* In many cases, multiple limitations need to be accommodated—such as a man who has *long-term memory loss and limited task-sequencing ability.*

**Remember, only functional limitations that affect the essential duties of the position sought need to be considered when making job accommodations.** If you have the limitation of climbing, for instance, and the position you're seeking is an automobile parking attendant where climbing isn't an essential function, that limitation does not need to be addressed.

## EXPLORING TYPES OF ACCOMMODATIONS

Job accommodations may take many forms. Here we'll explore several types of accommodations that an employer may make for an individual with a disability:

- Making workplace facilities accessible
- Modifying work schedules
- Restructuring jobs
- Acquiring or modifying equipment or devices
- Providing qualified support services assistants
- Changing job locations
- Retraining and/or reassigning employees to vacant positions

## Making Workplace Facilities Accessible

Many people benefit from accessible buildings. If you're visually impaired, have difficulty walking or climbing stairs, use a wheelchair for mobility, or are a person of small or short stature, accessibility to workplace facilities is a primary consideration in your employment. Here are examples of modifications employers are making to existing buildings or incorporating into new building designs:

- Reserve extra-wide spaces near building entrances
- Remove shrubbery and signs that obstruct walkways
- Ramp stairs
- Regrade entranceways
- Install wheelchair lifts
- Widen entrance doors
- Install automatic door openers or lever doorknobs to ease opening
- Install brailled or large, raised lettered directional signs and elevator controls
- Install elevators with lowered controls
- Provide accessible restrooms
- Provide accessible break rooms, lunch rooms, and training rooms
- Keep hallways and aisles to the job site clear
- Leave floors bare or install low-pile carpeting

When Lockheed Missiles & Space Company in Sunnyvale, California, hired astrophysicist Michael Munn, "everyone was aware of the disability (limb-girdle muscular dystrophy), but it was not a limitation that affected my job," says Dr. Munn. He was mobile and could still climb steps. Eventually, as his muscular dystrophy progressed, Dr. Munn had to ask the company to remove a step he couldn't get over. Lockheed did it "as fast as you can say Jack Spratt!" Dr. Munn exclaims.

## Modifying Work Schedules

Does a forty-hour work week, a daily nine-to-five schedule, or rush-hour traffic make employment difficult or impossible for you? A simple, yet often overlooked accommodation is modifying a work schedule. An employer may be willing to offer you *part-time work*, a *flexible schedule*, or *time off*:

- Split the position into multiple part-time jobs
- Adjust hours to lessen commuting problems
- Allow rest periods during the day that may be made up at the beginning or end of the day

- Provide a regular schedule for a worker who requires a specific eating or sleeping schedule
- Allow time off for regular medical treatments or therapy
- Permit occasional time off for brief periods of hospitalization

"Sure, there were many accommodations made to let me fit in," says Bill McGrath, a retired computer-software engineer at Eastman Kodak Company in Rochester, New York, who has multiple sclerosis, "but they were just tools to let me do the job." The largest part of McGrath's accommodation was Kodak's commitment. "I was given job assignments that provided the necessary flexibility to attend rehabilitation and medical appointments," he says.

## Restructuring Jobs

Job restructuring may be an appropriate accommodation for almost any functional limitation. If you have a hearing, speech, visual, or mobility impairment or a chronic illness or emotional disorder, you may benefit greatly if an employer can redistribute job functions. In restructuring, a *nonessential* job function that you cannot perform is reworked so you can perform it or is reassigned to another employee or employees, usually in exchange for tasks that you can perform.

Here are some examples of functions that may be able to be reworked or reassigned if you are unable to perform them and they are nonessential to the position:

- Less frequent travel
- Deliver in-house mail
- Computerize records instead of writing
- Telephone work
- Less busy sales region
- Keyboard
- Heavy lifting
- Reschedule morning tasks to afternoon
- File
- Greet visitors
- Drive
- Transcribe dictation

Parkinson's disease keeps Virginia Krohnfeldt from hand writing contracts but not selling real estate. A top-selling Prudential agent in Washington, D.C., Krohnfeldt works as a team with another realtor. "Our skills are very compatible," says Krohnfeldt. "Mary writes the contracts while I do property searches in the computer."

## Acquiring or Modifying Equipment or Devices

When many employers hear "reasonable accommodation" they immediately see dollar signs and visualize elaborate assistive equipment and devices. "Assistive technology ranges from high tech to no tech and costly to cost free," says Dr. John Leslie, Jr., executive vice president of the Cerebral Palsy Research Foundation of Kansas.

Although items may be newly purchased, some the employer currently owns may be modified or added on to to accommodate your specific functional limitation. Your limitation may require a *job site modification* or it may call for an *auxiliary aid*:

- Rearrange files or shelves
- Place brailled labels or tactile cues on shelves
- Provide large-button touch-tone telephone
- Purchase desktop turntable organizer
- Lower postage meter and copy machine
- Provide weighted pens to increase legibility
- Purchase talking calculator
- Replace small knobs and switches with larger, easier-to-grasp handles
- Purchase hand-held or table magnifier
- Install text telephone (TT)
- Organize desks for face-to-face communication
- Provide one-handed typewriter
- Replace voice communication with fax
- Shield unneeded computer keys
- Relocate desk to accessible area
- Provide machines and tools with brailled or notched markings
- Purchase voice-activated dictation machines
- Add braille printer to existing computer

Now may be a good time to refocus your attention on the concept of functional limitations. Accommodations using new or modified equipment or devices that have been made for real people in real jobs are sampled in the chart that begins on the next page.

# Adaptive Solutions
## Using New or Modified Equipment/Devices

| Job Goal | Job-Related Functional Limitations | Accommodation | Approximate Cost |
|---|---|---|---|
| | | **SEEING** | |
| Receptionist | Total loss of vision | Light probe auditorily identifies which telephone lines are ringing, on hold, in use | $45 |
| Police officer | Dyslexia | Tape recorder; secretary types daily reports | $50 |
| Computer operator | Partial loss of vision | Voice synthesizer and software added to existing computer to allow data input and file reading | $1,000 |
| Receptionist | Total loss of vision | Small pressure-sensitive floor mat activates door chime, notifying receptionist of guest's presence | $50 |
| Computer operator | Eye fatigue | Anti-glare computer screen | $39 |
| Data entry operator | Partial loss of vision | Changed desk layout from right to left side | $0 |
| Civil engineer | Dyslexia | Added word processing software with spell check and voice output to existing computer | $1,000 |
| | | **HEARING** | |
| Plant worker | Partial loss of hearing | Telephone amplifier designed to work in conjunction with hearing aids | $24 |
| Medical technician | Total loss of hearing | Timer with indicator light notifies when lab test complete | $100 |
| Foundry plant worker | Partial loss of hearing | Strobe light hardwired into building's emergency alarm system | $40 |
| Laboratory worker | Partial loss of hearing | Vibrating wrist alert system notifies when lab tests complete and warns of emergency alarms | $400 |
| | | **MOBILITY** | |
| Engineer | Mobility impairment | Light installed to alert security guard of needed assistance with high security door | $50 |

*(continued)*

# Adaptive Solutions *(cont'd.)*

| Job Goal | Job-Related Functional Limitations | Accommodation | Approximate Cost |
|---|---|---|---|
| **MOBILITY** *(cont'd.)* | | | |
| Secretary | Mobility impairment | Raised desk using scrap wood blocks with holes bored in them to hold legs stable | $0 |
| Accounting clerk | Mobility impairment | Relocated calculator, telephone, and computer terminal from three separate workstations and organized on single turntable at clerk's workstation | $400 |
| **MANUAL TASKS** | | | |
| Groundskeeper | Grasping, limited use of one arm | Detachable extension arm on rake allows worker to grasp extension handle with limited-use arm and control rake with functional arm | $20 |
| Employment consultant | Limited use of both upper extremities, especially left side | Worker allowed to dictate notes because handwriting them was extremely difficult | $0 |
| Insurance agent | Pronounced limitation in use of hands | Drafting table with tilt top for wheelchair access, page turner, and pressure sensitive tape recorder | $800 |
| Data entry clerk | Handling, operating foot pedal | "No hands" electric copy holder holds document and moves line finder; activate switch with right index finger instead of foot pedal | $230 |
| Clerk | Two large fingers instead of four fingers and thumb, each hand, and very short arms | Strap-on hand stylus to enable typing and large button telephone overlay | $13 |
| Electro-mechanical assembly crew person | Handling and fingering | Rechargeable electric motorized screw driver to reduce repetitious twisting tasks | $65 |
| Clerk | Limited use of hands | Lazy Susan file holder for desk | $85 |

*(continued)*

# Adaptive Solutions *(cont'd.)*

| Job Goal | Job-Related Functional Limitations | Accommodation | Approximate Cost |
|---|---|---|---|
| | | **MANUAL TASKS** *(cont'd.)* | |
| Photographer | Use of one hand | Waist pod (such as used to carry flags) allows camera manipulation with one hand | $50 |
| Seamstress | Carpal tunnel syndrome | Pair of spring-loaded ergonomically designed scissors | $18 |
| Food service worker | Limited use of one hand | One-handed can opener | $35 |
| Numerical data entry | Amputation of left arm above the elbow | Changed workstation layout from left to right | $0 |
| Truckdriver | Limited wrist movement | Special wrist splint and glove designed for skin divers | $50 |
| Sales agent | Use of arms and hands | Automatic page turner and voice-activated tape recorder | $600 |
| Manufacturing assembler | Limited wrist and hand movement | Redesigned workstation, placing shallow parts-storage bins on each side of worker, located at table height | $100 |
| Insurance salesperson | Difficulty holding telephone and writing | Telephone headset | $50 |
| Machinist | Limited manual dexterity, right | Commercially available one-handed center punch | $9 |
| Claim service representative | Weakness and numbness in left arm and hand, some restriction of upper-body movement | Telephone headset, rearranged work and resource materials on desk for right-handed use, shifted desk so worker could see others entering office without changing body position | $100 |
| Photographer | Grasping, fingering | Modifications to camera controls allow worker to push with side of hand or fingers; camera support mounted to wheelchair for stability | $150 |

*(continued)*

# Adaptive Solutions *(cont'd.)*

| Job Goal | Job-Related Functional Limitations | Accommodation | Approximate Cost |
|---|---|---|---|
| **MANUAL TASKS** *(cont'd.)* | | | |
| Plastic tubing inspector | Limited manual dexterity, left | Series of fixtures to hold gauges so worker can perform task with one hand | $200 |
| Sewing machine operator | Inability to operate foot pedal, both legs | Machine foot pedal replaced with pneumatic cylinder, operated by head control; leaves hands free to manipulate garment being sewn | $450 |
| Truckdriver | Inability to operate foot pedal, left leg | Hand control to operate truck clutch | $100 |
| **SEATING** | | | |
| Steno clerk | Need neck support, ability to recline for relief, and armrests to relieve gravitational pull on shoulders | Chair with neck support, arm rests, and recline feature | $399 |
| Barber | Limitation of stamina | Fasten revolving stool to base of barber chair; worker can sit and take load off leg prosthesis | $100 |
| Copy machine operator | Limited movement of spine, difficulty reaching | Height adjustable stool with full back support and foot rest | $350 |
| Secretary | Severe low back pain | Pneumatic height adjustable chair with back support allows worker to move from different-height desk to computer workstation | $300 |
| Data entry operator | Difficulty carrying out tasks because of extremely small size | Pneumatic height adjustable chair with moveable footrest | $300 |
| Cosmetologist | Limited reach | Manual wheelchair with a power-lifting feature allows worker to attain a standing position | $3,000 |

*(continued)*

| Adaptive Solutions *(cont'd.)* | | | |
|---|---|---|---|
| **Job Goal** | **Job-Related Functional Limitations** | **Accommodation** | **Approximate Cost** |
| **LIFTING AND CARRYING** | | | |
| Office cleaning person | Carrying, squatting, bending, and kneeling, primarily right side | Moved mop bucket from a storage closet downstairs to an upstairs location closer to water source and cleaning site; added rubber hose extension on water faucet so bucket can be filled with one hand | $2 |
| Process engineer | Paralyzed right arm | Pneumatic mechanism to lift and tilt cart so scraps of polystyrene can be raked with one hand into throat of granulator | $400 |
| Television service technician | Limited strength in legs | Free-standing electronic platform lift to raise and lower television sets | $450 |

# Providing Qualified Support Services Assistants

If you have a visual, hearing, speech, or mobility impairment, the job accommodation that enables you to work may be a person—a qualified support services assistant. You may need a *reader* or an *interpreter*. You may need a driver if you have limited mobility or if you are blind.

Sometimes assistants are needed on a daily basis. Other times they are needed only during the initial period of job adjustment and at large meetings or classes. Fellow workers may be able to fill the role of reader or driver when needed. Some companies offer free sign language classes during lunch periods so interested employees can more easily communicate with co-workers who are hearing impaired and speech impaired.

An assistant must *assist* you in performing your job—such as driving you to work and on calls if you're an insurance salesperson. If an assistant performs the essential functions of the job—such as driving you around town to make deliveries if you're a delivery person—the assistant is actually doing your job rather than assisting you.

Here are some examples of the types of support services assistants that an employer may be able to provide:

- Interpreter at interviews, training sessions, company meetings, and conferences

- Hearing employees to take notes during meetings
- Travel assistant on occasional business trips
- Part-time interpreter
- Reading assistants
- "Buddy" to alert to an emergency
- Page turner
- Co-worker to drive to and from work
- Employee volunteers to learn how to carry should it be necessary in an emergency
- Full-time reader

Phifer Wire Products factory in Tuscaloosa, Alabama, provided Ivan Fields, a screen weaver who is deaf, with an interpreter during training. The company also requires Fields and other plant employees who are deaf to wear special red shirts. Why? To warn fellow workers that they can't hear the horns and bells of oncoming equipment.

## Changing Job Locations

A very attractive accommodation option that may enable you to perform a job is a change of work location. If you have a mobility or a visual impairment, changing to *another business location* or *telecommuting* may be your ticket to employment:

- Allow to perform telemarketing work from home
- Permit to work at company office closest to public transportation line
- Hire to work at home, writing company policy and procedure manuals
- Change job location from downtown office to satellite office nearer home
- Provide computer and modem to input data at home and transmit it to the office over telephone lines
- Hire rehabilitation center resident to telecommute

On days that Harry Chandler, a computer programmer, can't get to his Chicago office, he works at home. Chandler, who is paralyzed as a result of a body-surfing accident, is one of several Allstate Insurance Company employees who has the option of working at home on a personal computer that dials into the company's mainframe network. Chandler isn't home alone.

California's Roxanne J. Cox-Drake put 300,000 miles on her Jeep Cherokee in a six-year period of working as an information services manager for Southern California Edison, the area's energy utility. Heaven knows what stress units she tallies running the roads on a 120-mile roundtrip commute from home in Moreno Valley to her job in Rosemead.

Most people, like Roxanne Cox-Drake, with jobs in Los Angeles or its most crowded suburbs, cannot afford to buy a home close to work. She says some days it has taken her three hours to get home. Her ordeal is being eased by the nation's first telecommuting center, an 8,100-square-foot building in Riverside County ten minutes from Cox-Drake's home and seven minutes from where her four children are in daycare.

Cox-Drake's company is trying a new arrangement that will allow her to work at the Riverside center one day a week. Other companies are expected to join in relocating some workers in the telecommuting center as a way to reduce freeway traffic and air pollution in a region where businesses are subject to fines if their workers drive too many miles to their work sites.

The telecommuting center is only one reflection of the home working arrangements made possible by the advent of the personal computer and related technology a decade ago. What's driving the trend, says Thomas E. Miller, vice president of Link Resources, a consulting firm in Manhattan, is dual-career families, particularly those with children, who prefer to work at or near home. Link believes that by the year 2000, at least eleven million people (of the 150 million working Americans) will work at home by electronic link.

But working at home—as an employee, not an entrepreneur—is more easily desired than accomplished. Only about 5 percent of the work force has managed to do so thus far.

The vast majority of home workers are managerial, professional, technical, sales, or administrative people. Only a small percentage are precision production, repair, service, or machine operators.

The companies most apt to hire home workers are either very large corporations or very small companies. In *Work-at-Home Jobs,* the authors, Joyce Lain Kennedy and Lynie Arden, say that information-intensive industries—such as banks, insurance companies, publishers, software developers, and even retail companies—are prime candidates because so much of their work is done via computer and telephone.

If you decide that you want to make your mark in the business world from your home, a good place to start finding job leads is your state department of vocational rehabilitation.

Some of the best opportunities are computer related. Popular ways computers are used to make money at home are typesetting, bookkeeping, writing, desktop publishing, information research, work processing, mailing list services, customer programming, data entry and processing, and computer consulting.

Lynie Arden's *The Work-at-Home Sourcebook* includes information on hundreds of companies nationwide that use homeworkers. Dozens of job categories are included and are cross-indexed by location.

Advertising is another source of job leads. But here a word of caution. Beware of envelope stuffing schemes and other scams where work at home is concerned.

If you read the envelope stuffing ads carefully, you'll see that the details of how you can make money are fuzzy. To lower your guard, many of the frauds advertise that "You may have been ripped off before by false schemes, but this is different."

Don't you believe it. The last time the Council of Better Business Bureaus investigated randomly selected advertisements promoting envelope stuffing schemes was in 1980, but all fifty-five cases—think of it, all fifty-five!—were found to be deceptive. Most commercial envelope stuffing is done by machine today.

Other ploys revolve around crafts—such as toys, plaster statues, and artificial flowers. In most cases you make the products and sell them to the advertiser. Of course, you must pay for materials and instruction in advance. The strange thing is that your work is never up to snuff. You receive a form letter telling you that your work doesn't cut it, that it isn't up to the company's "high standards," and that no payment will be forthcoming.

"Work-at-home schemes have been around a long time, and no doubt those who run them will continue to try to victimize persons most in need of additional income," says Dianne Ward, the Council of Better Business Bureaus' director of public affairs in Arlington, Virginia. "It may be a scheme we've heard of before, or a more creative hybrid. Con artists continue to come up with new angles and twists to overcome common-sense objections." The deceptions you may encounter are limited only by the fertile imagination of grifters who prey on those who can least afford to lose money.

"Look for the *generic characteristics* of a scam," advises Ward. "The red flag should go up if an advertisement promises a **very healthy income**, if not huge profits, for work done **in the comfort of your own home** where **little or no experience** is required. Look out for ads with an implied, if not outright promise, of a guaranteed market—and no way for you to lose. Take care if you're asked to **pay something up front**."

If you're looking into a work-at-home offer and you think it passes the generic characteristics test, Ward says to ask yourself: "If their idea is so great and can make so much money, why would they be foolish enough to let anyone in on it?"

Suppose you find an advertisement that passes the generic characteristics. Call your Better Business Bureau, your state or local department of consumers affairs, or your post office mail fraud inspector and check it out.

Finding a job to do at home remains a vexing problem for many. And although the forecast for work-at-home opportunities is generally hazy, the cloud of air pollution may come with a silver lining. Because of worsening smog and congestion in many metropolitan areas, employers may soon have to resort to a degree of telecommuting. Good news for workers with limited mobility.

## Retraining and/or Reassigning Employees to Vacant Positions

*Retraining* and *reassignment to a vacant position* are two job accommodations available to employees but not to applicants. If you are working and you become injured or ill, when you're ready to return to work you may be able to step right back into your current position.

If, because of your injury or illness, you're not able to pick up where you left off, you may need to be retrained in the same job functions you were performing before the injury or illness occurred. Your employer should do this as long as the retraining does not cause an undue hardship to the business. Another possibility is that—even with a reasonable accommodation—you can no longer perform the essential functions of your current job. In that case, alternative job placement options must be fully explored before you can be medically terminated.

*The law states that you are only eligible to be reassigned to those jobs for which you are a qualified individual. And the only alternative placement positions that you will be considered for are those that are vacant—or will be vacant within a reasonable amount of time.*

Is an employer required to reassign you to a position in the same class or at the same salary level as your current job? No, you may be transferred to an equivalent position, assigned to a lower-graded position, or given a position at a higher grade if you are qualified. The salary and benefits of the new position will apply to you as it would to any other employee changing positions with your employer. The following examples illustrate:

- A librarian who now uses a wheelchair as a result of a car accident is reassigned from the music department on the second floor to the reference department on the first floor. The building does not have an elevator and it would be an undue hardship on the employer to install one.
- A line installer who is paralyzed as a result of a fall from a telephone pole is promoted to a customer service position.
- A senior flight attendant for a major airline transfers to a reservation agent position after an illness resulting in a mobility impairment. She takes a salary cut but keeps her travel benefits.
- A toll collector who has a closed head injury is retrained for his current position.
- A long-distance truckdriver for a food chain is no longer able to ride the big rigs on long runs because of kidney disease. He is advanced and retrained as a truck dispatcher, coordinating the movement of trucks and freight between cities.

A motorcycle racing accident grounded Pacific Bell maintenance splicing technician Chuck McAvoy. After ten weeks of hospitalization and rehabilitation, McAvoy, of Rancho Cordova, California, was ready to return to work. "I looked around the company for a job that I could do from a wheelchair," he says. Spotting job openings in a newly formed department, McAvoy put in for a transfer. "I passed the qualification test, completed twelve weeks of training, and began a new job as testing technician in the special services department."

## FINDING ADAPTIVE SOLUTIONS

No two individuals with disabilities are alike—nor are their abilities and disabilities alike. Add occupations and specific positions to the mix and you have unique worker-job situations.

That's why, generally speaking, when seeking adaptive solutions to functional limitations it's a good idea for *you* to assume a major portion of the responsibility, rather than placing the entire burden on the employer. No one knows better than you your job skills and functional limitations. If you're a qualified applicant, you should also know the general requirements of the occupation and of the position. As you assess the situation, the employer's input will be valuable for information such as job specifics and equipment already owned.

Is it ever advisable *not* to develop the job accommodation game plan yourself? Yes, when the employer wants to be the coach. Never attempt to seize control when it's clear that the employer has definite ideas about how an accommodation may be made.

There will be instances when you and the employer want help coming up with appropriate and reasonable accommodation alternatives. To whom do you turn? Job accommodation professionals are your first resort.

### Job Accommodation Network (JAN)

If you're deaf and you want to be a meter reader, a mail carrier, or a door-to-door surveyor, for example, but the employer is worried about an increased risk of dog bites, Larry Littleton's adaptive solution may work for you. Littleton advanced to a job as a meter reader with Southern California Edison Company with the assistance of a small device that attaches to his waist. The device registers sound vibrations—including canine movements—in the immediate area, which Littleton in turn feels through another small device on his wrist. (Still with Southern California Edison Company in Santa Barbara, California, Littleton has been promoted to energy services representative.)

Good for Littleton, but how would you find out about his adaptive solution—or any other solution you may want to copy? The same way Littleton discovered it—call the Job Accommodation Network (JAN) in Morgantown, West Virginia. JAN was created in 1984 by the President's Committee on Employment of People with Disabilities, located in Washington, D.C., and is an international information, referral, and consulting network. Who can access the JAN network? Rehabilitation professionals, employers, employees with disabilities, and job applicants with disabilities can call for individualized accommodation solutions.

When you call JAN, a consultant gathers information about the employer's operation, the job, and you. The consultant makes an assessment of your situation and searches JAN's computer database—of thousands of job accommodations—for practical ideas to enable your hiring, retraining, or promotion.

JAN Project Manager Barbara Judy says that "70 percent of the calls we receive result in the placement or retention of someone with a disability. More often than not, we can answer the question while the caller's on the phone. But if, for example, we have to research a product to see if it's still being made, we try to get back with the answer within twenty-four hours."

JAN is not the only job accommodation expert in the field—but it is the most comprehensive resource currently available. The price can't be beat either—all services are free, including the telephone call.

### Disability-Specific Assistance

Other national organizations are more disability specific in the accommodations assistance they provide. AT&T National Special Needs Center in Parsippany, New Jersey, offers help with assistive devices for individuals with speech and hearing impairments. The National Center on Employment of the Deaf in Rochester, New York, serves the hearing-impaired community, and the Braille Institute of America in Los Angeles offers specialized assistance to individuals who are visually impaired.

### Cross-Disability Assistive Devices

Clearinghouses with extensive databases on cross-disability assistive devices are certain to increase as the field of adaptive technology explodes. "RESNA is the cream of assistive technology," says Dr. John Leslie, Jr. of the Cerebral Palsy Research Foundation of Kansas. Located in Washington, D.C., RESNA's initials are no longer an acronym, but the complete name of the organization. ABLEDATA, another clearinghouse on assistive products, located in Newington, Connecticut, should also be on your "must contact" list.

### Computer-Based Accommodations

Information on computer-based accommodations for solving specific hardware and software problems is available from IBM National Support Center for Persons with Disabilities in Atlanta. You can also contact Apple Computer's Worldwide Disability Solutions Group in Cupertino, California.

### Regional Level Assistance

The National Institute on Disability and Rehabilitation Research of the U.S. Department of Education in Washington, D.C., has established ten regional centers to provide training and technical assistance on ADA. The Regional Disability and Business Accommodation Centers grantees are designed to build a partnership between the disability and business communities. Check Appendix A3 to find the ADA Technical Assistance Program in your region, and contact them directly to find out what services they offer.

### State Level Assistance

At the state level, most agencies that serve individuals with disabilities have staff specialists trained to help their clients enter or re-enter the work force. Contact the governor's committee on employment of people with disabilities (the state counterpart to the President's Committee), the state vocational rehabilitation agency, and the public employment service office. Keep in mind that states use different terms for these agencies. Check the state government section of your telephone directory for terms your state uses and Appendix A5 for Governors' Committees.

The *Technology-Related Assistance for People with Disabilities Act of 1988* provides for the establishment of consumer responsive projects in each of the fifty states and territories of the United States. The purpose of these projects is to facilitate the acquisition of assistive technology for all people with disabilities. The National Institute on Disability and Rehabilitation Research of the U.S. Department of Education in Washington, D.C., administers the program.

**Local Level Assistance**

Need more resources for job-finding help? Locally, check for a mayor's committee on employment of people with disabilities. Independent living centers, which offer a variety of employment services, are also great sources, as are occupational therapy departments at rehabilitation hospitals.

## FINANCING JOB ACCOMMODATIONS

Many accommodations are surprisingly easy and inexpensive. A recent nationwide Louis Harris study conducted for the International Center for the Disabled in New York reports that 81 percent of top managers say that the average cost of employing a worker with a disability is about the same as the cost of employing a worker without a disability.

"Eighty-eight percent of the changes that firms make to accommodate employees with disabilities cost less than $1000," says Barbara Judy of JAN, "and of those, 31 percent cost absolutely nothing."

"It's interesting to note that these figures are pre-ADA (Americans with Disabilities Act)," Judy says. "They're based on the Rehabilitation Act when employers had to make physical changes to buildings to get people in to employ them. *Now ADA says physical changes must be made for public access. Employers who operate public places will already have accomplished access, which will lower future job accommodation costs.*"

Another study of job accommodation costs, done by Berkeley Planning Associates in Oakland, California, reaches virtually the same conclusions as JAN's—except the Berkeley study reports that half of the accommodations cost nothing.

If you need a job accommodation, by law most employers are required to provide it for you. But realistically, you may put yourself

| JAN<br>Job Accommodations Study | |
|:---:|:---:|
| **Cost** | **Percent** |
| 0 | 31% |
| under $50 | 50% |
| under $500 | 69% |
| under $1000 | 88% |

**Note:** Percentages do not total 100%; aggregates are most useful as educational tools.

Based on the *Job Accommodation Network Evaluation Survey,* 1987.

at a disadvantage if you ask the employer to part with big bucks for the privilege of hiring you. Put yourself in the interviewer's chair. If an applicant asked you to purchase equipment that costs many times over the salary for the job sought, what would you do? You'd probably look hard for a reason to disqualify that applicant and move on to someone else.

To encourage an employer to break open the checkbook, look for available sources of financial assistance to pay for appropriate and reasonable job accommodations. Here are some money wells you may be able to tap.

### Agency Assistance

State and local vocational rehabilitation agencies are good sources of both assistance in providing successful accommodations and in paying for some of them. Agencies dealing with specific disabilities, such as a state commission for the blind and visually impaired, should also be contacted for assistance.

### Vendor Discounting

Do you know that you can get a discount on equipment purchased through some vendors because you have a disability? You can—and it's important to bring that to an employer's attention.

Suppose you tell an employer that as an accommodation for

your visual impairment you need an optical character reader (OCR)—which converts typed text into computer language. Since many employers—including those without workers who are visually impaired—use OCRs, the employer may have some idea of the retail price of this equipment. What if the employer wants an OCR but hasn't purchased one because they're too expensive? Make it known that the employer may be able to buy the OCR at a substantially reduced cost because of your disability. Take advantage of this opportunity to turn a possible negative into a positive by saying: *To get a large discount the equipment must be used by a worker with a disability, but the OCR would actually be available for the entire company's use.*

## Health Insurance Benefits

Some health insurance companies cover communication systems and other assistive devices as a benefit. Ask your insurance representative what your policy covers. Don't be put off too easily. If you're told the equipment you need isn't covered in your policy, ask for the decision in writing so you have a basis on which to challenge the negative response.

## IRS Tax Incentives

Before totaling the available accommodation resources, seek help from your favorite uncle—Uncle Sam. The Internal Revenue Service has three business tax incentives to encourage employers to hire workers with disabilities: 1) a deduction for the cost of making facilities and vehicles accessible; 2) a tax credit to small businesses providing job accommodations; and 3) a tax credit for employers who hire individuals with disabilities. Tactfully mention this financial benefit to employers—most relish getting any kind of break from the IRS. (Call the IRS for a copy of the *Tax Information for Persons with Handicaps or Disabilities* pamphlet.)

## Employee Assistance

Finally, as part of reasonable accommodation, the employer must allow you the opportunity to pay for the portion of a job accommodation that proves undue hardship to the business. See Chapter 2 for suggestions on how to broach this topic with the employer.

## Loans

What do you do if the employer says you can have the job if you pay for the accommodation, or a portion of it, yourself—but you don't have the money? You may want to consider a loan. Once you start banking paychecks, you can pay it back in a lump sum or in monthly installments.

Compare loan fees and interest rates at local banks, savings and loan institutions, and credit unions. Don't overlook Computer-Assisted Technology Services (CATS), a program of the National Easter Seal Society. CATS is the first national loan fund to help people with disabilities buy computer-assistive and other technologies that enable them to work.

## GETTING IN THE TEAM SPIRIT

As you discuss reasonable accommodation with an employer, it's only fair to differentiate between accommodations that are necessities and those that are luxuries.

If you use a wheelchair for mobility, for example, you may decide that it's a necessity to have access to a restroom, the lunch room, and the library, but that access to the photocopy room and the conference room is not critical. You may also postpone requesting a long, short bookcase to replace the seven-foot-tall bookcase currently in the office.

An approach that worked for Cherrie Handy Pomerantz, a program specialist in the corporate human resources department at National Medical Enterprises in Santa Monica, California, was to start out supplying her own items. "When I joined NME, I brought in all my own adaptive equipment," says Pomerantz, who is blind. "Within six months, the company had provided me with the basic tools that anyone in my position would have, as well as a speech synthesizer to permit me to use the computer."

Another smart strategy to accommodation is waiting until you're on the job to assess your needs. After working in a position for a week or two, it may be clearer which items belong on your need list and which on your want list. Unfortunately, this opportunity won't be available often since most employers will need to know up front what the accommodation will cost to see if it passes the reasonable test.

## FINDING A WAY

Robbie Thomas, who uses a wheelchair for mobility, teaches physical education at Parkridge Elementary School and coaches varsity soccer at Stafford Senior High School in Stafford, Virginia. Isn't being a wheelchair-user a disadvantage for a PE teacher? Not for Thomas. He's always in the heat of the action, playing sports alongside his students. Thomas thinks of his wheelchair as an advantage because it allows him to see eye-to-eye with his young charges, creating a greater intimacy than if he were standing.

"Don't limit yourself," says Thomas, who has no feeling or movement in his right leg and very limited use of his left leg as a result of a car accident when he was a teenager. "There's always an alternative way of doing something," Thomas says, "If you can't walk, you use a wheelchair. If one method of teaching doesn't work, switch to another. It's the same for any occupation."

Functional limitations that initially appear as insurmountable as the Great Divide can many times be reduced to a molehill with reasonable accommodation. Dr. I. King Jordan, president of Gallaudet University in Washington, D.C., puts it like this:

*Deaf people can do anything but hear.*

# 6

# Job clans: understanding them can help you make a great alternative career choice

By knowing more about occupations than the average person, you'll also know when it's realistic to back off and say, "Okay, this occupation is out of my range, but I am going to look for a related occupation that I can do."

Forgoing your first choice of careers is not necessarily a bad thing, says Illinois State University counselor educator Dr. David L. Livers, an acknowledged authority on career selection. "Second or third career choices often prove to be more satisfactory than initial choices made for the wrong reasons," says Dr. Livers.

"Harry, a young man who came to our university center for counseling, has cerebral palsy," Dr. Livers explains. "Harry was fascinated by the glamour of becoming a sports announcer, but his speech was severely impaired. Believing it to be an inappropriate choice, we suggested he examine the realities for himself. We turned down the audio on a televised football game and asked Harry to record his own play-by-play announcing. Upon hearing his tape, Harry realized he lacked the verbal skills to compete with sportscasting professionals. After researching related occupations,

Harry, who is adept with numbers, discovered the occupation of sports statistician. Today Harry says he's elated with his choice, that combining the world of sports and numbers opened vistas far wider than merely calling the plays."

You say you have a dream occupation in mind, and you don't want to give it up because it's "perfect for you"?

"The notion of the 'right career' is a myth," says Dr. Livers. "Each of us would be equally happy in a half-dozen or more occupations. It's a good thing, too, because we are changing jobs and occupations more rapidly than ever as technology creates new opportunities and retires old ones."

## UNDERSTANDING JOB FAMILIES AND CAREER CLUSTERS

To make the study of thousands of occupations a more manageable task, they generally are grouped into career clusters and subdivided into job families. For example, **transportation** is a career cluster; within the cluster are the job families of *highway transport, rail transport, aviation transport, pipeline transport,* and *water transport.*

Each job family includes entry-level, skilled, technical, paraprofessional, and professional occupations in what is sometimes called a career ladder. In the *legal occupations* job family, for example, we find general office clerk, legal secretary, paralegal, and lawyer, to mention a few.

Job families and career clusters are a way to help you find what you want. An analogy might be if you entered an office with papers strewn everywhere—as if a tornado had blown through. It would take luck and time to locate what you sought. But imagine that same office after a clean-up crew neatly categorized all the papers into easily accessible files. You could go straight to the data and pull it out.

Think of occupational relationships like this: job families include immediate family members such as brothers and sisters; whereas career clusters include not only brothers and sisters, but also cousins, aunts, and uncles.

As Dr. Livers notes, job families and career clusters make career selection easier for everyone, but for people with disabilities they're invaluable. If, because of limited mobility, you cannot be an outside sales representative, perhaps you can be an inside sales representative. If you cannot sustain adequate education to become an oral surgeon, perhaps you can become a dental

# Career Ladders:
# The Path to Your Future

There are many different kinds of career ladders, depending upon your job family. Illustrated below is a general ladder in the administrative area. The timing between steps in the ladder varies by the individual, and most people, of course, never reach the top rung but find a level at which they feel comfortable in their job.

**Chief Executive Officer.** Top official in organization. Faces a variety of competing pressures from inside and outside (clients, government, employees, owners, competition, etc.).

**Executive.** Directs teams of workers. Has responsibility for personnel, budget, and production of units directed. Under considerable pressure to improve performance.

**Manager.** Coordinates activities of a number of units and individuals, generally in a specialized area. Makes general work assignments and follows up.

**Supervisor.** Responsible for work of a small team or branch, often works alongside of others. Performance is evaluated upon how well subordinates handle their jobs.

**Senior Professional/Master Craftsworker.** An expert in area. May work independently with little supervision. Often called upon to provide technical support for others.

**Professional/Journeyworker.** Fully trained and productive worker. Expected to accept responsibility for tasks and to carry them out with a minimum of supervision. Many careers plateau here, go no further.

**Junior Professional/Senior Apprentice.** Assigned individual responsibilities but still highly supervised. Increasingly expected to assume a full work load. Carefully evaluated.

**Entry Level/Trainee/Apprentice.** In a learning mode. First assignments combine doing with learning. Closely supervised and frequently evaluated.

laboratory technician. If you do not have the stamina to become a creative writing teacher, perhaps you can become a script reader.

"When you need to veer off in another direction, start with the job family you have targeted," says Dr. Livers. "See if any 'brother' or 'sister' occupations will work for you. If the family doesn't include a suitable occupation, move to the larger career cluster and look around for 'cousin', 'aunt', and 'uncle' occupations."

Your strategy is clear: If you cannot zig, perhaps you can zag.

## EXAMPLES OF USING JOB FAMILIES WHEN YOUR FIRST CHOICE OF CAREERS ISN'T POSSIBLE

We'll start with *aviation*. No matter how badly a person who is blind wants to be a commercial pilot, he or she isn't going to be able to make it a career. Following the hypothetical situation in which you're blind and your first choice of careers is pilot, here's how you'd search for a closely related career. Run down the list of occupations in the *aviation* job family of the **transportation** career cluster, asking yourself if you are able to perform the jobs—with or without reasonable accommodation. Your choice of answers may be "no," "probably not," "possibly," and "yes." Suppose the following are your responses.

### CAN I BE A:

| | |
|---|---|
| pilot? | No |
| air traffic controller? | No |
| flight attendant? | Probably not |
| airport ground equipment supervisor? | Possibly |
| aircraft mechanic? | Possibly |
| reservation agent? | Possibly |
| airport manager? | Possibly |
| aircraft company president? | Yes |
| aviation academy president? | Yes |

After answering whether or not you may be able to perform in each occupation given the disability of blindness, examine the occupations to which you gave any answer except "no." Do any of these occupations interest you? Do you have an aptitude for or skill in any of these occupations? Even though you won't be flying in the pilot's seat, you may be able to pursue a career in the *aviation* job family.

Let's try another example. Suppose your target career is professional football player and you have a lower-limb amputation. Run down the list of occupations in the *sports* job family of the **hospitality and recreation** career cluster, asking yourself if you are able to perform these jobs—with or without reasonable accommodation. The following may be your responses.

### CAN I BE A:

| | |
|---|---|
| professional football player? | No |
| sports coach? | Yes |
| time keeper? | Yes |
| equipment manager? | Possibly |
| athletic trainer? | Possibly |
| athletic director? | Yes |
| referee/umpire? | Probably not |
| pro sports scout? | Yes |

If you find an occupational match in this group, you may be able to pursue a sports career even when you're not physically running the ball.

Some people merely make slight adjustments in their choice of careers—such as Dr. Charles Ward, whose first career pick was to be a large animal veterinarian and whose second pick was to be a small animal veterinarian. Ward, who held a bachelor's degree in mammalian physiology and had completed his second year of veterinary college, was working during the summer for a veterinarian with an equine practice when he fell from a tree and broke his neck. In his own words, "It blew me away for a while."

After two years of physical rehabilitation, Ward returned to school and earned a doctorate in veterinary medicine. Although his first choice was treating horses, the animals' size, overpowering physical strength, and concern for his personal safety put that goal out of reach. That's when Ward turned to making house calls, in a wheelchair, to minister to small companion animals. Today Ward owns a thriving practice in Carrboro, North Carolina, with two veterinary hospitals that provide everything from emergency treatment to grief counseling.

## FIRST CAREER, NEXT CAREER

When an individual's disability progresses or when a person without a disability becomes a person with a disability, things change. But change doesn't always mean you must jump tracks and catch a career train going in another direction. It may be possible to transfer to a closely related occupation in the same job family that calls for abilities used in your previous occupation.

Suppose a surgeon is losing her sight. Because of her new visual limitations, she has lost her ability to be a surgeon. She has *not* lost her ability to be a doctor, counseling other doctors on surgical procedures or consulting on patient cases. Nor has she lost her ability to use her expertise in writing for medical journals.

A roofer has arthritis. The inflammation in his low back has become so painful he is unable to carry equipment and material or to bend for long periods. He has lost his ability to continue as a roofer. But he may have the ability needed to become an estimator for a roofing contractor.

A concert violinist's left arm is amputated as the result of cancer. He may be able to be a composer or an arranger. He may make a great teacher or music therapist.

As mentioned earlier, a number of job families make up a career cluster—that's what we'll look at now.

## A SIMPLE SYSTEM OF CAREER CLUSTERS

Among several commonly encountered career clustering systems, the one chosen for this chapter is found in many educational settings. More complex ways to identify alternative occupations in a career cluster exist, but they defy brief explanation. Many occupational capsules include a section that describes related occupations. A career counselor can help you with occupational grouping systems found in various guides to worker trait groups and in such books as *Occupational Outlook Handbook, Standard Occupational Classification Manual,* and *Dictionary of Occupational Titles.*

In the clustering system that follows, each occupation has specific skills. At first glance the relationships may not be self-evident, but a breakout of the skills and requirements for each occupation would reveal why they are related in some way.

Here's a mini-sampling of the hundreds (and sometimes thousands) of occupations found in each career cluster:

## Agriculture
## (including Agribusiness)
agricultural economist
agricultural research chemist
beekeeper
dairy technologist
farm appraiser
farm manager
florist
food technologist
greenhouse superintendent
irrigation engineer
soil scientist
veterinarian

## Business and Office
accountant
administrative assistant
computer operator
credit officer
human resources director
immigration attorney
insurance sales agent
job retraining specialist
legal secretary
paralegal
systems analyst
technical services manager

## Communication and Media
camera operator
critic
electronic communications
    technician
foreign language teacher
interpreter
newspaper syndicate executive
phototypesetter
proofreader
recording engineer
special events director
television reporter
video-taping service owner

## Construction
architectural drafter
building trades union leader
cabinetmaker
civil engineer
construction engineering
    professor
construction project manager
custom home builder
heavy equipment operator
pipefitter
sandblaster
solar heating installer
surveyor

## Consumer and Home Economics
Better Business Bureau
    manager
cafeteria food operations
    manager
childcare service owner
customer service
    representative
fashion designer
food photography stylist
home economics instructor
nutritionist
preschool teacher
product information manager
retirement planner
test kitchen researcher

## Environment and Natural Resources
## (including Marine Science)
astronomer
chemical engineer
environmental physicist
exterminator
fisher
forestry technician
marine animal trainer
oil company executive
seismologist
solar energy engineer
timber buyer
wind energy systems engineer

## Fine Arts and Humanities
actor
archaeologist
art dealer
cartoonist
cinematographer
comedian
creative writing teacher
film editor
historian
musical instrument maker
photographer
special effects technician

## Health
cardiologist
child abuse therapist
dialysis technician
emergency medical technician
hospital administrator
medical assistant
medical laboratory technician
oral surgeon
pharmacist
radiologic technologist
registered nurse
sonographer

## Hospitality and Recreation
caterer
convention manager
cruise director
lifeguard
professional athlete
restaurant manager
sports coach
stunt performer
theme park manager
tour guide
travel agency owner
youth program director

## Manufacture and Repair
computer games manufacturer
computer service technician
farm equipment mechanic
fiber-optics researcher
laser technician
materials manager

mechanical engineer
planning and scheduling
    manager
quality control supervisor
robotic line supervisor
tool designer
watch repairer

## Marketing and Distribution
auctioneer
computer software distributor
direct mail entrepreneur
import-export agent
inventory control supervisor
marketing research analyst
package designer
product demonstrator
real estate sales agent
retail buyer
sales manager
television time sales
    representative

## Personal Services
bodyguard
career adviser
carpet cleaning contractor
custom tailor
domestic cook
hairstylist
home attendant
personal driver
pet grooming shop owner
shoeshine stand owner
social secretary
wedding consultant

## Public Service
CIA intelligence specialist
college alumni director
coroner
correction officer
equal opportunity
    representative
Internal Revenue Service
    agent
judge
mail carrier
police officer

school guidance counselor
U.S. senator
volunteer services coordinator

**Transportation**
air traffic controller
busdriver
corporate airplane pilot
cruise ship captain

diesel mechanic
flight attendant
flight test engineer
hot-air balloon operator
locomotive engineer
long-distance truckdriver
motorcycle mechanic
space mission specialist

## WISE ALTERNATIVE CHOICES

Making good choices in your life's work means refusing to become discouraged merely because your dream career seems impossibly distant. If you determine that even with accommodations there's no way you can achieve Choice Number One, investigate alternatives within the same job family. Perhaps you'll find an occupation that sparks a similar or even greater interest. If you come up empty handed, turn to the career cluster in which the job family is located and look for ways to renew your enthusiasm.

Still no luck with a choice? Investigate another career cluster. Another. And still another. The right alternative for you is waiting to be found.

As Louisa May Alcott, author of *Little Women*, once said about the usefulness of finding alternative choices:

*I can't do much with my hands; so I will make a battering-ram of my head and make a way through this rough-and-tumble world.*

# 7

# Putting it all together

Now that you have a clear picture of job trends, job accommodations, and job families and career clusters, as well as what makes you desirably unique, let's put it all together. Remember, your final career choice may be your first pick, your first pick with an accommodation, or your second or third or even fourth pick (with or without an accommodation).

The only career that Robert Thome of Montebello, California, one of the country's finest mouth painters, ever dreamed of was drawing—until his spinal cord was severed during a high school football scrimmage. "Then everything ended," says Thome, who is paralyzed and has no feeling below his collar bone. "When the therapist said I could draw with a mouthstick, I didn't want to because I remembered what I could do with my hands. To draw, and not be so good, frightened me."

The images in Thome's head begged to come out, and soon he succumbed and started drawing by mouth. "At first I was really terrible," says Thome, "but it was my way of competing with other people on an equal level. I got better and won awards for my work, and no one who saw my paintings knew I was disabled."

As we work to put it all together, it's good to remind ourselves that there's more than one way to paint a picture.

## MATCHING YOURSELF WITH
## THE WORLD OF WORK

The chart that begins on the next page is based on a clustering system used by the U.S. Department of Labor. (Don't become confused because the grouping differs somewhat from the clustering system described in the previous chapter.) This chart is designed to help you compare general occupational characteristics, job requirements, and work environments with your skills, interests, and values.

Keep in mind that while the information listed is for a typical job in the occupation, all jobs in the occupation are not alike. Jewelers generally work full time, for example, but that doesn't mean you should cross jeweler off your list of possible occupations simply because you want to work part time. Before you do, research the job market for part-time jewelers.

**Matching Yourself with the World of Work,** based on a report in the Department of Labor's *Occupational Outlook Quarterly,* contains a sampling of 200 occupations that you can use in several exploratory ways.

- *If you've finished your self-assessment but haven't started your search for an occupation,* the chart can propose several occupations for which you may be a match.
- *If you've decided on a general field of work—such as health or business and office—but not on an occupation,* the chart can help you learn about different jobs in that cluster.
- *If you have already narrowed your career options,* the chart reveals general characteristics of the occupations you're considering.

As you read through the chart, put a check mark next to the occupations that most interest you.

---

Take Time Now
to Review
**Matching Yourself with the World of Work**

---

## NARROWING YOUR CAREER OPTIONS

Most of this book encourages you to widen your horizons, but now it's time to narrow your focus. Try to trim your preferences to about three options as you work your way through the job-matching process. Consider carefully the occupations you checked as you went through the **Matching Yourself with the World of Work** chart.

For many, decision making is the most difficult part of the career development process. If you're stuck, read on to find solutions.

Reading saved Robert Howard Allen of west Tennessee. Allen does not have a disability, but his story is an electrifying example of

*(continued on page 123)*

# Matching Yourself with the World of Work

| | Job requirements | | | | | | | | | Work environment | | | Occupational characteristics | | |
|---|---|---|---|---|---|---|---|---|---|---|---|---|---|---|---|
| | 1. Leadership/persuasion | 2. Helping/instructing others | 3. Problem-solving/creativity | 4. Initiative | 5. Work as part of a team | 6. Frequent public contact | 7. Manual dexterity | 8. Physical stamina | 9. Hazardous | 10. Outdoors | 11. Confined | 12. Geographically concentrated | 13. Part-time | 14. Earnings | 15. Entry requirements |
| **Executive, Administrative, and Managerial Occupations** | | | | | | | | | | | | | | | |
| **Managers and Administrators** | | | | | | | | | | | | | | | |
| Bank officers and managers | • | • | • | • | • | • | | | | | | • | | H | H |
| Health services managers | • | • | • | • | • | • | | | | | | | | H | H |
| Hotel managers and assistants | • | • | • | • | • | • | | | | | | | | 1 | M |
| School principals and assistant principals | • | • | • | • | • | • | | | | | | | | H | H |
| **Management Support Occupations** | | | | | | | | | | | | | | | |
| Accountants and auditors | | • | • | | • | • | | | | | | • | | H | H |
| Construction and building inspectors | | • | • | • | • | | • | | | • | | | | M | M |
| Inspectors and compliance officers except construction | | • | • | • | • | | • | | | • | | | | H | M |
| Personnel, training, and labor relations specialists | • | • | • | • | • | • | | | | | | | | H | H |
| Purchasing agents | • | | • | | • | • | | | | | | | | H | H |
| Underwriters | | | • | | | | | | | | | | | H | H |
| Wholesale and retail buyers | • | | • | • | • | | | | | | | | | M | H |
| **Engineers, Surveyors, and Architects** | | | | | | | | | | | | | | | |
| Architects | | • | • | • | • | • | | | | | | | | H | H |
| Surveyors | • | | | | • | | • | • | | • | | | | M | M |
| **Engineers** | | | | | | | | | | | | | | | |
| Aerospace engineers | | • | • | • | | | | | | | | • | | H | H |
| Chemical engineers | | • | • | • | | | | | | | | | | H | H |
| Civil engineers | | • | • | • | | | | | | | | | | H | H |
| Electrical and electronics engineers | | • | • | • | | | | | | | | | | H | H |
| Industrial engineers | | • | • | • | | | | | | | | | | H | H |
| Mechanical engineers | | • | • | • | | | | | | | | | | H | H |
| Metallurgical, ceramics, and materials engineers | | • | • | • | | | | | | | | | | H | H |
| Mining engineers | | • | • | • | | | | | | | | | | H | H |
| Nuclear engineers | | • | • | • | | | | | | | | | | H | H |
| Petroleum engineers | | • | • | • | | | | | | | | • | | H | H |
| **Natural Scientists and Mathematicians** | | | | | | | | | | | | | | | |
| **Computer and Mathematical Occupations** | | | | | | | | | | | | | | | |
| Actuaries | | | • | • | | | | | | | • | • | | H | H |
| Computer systems analysts | • | • | • | • | • | | | | | | | • | | H | H |
| Mathematicians | | | • | • | | | | | | | | | | H | H |
| Statisticians | | | • | • | | | | | | | | | | H | H |
| **Physical Scientists** | | | | | | | | | | | | | | | |
| Chemists | | | • | • | | | | | | | | | | H | H |
| Geologists and geophysicists | | | • | • | • | | | | | | • | | • | H | H |

1 Estimates not available.

Based on "The World of Work," by Melvin Fountain, *Occupational Outlook Quarterly.*

# Matching Yourself with the World of Work (con't.)

Column key — **Job requirements:** 1. Leadership/persuasion; 2. Helping/instructing others; 3. Problem-solving/creativity; 4. Initiative; 5. Work as part of a team; 6. Frequent public contact; 7. Manual dexterity; 8. Physical stamina; 9. Hazardous; 10. Outdoors; 11. Confined; 12. Geographically concentrated. **Work environment:** 13. Part-time. **Occupational characteristics:** 14. Earnings; 15. Entry requirements.

| Occupation | 1 | 2 | 3 | 4 | 5 | 6 | 7 | 8 | 9 | 10 | 11 | 12 | 13 | 14 | 15 |
|---|---|---|---|---|---|---|---|---|---|---|---|---|---|---|---|
| Meteorologists | | | • | • | | | | | | | | | | H | H |
| Physicists and astronomers | | | • | • | | | | | | | | | • | H | H |
| **Life Scientists** | | | | | | | | | | | | | | | |
| Agricultural scientists | | | • | • | | | | | | | | | | H | H |
| Biological scientists | | | • | • | | | | | | | | | | H | H |
| Foresters and conservation scientists | | • | • | • | • | | | • | • | • | | | | H | H |
| **Social Scientists, Social Workers, Religious Workers, and Lawyers** | | | | | | | | | | | | | | | |
| Lawyers | • | • | • | • | • | • | • | | | | | | | H | H |
| **Social Scientists and Urban Planners** | | | | | | | | | | | | | | | |
| Economists | | | • | • | | | | | | | | | | H | H |
| Psychologists | | • | • | • | | • | | | | | | | | H | H |
| Sociologists | | | • | • | | • | | | | | | | | H | H |
| Urban and regional planners | • | | • | • | • | • | | | | | | | | H | H |
| **Social and Recreation Workers** | | | | | | | | | | | | | | | |
| Social workers | • | • | • | • | • | • | | | | | | | | M | H |
| Recreation workers | • | • | • | • | • | • | • | • | • | | • | | • | L | M |
| **Religious Workers** | | | | | | | | | | | | | | | |
| Protestant ministers | • | • | • | • | • | • | | | | | | | | L | H |
| Rabbis | • | • | • | • | • | • | | | | | | | | H | H |
| Roman Catholic priests | • | • | • | • | • | • | | | | | | | | L | H |
| **Teachers, Counselors, Librarians, and Archivists** | | | | | | | | | | | | | | | |
| Kindergarten and elementary school teachers | • | • | • | • | • | • | • | • | | | | | | M | H |
| Secondary school teachers | • | • | • | • | • | • | | • | | | | | | M | H |
| Adult and vocational education teachers | • | • | • | • | • | • | • | • | | | | | • | M | H |
| College and university faculty | • | • | • | • | • | • | | • | | | | | • | H | H |
| Counselors | • | • | • | • | • | • | | | | | | | | M | H |
| Librarians | • | • | • | • | • | • | | • | | | | | • | M | H |
| Archivists and curators | | | • | • | • | | | | | | | | | M | H |
| **Health Diagnosing and Treating Practitioners** | | | | | | | | | | | | | | | |
| Chiropractors | • | • | • | • | • | • | • | | | | | | | H | H |
| Dentists | • | • | • | • | • | • | • | | | | | | | H | H |
| Optometrists | • | • | • | • | • | • | • | | | | | | | H | H |
| Physicians | • | • | • | • | • | • | • | | | | | | • | H | H |
| Podiatrists | • | • | • | • | • | • | • | | | | | | | H | H |
| Veterinarians | • | • | • | • | • | • | • | • | • | | | | | H | H |
| **Registered Nurses, Pharmacists, Dietitians, Therapists, and Physician Assistants** | | | | | | | | | | | | | | | |
| Dietitians and nutritionists | • | • | • | • | • | • | | | | | | | | M | H |
| Occupational therapists | • | • | • | • | • | • | • | • | | | | | | ¹ | H |
| Pharmacists | • | • | • | • | • | • | | | | | | • | | H | H |

¹Estimates not available.

# Matching Yourself with the World of Work *(con't.)*

| | Job requirements | | | | | | | | | Work environment | | | | Occupational characteristics | |
|---|---|---|---|---|---|---|---|---|---|---|---|---|---|---|---|
| | 1. Leadership/persuasion | 2. Helping/instructing others | 3. Problem-solving/creativity | 4. Initiative | 5. Work as part of a team | 6. Frequent public contact | 7. Manual dexterity | 8. Physical stamina | 9. Hazardous | 10. Outdoors | 11. Confined | 12. Geographically concentrated | 13. Part-time | 14. Earnings | 15. Entry requirements |
| Physical therapists | • | • | • | • | • | • | • | • | | | | | | M | H |
| Physician assistants | • | • | • | • | • | • | • | | | | | | | M | M |
| Recreational therapists | • | • | • | • | • | • | • | • | | • | | | | M | M |
| Registered nurses | • | • | • | • | • | • | • | • | • | • | | | • | M | M |
| Respiratory therapists | • | • | • | • | • | • | • | | | | | | | M | L |
| Speech pathologists and audiologists | • | • | • | • | • | • | | | | | | | | M | H |
| **Health Technologists and Technicians** | | | | | | | | | | | | | | | |
| Clinical laboratory technologists and technicians | | • | | • | | • | | | | | | • | | L | |
| Dental hygienists | | • | | • | • | • | • | | | | | | • | L | M |
| Dispensing opticians | | • | • | • | • | • | • | | | | | | | M | M |
| Electrocardiograph technicians | | • | • | | • | • | • | | | | | | | ¹ | M |
| Electroencephalographic technologists and technicians | | • | • | | • | • | • | | | | | | | ¹ | M |
| Emergency medical technicians | • | • | • | • | • | • | • | • | • | • | • | | | L | M |
| Licensed practical nurses | | • | | • | • | • | • | • | | | | | • | L | M |
| Medical record technicians | | | | • | | | | | | | | • | | L | M |
| Radiologic technologists | | • | | • | • | • | | | • | | | | | L | M |
| Surgical technicians | | • | | • | • | • | | | | | | | | L | M |
| **Writers, Artists, and Entertainers** | | | | | | | | | | | | | | | |
| **Communications Occupations** | | | | | | | | | | | | | | | |
| Public relations specialists | • | | • | • | • | • | | | | | | | | H | H |
| Radio and television announcers and newscasters | • | • | | • | • | • | | | | | | • | | L | H |
| Reporters and correspondents | • | | • | • | • | • | | | | | | | | ¹ | H |
| Writers and editors | • | | • | • | | | | | | | | • | • | ¹ | H |
| **Visual Arts Occupations** | | | | | | | | | | | | | | | |
| Designers | | | • | • | • | • | • | | | | | | | H | H |
| Graphic and fine artists | | | • | • | | | | | | | | | | | |
| Photographers and camera operators | | | • | • | | • | • | | | | | | • | M | M |
| **Performing Arts Occupations** | | | | | | | | | | | | | | | |
| Actors, directors, and producers | | | • | • | • | • | • | • | | | | • | • | L | M |
| Dancers and choreographers | | | • | • | • | • | • | • | | | | • | • | L | M |
| Musicians | | | • | • | • | • | • | • | | | | • | • | L | M |
| **Technologists and Technicians Except Health** | | | | | | | | | | | | | | | |
| **Engineering and Science Technicians** | | | | | | | | | | | | | | | |
| Drafters | | | • | | • | | | | | | | • | | M | M |
| Electrical and electronics technicians | | | • | | • | | • | | | | | | | M | M |
| Engineering technicians | | | • | | • | | • | | | | | | | M | M |
| Science technicians | | | • | | • | | • | | | | | | | M | M |
| **Other technicians** | | | | | | | | | | | | | | | |
| Air traffic controllers | • | • | • | • | | • | | | | | | • | | H | H |
| Broadcast technicians | | | • | | • | | • | | | | | • | | M | M |

¹Estimates not available.

# Matching Yourself with the World of Work *(con't.)*

| | Job requirements | | | | | | | | | Work environment | | | Occupational characteristics | | |
|---|---|---|---|---|---|---|---|---|---|---|---|---|---|---|---|
| | 1. Leadership/persuasion | 2. Helping/instructing others | 3. Problem-solving/creativity | 4. Initiative | 5. Work as part of a team | 6. Frequent public contact | 7. Manual dexterity | 8. Physical stamina | 9. Hazardous | 10. Outdoors | 11. Confined | 12. Geographically concentrated | 13. Part-time | 14. Earnings | 15. Entry requirements |
| Computer programmers | | | • | | • | | | | | | | | • | H | H |
| Legal assistants | | | | 2 | • | 2 | | | | | | | | M | L |
| Library technicians | | • | | | • | • | • | | | | | | • | L | L |
| Tool programmers, numerical control | | | • | | | | • | | • | | | | | M | M |
| **Marketing and Sales Occupations** | | | | | | | | | | | | | | | |
| Cashiers | | • | | | | • | • | | | | • | | • | L | L |
| Insurance sales workers | • | • | • | • | | • | | | | | | | • | M | M |
| Manufacturers' sales workers | • | • | • | • | | • | | | | | | | | H | H |
| Real estate agents and brokers | • | • | • | • | | • | | | | • | | | • | M | M |
| Retail sales workers | • | • | | • | | • | | | | | | | • | L | L |
| Securities and financial services sales workers | • | • | • | • | | • | | | | | | | • | H | H |
| Travel agents | • | • | • | • | | • | | | | | | | 1 | M |
| Wholesale trade sales workers | • | • | • | • | | • | | | | | | | | M | M |
| **Administrative Support Occupations, Including Clerical** | | | | | | | | | | | | | | | |
| Bank tellers | | | | | • | • | | | | | • | | • | L | L |
| Bookkeepers and accounting clerks | | | | | • | | | | | | • | | • | L | L |
| Computer and peripheral equipment operators | | • | | | • | | • | | | | • | | | L | M |
| Data entry keyers | | | | | • | | • | | | | • | | | L | L |
| Mail carriers | | | | | | • | • | • | | • | | | | M | L |
| Postal clerks | | | | | | • | • | • | • | | • | | | M | L |
| Receptionists and information clerks | | • | | | • | • | | | | | • | | • | L | L |
| Reservation and transportation ticket agents and travel clerks | • | • | | | • | • | | | | | • | | | M | L |
| Secretaries | | | • | • | • | • | | | | | | | | L | L |
| Statistical clerks | | | | | • | | | | | | • | | | L | L |
| Stenographers | | | • | • | • | • | | | | | | | | L | L |
| Teacher aides | • | • | | | • | • | • | • | | | | | • | L | L |
| Telephone operators | | • | | | | • | | | | | • | | | L | L |
| Traffic, shipping, and receiving clerks | | | • | • | • | | | | | | | | | L | L |
| Typists | | | | | | • | | | | | • | | • | L | L |
| **Service Occupations** | | | | | | | | | | | | | | | |
| **Protective Service Occupations** | | | | | | | | | | | | | | | |
| Correction officers | • | • | | | • | | | • | • | | • | | | M | L |
| Firefighting occupations | | • | • | | • | • | • | • | • | • | • | | • | M | L |
| Guards | | | | | | • | • | • | • | • | • | | • | L | L |
| Police and detectives | • | • | • | • | • | • | • | • | • | • | • | | | M | L |
| **Food and Beverage Preparation and Service Occupations** | | | | | | | | | | | | | | | |
| Bartenders | | | • | | | • | • | • | | | • | | • | L | M |

¹Estimates not available.

²Vary, depending on job.

# Matching Yourself with the World of Work *(con't.)*

| | 1. Leadership/persuasion | 2. Helping/instructing others | 3. Problem-solving/creativity | 4. Initiative | 5. Work as part of a team | 6. Frequent public contact | 7. Manual dexterity | 8. Physical stamina | 9. Hazardous | 10. Outdoors | 11. Confined | 12. Geographically concentrated | 13. Part-time | 14. Earnings | 15. Entry requirements |
|---|---|---|---|---|---|---|---|---|---|---|---|---|---|---|---|
| | \<-- Job requirements --> | | | | | | | | | Work environment | | | Occupational characteristics | | |
| Chefs and cooks except short order | | | • | | | • | • | | | | • | | • | L | M |
| Waiters and waitresses | | | • | | • | • | • | | | | | | • | L | L |
| **Health Service Occupations** | | | | | | | | | | | | | | | |
| Dental assistants | | • | | | • | • | • | • | | | | | • | L | L |
| Medical assistants | | • | | | • | • | • | | • | | | | | L | L |
| Nursing aides | | • | | | • | • | • | • | • | | | | • | L | L |
| Psychiatric aides | | • | | | • | • | | • | • | | | | | L | L |
| **Cleaning Service Occupations** | | | | | | | | | | | | | | | |
| Janitors and cleaners | | | | | | | • | | | | | | • | L | L |
| **Personal Service Occupations** | | | | | | | | | | | | | | | |
| Barbers | | | | | • | • | • | | | | • | | • | L | M |
| Childcare workers | • | • | | • | | • | • | | | | | | • | L | L |
| Cosmetologists and related workers | | | | | • | • | • | • | | | • | | • | L | M |
| Flight attendants | | • | | | • | • | • | • | | | | | | M | L |
| **Agricultural, Forestry, and Fishing Occupations** | | | | | | | | | | | | | | | |
| Farm operators and managers | • | • | • | • | • | | • | • | | • | | | | M | L |
| **Mechanics and Repairers** | | | | | | | | | | | | | | | |
| **Vehicle and Mobile Equipment Mechanics and Repairers** | | | | | | | | | | | | | | | |
| Aircraft mechanics and engine specialists | | • | | • | | • | • | • | • | | | • | | H | M |
| Automotive and motorcycle mechanics | | • | | | • | • | • | • | | | • | | | M | M |
| Automotive body repairers | | • | | | | • | • | • | | | • | | | M | M |
| Diesel mechanics | | • | | | • | • | • | • | | | • | | | M | M |
| Farm equipment mechanics | | • | | | | • | • | • | • | | | | | M | M |
| Mobile heavy equipment mechanics | | • | | | | • | • | • | | | • | | | M | M |
| **Electrical and Electronic Equipment Repairers** | | | | | | | | | | | | | | | |
| Commercial and electronic equipment repairers | | • | • | | • | • | | | | | | | | L | M |
| Communications equipment mechanics | | • | • | | • | • | | | | | | | | M | M |
| Computer service technicians | | • | • | | • | • | | | | | | | | M | M |
| Electronic home entertainment equipment repairers | | • | • | | • | • | | • | | | | | • | M | M |
| Home appliance and power tool repairers | | • | • | | • | • | | | | | | | | L | M |
| Line installers and cable splicers | | • | | • | | • | • | • | • | | | | | M | L |
| Telephone installers and repairers | | • | | • | • | • | • | • | | | | | | M | L |
| **Other Mechanics and Repairers** | | | | | | | | | | | | | | | |
| General maintenance mechanics | | • | | | | • | | • | | | | | | M | M |
| Heating, air-conditioning, and refrigeration mechanics | | • | | | | • | | • | | | | | | M | M |
| Industrial machinery repairers | | • | | | | • | • | • | | | | | | M | M |
| Millwrights | | • | | | | • | | • | | | | | | H | M |

# Matching Yourself with the World of Work *(con't.)*

| | 1. Leadership/persuasion | 2. Helping/instructing others | 3. Problem-solving/creativity | 4. Initiative | 5. Work as part of a team | 6. Frequent public contact | 7. Manual dexterity | 8. Physical stamina | 9. Hazardous | 10. Outdoors | 11. Confined | 12. Geographically concentrated | 13. Part-time | 14. Earnings | 15. Entry requirements |
|---|---|---|---|---|---|---|---|---|---|---|---|---|---|---|---|
| Musical instrument repairers and tuners | | | | | | | • | | | | | | | L | M |
| Office machine and cash register servicers | | | • | • | • | | • | | | | | | | M | M |
| Vending machine servicers and repairers | | | • | • | | | • | | | | | | | ¹ | M |
| **Construction and Extractive Occupations** | | | | | | | | | | | | | | | |
| **Construction Occupations** | | | | | | | | | | | | | | | |
| Bricklayers and stonemasons | | | • | | • | | • | • | • | • | | | | M | M |
| Carpenters | | | • | | • | | • | • | • | • | | | | M | M |
| Carpet installers | | | • | | • | • | • | • | | | | | | M | M |
| Concrete masons and terrazzo workers | | | • | | • | | • | • | • | • | | | | M | M |
| Drywall workers and lathers | | | • | | • | | • | • | • | | | | | M | M |
| Electricians | | | • | | • | | • | • | • | • | | | | H | M |
| Glaziers | | | • | | • | | • | • | • | • | | | | M | M |
| Insulation workers | | | • | | • | | • | • | • | | | | | M | M |
| Painters and paperhangers | | | • | | • | • | • | • | • | • | | | | M | M |
| Plasterers | | | • | | • | | • | • | • | | | • | | M | M |
| Plumbers and pipefitters | | | • | | • | • | • | • | • | • | | | | H | M |
| Roofers | | | • | | • | | • | • | • | • | | | | L | M |
| Sheetmetal workers | | | • | | • | | • | • | • | | | | | M | M |
| Structural and reinforcing metalworkers | | | • | | • | | • | • | • | • | | | | H | M |
| Tilesetters | | | • | | • | | • | • | | | | | | M | M |
| **Extractive Occupations** | | | | | | | | | | | | | | | |
| Roustabouts | | | | | • | | • | • | • | • | | • | | M | L |
| **Production Occupations** | | | | | | | | | | | | | | | |
| Blue-collar worker supervisors | • | • | • | • | • | | • | | • | | | | | M | M |
| **Precision Production Occupations** | | | | | | | | | | | | | | | |
| Boilermakers | | | • | | | | • | | • | | | | | M | M |
| Bookbinding workers | | • | | | • | | • | • | • | | | | • | L | M |
| Butchers and meatcutters | | | | | | • | • | • | • | | | | • | L | M |
| Compositors and typesetters | | | | | | | • | • | • | | | | • | L | M |
| Dental laboratory technicians | | | | | | | • | | | | | | • | L | M |
| Jewelers | • | • | • | • | • | • | • | | | | | • | • | L | M |
| Lithographic and photoengraving workers | | • | • | | • | | • | • | | | | | • | H | M |
| Machinists | | | • | | | | • | • | • | | | | • | M | M |
| Photographic process workers | | | | | | | • | | | | | | • | L | L |
| Shoe and leather workers and repairers | | • | | | • | • | • | | | | | | | L | M |
| Tool-and-die makers | | | • | | | | • | • | • | | | • | • | H | M |
| Upholsterers | | | | | | | • | • | | | | | • | L | M |
| **Plant and System Operators** | | | | | | | | | | | | | | | |
| Stationary engineers | | | • | | | | • | • | • | | | | | M | M |
| Water and sewage treatment plant operators | | • | • | | | | • | | • | • | | | | L | M |

¹Estimates not available.

# Matching Yourself with the World of Work *(con't.)*

| | Job requirements | | | | | | | | | Work environment | | | Occupational characteristics | | |
| --- | --- | --- | --- | --- | --- | --- | --- | --- | --- | --- | --- | --- | --- | --- | --- |
| | 1. Leadership/persuasion | 2. Helping/instructing others | 3. Problem-solving/creativity | 4. Initiative | 5. Work as part of a team | 6. Frequent public contact | 7. Manual dexterity | 8. Physical stamina | 9. Hazardous | 10. Outdoors | 11. Confined | 12. Geographically concentrated | 13. Part-time | 14. Earnings | 15. Entry requirements |
| **Machine Operators, Tenders, and Setup Workers** | | | | | | | | | | | | | | | |
| Metalworking and plastic-working machine operators | | | | | | • | • | • | | | • | • | | L | |
| Numerical-control machine-tool operators | | | • | | | • | • | • | | | • | | | M | M |
| Printing press operators | • | • | | • | | • | • | • | | | • | | | M | M |
| **Fabricators, Assemblers, and Handworking Occupations** | | | | | | | | | | | | | | | |
| Precision assemblers | | | | • | | • | • | | | | • | | | L | L |
| Transportation equipment painters | | | | | | • | • | • | | | • | | | M | M |
| Welders and cutters | | | | | | • | • | • | • | | | | | M | M |
| **Transportation and Material Moving Occupations** | | | | | | | | | | | | | | | |
| Aircraft pilots | • | • | • | | • | | | | | | • | | | H | M |
| Busdrivers | | • | | • | • | • | | | | | • | | • | M | M |
| Construction machinery operators | | | • | | | • | • | • | • | • | • | | | M | M |
| Industrial truck and tractor operators | | • | | | • | • | | | | | • | | | M | M |
| Truckdrivers | | • | | | • | • | | | | | • | | | M | M |
| **Handlers, Equipment Cleaners, Helpers, and Laborers** | | | | | | | | | | | | | | | |
| Construction trades helpers | | | • | | | • | • | • | • | • | | | | L | L |

the value of reading. Born into a broken home, at the age of six his mother abandoned him to elderly relatives. His uncle blocked authorities from enrolling him in school, decreeing it "a waste of time." Fortunately, his grandfather taught him to write, and an aunt taught him to read.

In a ramshackle farmhouse without indoor plumbing, Allen read. And read. And read. He read everything he could get his hands on, whether from a library or a yard sale. He read thousands upon thousands of books—from comics to Shakespeare to the Bible. Then he taught himself to read Greek and French so he could better absorb the original versions of classic works.

Never having seen the inside of a classroom but encouraged by a librarian, at age thirty-two Allen tried for his first formal education—college. After blowing the lid off his placement test, Bethel College in McKenzie, Tennessee, invited him to enter as a sophomore. Three years later, he graduated summa cum laude. Allen since has earned a master's degree and a Ph.D. in English from Vanderbilt University in Nashville. Dr. Allen is currently teaching English and humanities at Murray State University in Murray, Kentucky.

Reading can transform a person's life.

Today may be a good day to make a librarian your new best friend. A librarian can be your personal tour guide through the maze of career books, describing each book's specific purpose. Many large libraries carry reference books detailing occupations. They aren't meant to be read cover to cover, but rather to be explored and studied.

The U.S. Department of Labor publishes many books that are valuable to a career decision maker. The two most helpful are the *Occupational Outlook Handbook* and the *Dictionary of Occupational Titles.* The handbook details about 250 of the larger occupations (those with many workers), covering more than 100 million jobs—that's 85 percent of all jobs in the economy. What workers do on the job, working conditions, the training and education needed, earnings, and expected job prospects are described. The dictionary provides descriptions and a standardized coding system (used in many other books) for more than 20,000 job titles.

Once you narrow your choices to a few career fields, look for career-specific books. VGM Career Horizons/NTC Publishing Group has an excellent career series called "Opportunities In." Titles such as *Opportunities in Fashion, Opportunities in Business Management,* and *Opportunities in The Machine Trades* provide comprehensive information to help in making choices about education, the job situation, or career advancement.

Schools and libraries often have a treasure trove of materials describing what different occupations are like, including collections of occupational capsules such as those published by Chronicle Guidance and Vocational Biographies. Also check out the *Encyclopedia of Careers and Vocational Guidance,* J. G. Ferguson Publishing Company. Some have collections of videos with career information and computerized guidance systems. Remember, private career counselors, college and university counselors, and vocational rehabilitation counselors can offer advice and serve as sounding boards. Supplement your book research by trying to find people who are working in the occupation you want and ask them about it.

*Read, research, gather information, and talk to people until you are confident you've absorbed as much as you can.*

Has your career exploration left you confused or undecided about the career path that's best for you? Your own personal analysis chart may help to sort choices and make a career decision easier.

The **Career Analysis Work Sheet** on the following pages helps you compare the positive/negative points and the obstacles of each career. Make photocopies of the blank work sheet and fill out one for each occupation you're considering. Use the sample as a guide. Record the specific information you need to see how your career choices fit your Foremost Five work values, personal values, interests, personality traits, and skills that you listed on your **Equal-to-the-Task Composite** in Chapter 4 on self-assessment.

> Take Time Now
> to Review
> **Career Analysis Work Sheet**

## WHAT WILL HAPPEN IF I CHOOSE TO BE . . . ?

Which occupational choices appear to have the best possibilities of landing you a job that fulfills your needs and desires? Which ones offer the least possibilities?

The following work sheet titled **What Will Happen If I Choose to Be . . . ?** may help you answer these questions. Make photocopies of the blank work sheet and fill out one for each occupation you're still considering, using the sample as a guide. Be as specific as possible with your answers.

> Take Time Now
> to Review
> **What Will Happen If I Choose to Be . . . ?**

"Be confident about what you've learned you can do and don't get hung up on disability stereotypes," says Paul Scher, rehabilitation services consultant, employee benefits staff, at Sears, Roebuck, and Company in Chicago. "Your greatest asset may fall into what others perceive as a nontraditional job. So what, so long as you're a match." Scher, who is blind, says that job options should not be limited without fully investigating their potential.

Consider the following real people and their real career choices before wrapping up your personal career analysis.

# Career Analysis Work Sheet

Occupation: _____

Job Family: _____  Career Cluster:_____

Check boxes if you possess skills or education required
or
if the items listed are factors you find desirable

### Duties

- ☐ _____
- ☐ _____
- ☐ _____
- ☐ _____
- ☐ _____
- ☐ _____

### Physical/Mental Demands

- ☐ _____
- ☐ _____
- ☐ _____
- ☐ _____
- ☐ _____
- ☐ _____

### Aptitude/Skill Requirements

- ☐ _____
- ☐ _____
- ☐ _____
- ☐ _____
- ☐ _____
- ☐ _____

### Education/Entry Requirements

- ☐ apprenticeship
- ☐ vocational-technical program
- ☐ community college (2 yrs.)
- ☐ college (4 yrs.)
- ☐ advanced degree (study beyond bachelor's degree)
- ☐ professional degree (work-focused, e.g., physician, librarian, lawyer)

### Work Factors

- ☐ _____
- ☐ _____
- ☐ _____
- ☐ _____
- ☐ _____
- ☐ _____

### Where Employment Found

- ☐ _____
- ☐ _____
- ☐ _____
- ☐ _____
- ☐ _____
- ☐ _____

### Earnings/Employee Benefits

- ☐ _____
- ☐ _____
- ☐ _____
- ☐ _____
- ☐ _____
- ☐ _____

### Job Outlook

- ☐ _____
- ☐ _____
- ☐ _____
- ☐ _____
- ☐ _____
- ☐ _____

# Career Analysis Work Sheet

**Occupation:** Travel agent *(Sample)*

**Job Family:** Travel          **Career Cluster:** Hospitality/
                                                    Recreation

Check boxes if you possess skills or education required
or
if the items listed are factors you find desirable

## Duties

- ☑ Arrange business/personal travel
- ☑ Arrange business/personal
- ☐   accommodations
- ☐ Help customers with international
- ☐   travel
- ☐

## Physical/Mental Demands

- ☑ Sedentary
- ☑ Light lifting/carrying
- ☑ Communicating
- ☑ Keyboarding
- ☐
- ☐

## Aptitude/Skill Requirements

- ☑ Computer skills
- ☐ Influencing people
- ☑ Make evaluations based on
- ☐   sensory material
- ☐
- ☐

## Education/Entry Requirements

- ☐ apprenticeship
- ☐ vocational-technical program
- ☑ community college (2 yrs.)
- ☐ college (4 yrs.)
- ☐ advanced degree
- ☐ professional degree

## Work Factors

- ☐ Inside
- ☑ Travel sometimes required
- ☐ High pressure during vacation
- ☐   seasons
- ☐ May require long hours
- ☐

## Where Employment Found

- ☑ Suburbs, cities, small towns,
- ☐   rural
- ☑ Travel agencies
- ☐ Tour companies
- ☐ Many self-employed
- ☐

## Earnings/Employee Benefits

- ☐ Entry: $12,000/year (1986
- ☐   figures)
- ☐ Experienced: $21,000/year
- ☑ Managers:   $30,000/year
- ☑ Insurance coverage
- ☑ Paid vacation

## Job Outlook

- ☑ 13th fastest-growing occupation
- ☐   thru 2005
- ☐ 62 percent increase, 82,000 jobs
- ☐
- ☐
- ☐

# What Will Happen
# If I Choose to Be . . . ?

**Career Option:** _____

Fill out this work sheet assuming you've chosen this career option. Use the thought process outlined below to guide your decisions and to evaluate their potential outcomes. You will have to use your imagination in order to complete the decision-making process.

This occupation would be particularly satisfying to me because (I'll review my **Equal-to-the-Task Composite** for guidance here) _____

_____

_____

Education obstacles I must overcome: _____

How I will overcome education obstacles: _____

Other obstacles I must overcome: _____

_____

_____

How I will overcome other obstacles: _____

_____

_____

Occupational accommodations needed:_____

_____

_____

If this occupation and I aren't a match, these are related occupations I can consider: _____

_____

_____

_____

# What Will Happen
# If I Choose to Be . . . ?

**Career Option:** _Travel agent (Sample)_

Fill out this work sheet assuming you've chosen this career option. Use the thought process outlined below to guide your decisions and to evaluate their potential outcomes. You will have to use your imagination in order to complete the decision-making process.

This occupation would be particularly satisfying to me because (I'll review my **Equal-to-the-Task Composite** for guidance here) _____

_I like computer work_

_I enjoy working with people_

_I would like the opportunity to travel_

Education obstacles I must overcome: _Not enough training_

How I will overcome education obstacles: _Enroll in community college_ _program_

Other obstacles I must overcome: _Improve my selling skills_

How I will overcome other obstacles: _Practice influencing skills with_ _family and friends_

Occupational accommodations needed: _Use wheelchair for mobility;_ _before making each trip to familiarize myself with locations, airlines,_ _cruise ships, hotels, and special tour packages, research accessibility_

If this occupation and I aren't a match, these are related occupations I can consider: _Tour guide_

_Airline reservation agent_

_Travel counselor_

- The first job that Doreen Smith, an engineer who uses crutches as the result of polio, held with New England Telephone and Telegraph required her to descend ladders into manholes. "When I started the field job in 1978," says Smith of Boston, "not only was I a woman engineer, but a 'four-legged' one."
- Chad Moore, who is autistic, works as a full-time data entry clerk. Moore spent last year's vacation in Australia on money he saved working the past five years at a Chicago insurance company.
- Award-winning consumer reporter Ellen MacFarlane exposes consumer fraud and con artists on WCPX-TV in Orlando, Florida. MacFarlane, who has multiple sclerosis, chases down cheats with the aid of a scooter and her cameraman/best friend.
- Washington Water Power Company originally hired Craig Thomas as a drafter. The Spokane, Washington, company promoted Thomas, who lost both legs during the Vietnam War, to on-site construction coordinator and then on-site control analyst on a power plant construction project. Today Thomas, promoted again, is a contractor coordinator to corporate services.
- Darla Crowley's speech is punctuated with obscenities, racial slurs, sexual slurs, assorted yelps, and spitting. Crowley, whose Tourette syndrome is severe, is a security guard at the H.J. Heinz Company in Pittsburgh, where she has greeted hundreds of workers every day for more than ten years.

## YOUR CAREER DECISION

When you finish your in-depth study of the occupations that seem appropriate for you, you're ready to make a career choice.

If you need formal education/training before pursuing your career, you'll have to narrow your choice to that goal—engineering, business, or food service, for instance. But if you need no additional preparation, you may decide to target as many as three occupations and seek employment in any one of them. The important thing is to set goals—not just say you'll settle for any job that strays your way.

Before writing down your career decision in permanent ink, ask yourself each of these questions. Did I choose an occupation:

- that offers the type of work I like?
- in which there is likely to be an active demand for workers?

- after carefully thinking about other possible choices?
- freely without pressure from counselors, family, or friends?
- based on logic—adding instinct to tip the career scale?
- that uses my strengths and abilities?
- that makes use of the training or schooling I have or plan to acquire?
- that objectively takes into account my functional limitations?
- in which accommodations to meet my specific needs can be made?
- that makes me feel good about myself?

## MAKE AN ACTION PLAN

All that's left in the career decision-making process is to develop a plan of action and follow through with it. Decide what steps you need to take and set up a time line to reach your goal. Be specific as you set goals.

Read the following general goals and see how they become more motivating when they're made specific.

- Pursue more training to meet the requirements of the occupation I chose.

  *Begin welding class on January 11th.*
- Make arrangements for transportation.

  *Meet John on Tuesday to discuss payment for ride-sharing.*
- Check out general job accommodations for my specific occupation.

  *Call Job Accommodation Network tomorrow to find out where to buy a one-handed keyboard.*
- Begin my job search.

  *Call today and order daily newspaper delivery. Mark calendar nine to five on Monday, Tuesday, and Friday to write resume.*

## REMEMBER, WHAT YOU WANT COUNTS

At this point, you may want to reread this section on career choices for nuances overlooked the first time through. Even though you may or may not achieve your first (or even second or third) choice, it's important to know what you prefer, instead of humbly accepting whatever the world offers. All of us need a purpose in life and a few dreams jingling in our pockets.

# 8

---

# To disclose or
# not to disclose

Should you or shouldn't you? And, if so, when?

The issue of disclosure of your disability to prospective employers may be the single biggest question mark in your job search.

Mark Switzer didn't worry about disclosure of his disability when applying for his position as warehouse man at Thomas Distributing in Salem, Oregon. Switzer's mental disability was communicated to the prospective employer by a third party offering a referral—a co-worker of Switzer's at Goodwill Industries.

If you're among the lucky job seekers who get a foot in the employment door through a referral, as did Switzer, you probably won't lose sleep over whether or not to disclose your disability. Your third-party referrer undoubtedly will do it for you when recommending you to the employer.

But, if you're flying solo, more likely you will have to wrestle with this wrenching question: Even with a strong new federal law to protect you, do you tell all about your disability to prospective employers? The correct answer is: *Yes, no, maybe, sometimes.*

Street-smart job hunters know disclosure—and the timing of it—can have tremendous effects on the success of their job searches. They make an individual decision about disclosure for each job lead they pursue, keeping in focus the objective of landing jobs they want. The real litmus test of whether or not to disclose your disability should be:

*Does disclosure of my disability at this time and in this way support my objective of getting hired?*

Ask yourself this question as you evaluate each approach to disclosure for each job lead. If an employer will see your disclosure as a positive, volunteer it as soon as possible. If an employer may see it as a negative, hold back until the time is ripe.

When might employers see disclosure as a positive? Take a look at the categories of best prospects for employment in Chapter 11. But, in general, companies with established policies or programs for recruiting individuals with disabilities and companies with federal contracts are most likely to make special efforts to hire job seekers with disabilities. Other employers who might see disclosure as positive are organizations that serve people with disabilities. Many seek employees with similar disabilities.

The key is to research employers carefully. You may inadvertently cut yourself out of a job if you fail to disclose to a company or organization that welcomes workers with disabilities.

Once you make the decision to disclose, when do you do it and how? Because disclosure timing can color the employer's reaction to your disability, nine possible times to disclose during the job hunt are discussed in this chapter:

- Third-party referral
- Resume
- Cover letter
- Employer call for an interview
- Your call to disclose
- Application
- Interview—the moment of meeting
- Interview—preoffer
- Interview—postoffer, preacceptance

Read the following options. With each job lead, evaluate which timing will work best for you.

## THIRD-PARTY REFERRAL

This is the fairy tale come true of job hunting—and third-party referrers are the godparents of job seekers.

People who can supply third-party referrals have an "in" with prospective employers, so employers listen to what they say. While they're putting in a good word for you, they're bound to mention your disability in a positive way. How can you be sure? Your employment godparents wouldn't be referring you if they think your disability will be a problem on the job. And when third-party referrers don't think it will be an unsolvable problem, they probably can sell the prospective employer on that opinion.

## RESUME

If an employer falls into one of the most-likely-to-hire-individuals-with-disabilities category, find a positive way of disclosing your disability in your resume.

"From my experience, IBM doesn't have a quota to meet, but if it can hire a qualified minority, that's great," says Jim Haidinyak, a development engineer for International Business Machines in Austin, Texas. When Haidinyak applied for a transfer from Tucson, Arizona, recently, he disclosed in his resume under the personal activities category. He listed national competition in wheelchair tennis, IBM Representative to the Mayor's Council on Employment of People with Disabilities, and member of the Architectural Barriers Action League.

*If there's any chance that an employer will view your disability as a negative, don't disclose in your resume.*

## COVER LETTER

Disclosure in your cover letter should *only* be done if your disability helps meet one of the three major responsibilities of the position (as listed in recruitment materials or as commonly known for the occupation). If the American Burn Association were seeking a peer counselor, disclosure of your record of a burn injury would be an asset. In such instances, disclose positively, and make it shout "JOB MATCH!"

*Caution:* Don't disclose in your cover letter just because a company is an affirmative action employer, is a federal contractor, or has a hiring policy. Your disability is not a match for a job responsibility in this scenario. You're best served with disclosure at another time.

## EMPLOYER CALL FOR AN INTERVIEW

Many experts say the best time to disclose a visible disability is during the employer telephone call for an interview.

After reviewing your resume on the merits of your skills and accomplishments, suppose an employer telephones and says, "I'm favorably impressed with your resume and would like to meet you."

Schedule a mutually convenient time and find out if the caller is the person who will interview you. If so—in a confident manner— disclose your disability. *By the way, I use a wheelchair for mobility. Is your building accessible?* or *I want you to know I have a visual impairment. I wouldn't want Trump, my golden retriever, to surprise you when we meet on Friday.*

By waiting to disclose until *after* the employer schedules a meeting, you have virtually ensured the employer will go through with the interview. The employer has already admitted being impressed with your qualifications and has committed to a meeting. It would be obvious discrimination to make a 180-degree turn and cancel the interview at this time.

You've done another thing by disclosing during the call for an interview. You haven't waited so long as to make the employer think you've been trying to hide your disability.

Many employers say they prefer to avoid being startled by the unexpected. Michael Crawford is a Texas attorney who uses a wheelchair, and with his service dog, Neville, at his side, represents employers in employment discrimination claims. "Employers definitely want to know about your disability," Crawford says. "They want to meet everyone equally on paper, but they want the disability disclosed up front before they meet you in person. Employers say it alleviates the shock factor and avoids creating an obstacle during the interview."

Be alert to the position of the employer representative who is calling you to set the interview. Is the person a gatekeeper—a secretary or assistant? *Then don't disclose your disability, even a visible one, at this time.* **You** want to disclose your disability in your own carefully chosen words to the screening interviewer or hiring manager, not have it paraphrased, relayed, and possibly presented in a way that may hurt your employment chances.

## YOUR CALL TO DISCLOSE

You have one last chance before your face-to-face meeting to disclose a disability that's visible. If a gatekeeper called to set up your interview, take the opportunity to telephone the employer a few days before the interview to disclose.

Speak directly to the person who will be interviewing you. *Do not leave a message with a gatekeeper.*

Tell the interviewer you want to avoid any shock or awkwardness by mentioning before the interview that you have a disability. You can say: *I don't like surprises, and I bet you don't either.* Explain your disability in general terms, say that (perhaps with an accommodation) it will not affect your being able to do a good job, and express a willingness to answer any questions during the interview.

No matter that the law says you don't have to discuss your disability with a prospective employer except as it relates to your ability to perform job-related functions. The bottom line is, in many cases, you probably won't get the job if you don't. You must build the employer's comfort level, and if that means discussing your disability, do it. Help the employer understand and believe that you are equal to the task.

## APPLICATION

For various reasons, many organizations require job seekers to fill out applications for employment even when they have resumes.

If an application question asks, "Do you have any physical limitations that would hinder your performance in the position applied for?" and as you understand the duties you don't, answer *No.* It doesn't matter that you have a disability, as long as your disability will not keep you from performing the job duties.

If you're not sure if you have limitations that would affect your job performance, simply write *Will discuss.* Of course, if your disability will help you get the job, disclose. Discussion of your disability should be done when and how you choose. And you should choose the when and how that best support your objective of being hired.

## INTERVIEW—THE MOMENT OF MEETING

Disclosure of a visible disability at the moment of meeting at the interview carries a shock factor that employers may find hard to move beyond. But some job seekers, believing that the shock factor works in their favor, deliberately choose the first face-to-face encounter as the time to disclose their visible disabilities.

Heidi Vandewinckel, a social work supervisor at the Department of Veterans Affairs Medical Center in Northport, New York, explains why she sometimes waits for the moment of meeting to disclose during the job search. "Because I travel with a guide dog, obviously they know I'm blind when they first see me, and I like that surprise," Vandewinckel says. "I like the fact that it takes them off guard because my feeling is if they knew I was disabled before then, there would be a number of preconceived ideas that I would have to fight against.

"In the first few minutes of an interview I'm able to put stereotyped ideas to rest," says Vandewinckel. "Many employers, for example, are pleasantly surprised to see me wearing eye makeup and color-coordinated clothing. And many are disarmed by my professional but personable attitude, which projects the feeling of how comfortable I am with myself," says Vandewinckel. "What I look for then is any indication that the employer is uncomfortable with my disability. If so, I open up the discussion to questions about my blindness."

It takes a lot of inner confidence to use the shock treatment as Vandewinckel and other job seekers sometimes do. And it takes true grit to work through the employer's silence, embarrassment, and hostility that may arise when disclosure is approached this way. Further, it takes a strong personality to quickly refocus the employer on the interview and your job qualifications.

In a variation of the shock treatment, some job seekers subscribe to the model-of-resourcefulness approach to disclosure. They excel beyond their disability so the employer will take note.

Brian Welnack, a computer systems consultant in Dallas, is one of those people. When Welnack showed up for an interview at Texas Instruments (which resulted in his first after-college job), he hadn't disclosed his spinal cord injury. He also hadn't asked if the building was accessible. It wasn't.

With several stairs between Welnack and his job interview, the young candidate thought smart. "I had to go around to a side door where there were bushes," Welnack says. "I pulled myself up, sat on the porch, pulled my wheelchair up, and climbed back in." His interviewers were astonished and approving when they met him at the door—at the top of the stairs.

## INTERVIEW—PREOFFER

A disability requiring a job accommodation should be disclosed and the accommodation discussed at the interview *before an offer* is made. If you have a disability—whether visible or invisible—that will affect your work and you haven't previously disclosed it, this is the time to do so.

Prior to arrival, anticipate opportunities to discuss your disability in a positive way. Suppose you have a hearing loss and you are applying for a sales representative position. You may disclose with these comments: *I have a moderate hearing loss. I read lips, so dealing in person with co-workers and clients is generally not a problem. And I own an assistive listening device that I would be happy to bring to sales meetings. To allow me to call customers and keep in contact with the office while in the field, there are two essential pieces of equipment I'll need. A portable telephone amplifier and a tactile pager — a vibrating beeper — should fit the bill. Speaking of bills, do you know the federal government allows tax deductions for the purchase of these devices?*

Or your conversation may go something like this: *I had vertebra surgery last year and to prevent back pain when I sit for extended periods I need a special chair. Actually, it's just a pneumatic height adjustable chair—you may already have one at that desk.*

## INTERVIEW—POSTOFFER, PREACCEPTANCE

If you don't have a visible disability and your disability will not affect any job-related function or require any accommodation, waiting until *after an offer* is made—*but before acceptance*—may be the best time to disclose.

Employers may say they want to know about your disability before the interview, but your goal is to get the interview and then get the job offer. You have a better chance of doing this if you wait to disclose an invisible, non-job-related disability until after the offer. (The exception, of course, is when disclosure can help your position. But if that is the case, you'd probably have disclosed already in your résumé or cover letter.)

Suppose you have epilepsy that is controlled by medication. You require no accommodation of any kind, but you feel the employer should know. After the employer extends the offer, you can say: *I very much appreciate the offer, but before I consider it I would like to briefly discuss my disability with you.* Describe the disability as quickly as possible and explain that although it has no bearing on your ability to do the job or to be a model employee, as a courtesy you wanted to let the employer know. Then close by restating your skills and accomplishments that match the job's requirements.

*Caution:* Some experts warn this timing may backfire on you—even when your disability will not affect your ability to perform any job-related functions and will not require an accommodation of any kind. They say that if you wait until after an offer is extended, some employers may feel you have been deceitful and resent not being told sooner.

## THE CHOICE NOT TO DISCLOSE

If you have a record of a disability but no longer have the disability, or if you have an invisible disability that will not affect any job-related function or require any accommodation—and disclosure does not support your objective of getting hired—you may choose not to disclose at all.

Melanie Gall, regional coordinator of the Southwest Regional Brain Injury Rehabilitation and Prevention Center in Houston, has a record of a brain injury. She has disclosed her record when it was advantageous to her position. Gall, who was injured more than twenty-five years ago and has experienced extensive recovery, says she does not disclose unless it has job-related benefits and then she does so cautiously.

"It is absolutely amazing how it has worked against me," Gall says. "Time and time again, people look for the deficits they expect to find; I find this invasive. Even without proof, colleagues have been known to assume a deficit exists and have a hard time accepting otherwise. In the past, in jobs where I have disclosed, I have had to struggle to keep the focus on my abilities as opposed to the record of my disability. Consequently, even if disclosure may help me get a job, I would choose not to if I felt ill equipped to deal with a new employer's or colleague's need to discover how I am 'broken' and to create the proper perspective in the workplace."

## EACH CHOICE, YOUR CHOICE

Remember, these methods and timings of disclosure are merely generalized suggestions. Only you will have researched prospective employers, and so only you can best answer the pivotal question raised at the beginning of this chapter:

*Does disclosure of my disability at this time and in this way support my objective of getting hired?*

Never lose sight of the goal—*getting the interview and then getting the offer for the job you want.* It may mean allowing a third-party referrer to disclose for you as did Mark Switzer. It may mean disclosing your disability in your resume as Jim Haidinyak did, or in your cover letter. It may mean disclosing during an employer call for an interview or making a special call to an employer. It may mean disclosing on an application or even hoisting yourself up a few stairs in an inaccessible building as Brian Welnack illustrated. It may mean discussing job accommodation before a job offer is extended or disclosing an invisible, non-job-related disability after you receive an offer. Or it may mean never disclosing at all.

Although federal legislation states that you need not disclose your disability to prospective employers unless it affects your ability to perform a job-related function, it's a mistake to withhold

# Disclosure at a Glance
## General Guide to Disclosure Timing

| Method of Disclosure | Use When . . . |
|---|---|
| **Third-party referral** | Someone else can sell you |
| **Resume** | Employer will see it as a positive |
| **Cover letter** | It helps meet specific job responsibility |
| **Employer call for an interview** | You have a visible disability and want to avoid shock effect and awkwardness during interview |
| **Your call to disclose** | You have a visible disability and want to avoid shock effect and awkwardness during interview—use only when someone other than person who will interview you telephones for meeting |
| **Application** | Asked a direct "job performance limitation" question that you must answer *Yes* **and** you have already disclosed in your paperwork; if you must answer *Yes* but you haven't already disclosed, write *Will discuss* |
| **Interview—the moment of meeting** | You have a visible disability and you want surprise factor so employer doesn't have time to develop stereotyped ideas (*Caution:* employers may find it hard to move beyond shock and focus on your job qualifications) |
| **Interview—preoffer** | You have an invisible disability that may affect a job-related function or require accommodation |
| **Interview—postoffer, preacceptance** | You have an invisible disability that will not affect any job-related function nor require any accommodation; may choose not to disclose at all |

disclosure simply to follow the letter of the law. It's the spirit of the law—equal opportunities in employment for individuals with disabilities—that should be pursued.

Rather than arguing whether or not disclosure at a given time in the job search is legal, do what it takes to get the job—and then perform well at it. You will have done more to break down attitudinal barriers in the workplace and promote the equality of fellow citizens with disabilities than you ever could by refusing to discuss a disability.

All that said, first and foremost you must do what feels comfortable to you or you have no chance of putting the employer at ease. And if you don't put the employer at ease, there will be snow in the Caribbean before you get a paycheck from that organization.

# 9

# Creating standout resumes and cover letters

What are standout resumes and cover letters? The ones that employers move from the high screening stack to the short interviewing stack.

Jennifer Lee Robertson of Vista, California, is a personable young woman who sells computers and other high-tech equipment for a major California distributor. This was not her original career choice. Robertson's hearing loss led her to spend nearly six college years preparing to teach the deaf. But after an internship, she decided teaching really wasn't her preference. By following the exercises set forth in this chapter, Robertson organized her background and thoughts, set them on paper, and used her resume and networking techniques to obtain the job she now holds.

"I spent hours and hours preparing a strong resume and cover letters," Robertson explains. "All that work paid off, though. It helped me focus on what I really had to offer an employer other than a splendid education and, as an extra benefit, helped me sell myself not only on paper but in interviews as well."

The purpose of your job hunt paperwork is to get employers interested enough in you to invite you in for job interviews. With dozens, sometimes hundreds, of applicants for a job, screeners have little time to digest each resume. Of necessity, most resumes are skimmed, not read thoroughly. Your resume must convince an employer—sometimes within a mere *half-minute*—that investing time interviewing you is a wise business move. Standout resumes and cover letters shout "MEET ME!"

*In your resume and cover letter, focus on the employer's needs, not yours.* Remember, until you receive a job offer, the employer is the buyer and you are the seller.

Much as an advertiser markets a product to a consumer in a print ad, you market yourself to a prospective employer with your paperwork. A good advertisement makes a consumer want to try a product—a standout resume and cover letter make an employer want to try you in an interview.

Take a marketing tip from experts. Whether selling shampoo or selling job applicants, a basic rule applies: Products don't sell—*what products can do for buyers sells.* People buy shampoo because ads promise it will make their hair full and shiny like the models on television. Employers interview applicants because their resumes and cover letters present individuals with the prospect of becoming valuable employees who can meet their specific needs.

Profit or nonprofit, every organization works with a budget. Showing how you can become an asset, not a liability, to the organization is what impresses an employer and wins you an interview.

## DO YOU REALLY NEED A RESUME? A COVER LETTER?

Some people would have you believe resumes are useless, ineffective tools. Here's why it's dangerous to buy into that mindset.

**A resume is often your only chance to get that first interview.**

Except for a few unskilled, quick-turnover jobs (such as fast-food worker, laborer, and machine worker), resumes are used in job searching for positions ranging from an entry level slot to president of the company. Employers use them as tools to screen *out* job seekers—so if you don't have one, you may already be out.

You may have one basic resume, or you may have several resumes, each targeted to a particular type of job. A cover letter is attached to your resume and directly relates your qualifications for the job sought.

Even the world's best resume and cover letter will not get you a job offer. But good ones can get you an interview. Let's analyze what standout resumes and cover letters say.

## RESUMES AND COVER LETTERS MUST ANSWER EMPLOYER QUESTIONS

When screeners scan your paperwork, they're in search of a convincing answer to the question "Why should I interview this applicant?" To build a strong case for an interview, make your **resume and cover letter** answer "yes" to these concerns:

- Can you do the job?
- Do you have a positive work attitude?
- Do you work well with other people?

Resume and cover letter facts can affirm your ability to do the job. But every item also must suggest that you are an enthusiastic, hard worker with a personality that fits in well with others in the organization. If not, you'll miss your chance to prove these points later with references and a job interview.

In addition to job-related facts, remember to state contact facts clearly for the employer. If you forget to list a telephone number where someone or a machine can take a message if you're away, the employer may find it easier to move on to the next name on the list.

Your **resume** must answer these basics:

- Who are you?
- What job do you want?
- What do you know?
- What can you do?
- What have you done?

Your **cover letter** must answer these basic employer questions:

- Why are you writing?
- What do you want?
- Why are your qualifications of interest to our organization?
- How do you plan to follow up?

While answering these questions, seize every opportunity to include as many great job-related things about exceptional you as possible. That will make your resume and cover letter stand out from the pack and give you a better chance of making it onto the short list to be interviewed.

Molding your paperwork into an advertisement that says "This job and I are a match made in occupation heaven!" takes time and care.

## ONE—OR MORE—RESUMES?

When a single resume can't match the needs of all the employers to whom you're applying, you may need to write multiple resumes.

Here are two sample circumstances where more than one resume is called for.

**Circumstance #1: Never let an employer think you might want to be doing something other than the job for which you are applying.**

Suppose you're a qualified legal secretary and a qualified medical transcriber, and you would be happy in either occupation. Create two resumes—one patterned to a legal secretary position, one to a medical transcriber. If you don't do this and create one resume so general that you could be applying for either job, an employer may wonder which job you're applying for—and which job you really want.

**Circumstance #2: If disclosing your disability in your resume supports your objective of getting a job, do it. If not, don't.**

Have you read the pros and cons of disclosing your disability in your resume that was discussed in Chapter 8? If you have, you may have decided disclosure of your disability is to your advantage in applying for some jobs but not for others. In this case, prepare one resume disclosing your disability for employers—such as federal contractors and large corporations—who are likely to regard it as a positive. Prepare another, nondisclosing resume for employers to whom you wish to disclose your disability at a later time or not at all.

## ANATOMY OF A RESUME

Now, make up work sheets using standard-size sheets of paper (8½" x 11") or create new files on your personal computer to help you systematically gather and organize the information you'll use later to create your resumes. Title your work sheets:

- Heading
- Job Objective and Career Summary
- Employment Experience
- Education
- Accreditation and Licenses
- Military Service
- Volunteer Experience
- Professional Affiliations and Organization Memberships
- Special Abilities and Projects
- Personal Data
- References

Where do you get all the information to put on your work sheets? Your **Equal-to-the-Task Snapshots** for *work values, personal values,* *interests, personality traits, skills,* and *job requirement competencies* you filled out in Chapter 4 offer a wealth of data you can use.

On your work sheets, write profusely. Although you won't use all the information in your resumes, the exercise itself is a fine warm-up to talking about yourself in interviews.

*Regardless of your decision about disclosure, as you fill out work sheets for each resume category ask yourself:* **Is there a positive way to disclose my disability here?** Even if you don't disclose in your resume, knowing positive ways of doing so will help you to present yourself confidently in interviews.

Before considering how your resume will be structured, let's consider the content of each category. Read each section and then fill out your work sheet for that category.

# Heading

List the information employers need to identify and contact you. Include your name, home address, and telephone number(s). If you're not home during the business day and don't have an answering machine, use an alternate number that does.

# Job Objective and Career Summary

A one-line job objective gives the employer a quick focus on the job you want. A career summary outlines your experience and expertise. Combine the two at the top of your resume to immediately clue the employer to where you will fit in the organization. The employer doesn't like guessing games.

Using a fairly broad job objective in your resume has two benefits. First, you are not dropped from consideration for positions that may be closely but not exactly related to your objective. Second, you may avoid the need for multiple resumes. In this approach, you customize the job objective in cover letters.

The downside to a fairly broad objective is that it may be so nonspecific as to be useless. Employers want people to do specific tasks, not people who may be able to do many things but none of them expertly.

Your job objective and career summary may be simple, like this:

### SALES MANAGER—RETAIL STORE

More than five years' sales management experience in consumer products for a medium-sized organization.

Alternatively, it may be more definitive, like this:

**JOB OBJECTIVE:**

Direct sales career-track position for a fast-moving and innovative advanced technology manufacturer.

**CAREER SUMMARY:**

A high-performance, highly motivated, very energetic college graduate with more than two years' advanced technology sales experience.

A quick study with proven ability to adapt to a spectrum of challenges. Have strong persuasion, communication, and listening skills. Clients show loyalty with repeat business. A recent management evaluation rated me as the consummate professional with solid product knowledge.

- Consistently sell 40-50 percent above sales quotas even in down market.

- Have extensive customer contact. Make cold calls and field visits to dealers to increase sales productivity. Well-developed people skills have earned me a reputation for reclaiming lost accounts as well as originating new ones. In one instance, reactivated 40 inactive accounts. Restructured inventory control procedure.

- Created customized sales materials to respond to commonly asked technical questions. Prepared price lists for entire company.

## Employment Experience

Record all full- and part-time employment, as well as summer or student employment. List dates you worked, names of organizations, supervisors' names, job titles, accomplishments, skills learned, and major responsibilities and duties.

This category lends itself well to a positive disclosure statement. If your work history includes a job as a braille proofreader for National Braille Press and you are blind, this is your chance to disclose. As a concrete example of an accomplishment in that position you may be able to write: *Produced 10 percent more proofread braille copy than any other employee who is blind.*

Have you decided not to disclose your disability in your resume? If you don't want to inadvertently disclose without the benefit of giving it a positive spin, consider omitting past work experience with any disability organization that may cause employers to infer you have a related disability. Carefully weigh the value of including the experience against the risk of leaving it out. Ask yourself these questions:

- Would leaving this position out of my resume leave a noticeable time gap?
- Does this position contain important skills and experience— that I can't demonstrate elsewhere—related to getting the job I want?

If you answered "yes" to either question, excluding the experience may work against you. If you answered "no" to both questions, you may want to leave it out to avoid disclosure at this point in the job-finding process.

What if you're looking for your first paid position? What if you're changing occupations or industries? Never assume you're out of the running because you lack paid experience related to your goal. Often experience can be paid or unpaid. Here's where volunteer work, unpaid internships, and hobbies may pay off. That's why you'll fill out work sheets for these soon.

Even if you don't have any kind of related experience, do you have the functional and technical skills required to do the job? Does your repertoire include an abundance of good worker skills? If so, employers may have flexibility with experience demands for some positions.

**Employers are looking for assurance that you have the ability— or at least the potential and promise—to do the job.**

## Education

List degrees you have earned, institutions where you earned them, and dates of attendance, as well as special courses you've taken to upgrade or enhance skills that correlate to the job you want. Relevant special school projects and internships should be included. List honors, awards, impressive grade point averages, and high class standings.

Stress your highest level of education. If you are a high school graduate, skip details of your elementary school years. If you are a college or vocational-technical school graduate, don't mention your high school experiences. If you have a graduate degree, list it first and your undergraduate degree second.

Although the focus here is on your highest level of education, if at a lower level you accomplished something that will sell the employer on you, include it. Suppose you earned a degree in journalism, but you lack related paid experience. If you were editor of the high school newspaper, an employer will want to know, so list your undergraduate degree first and your high school record second.

The education category is another place the fates may decide the disclosure issue for you. If you earned your degree from Gallaudet University, most employers will presume you are hearing impaired. If you're absolutely set on not disclosing in your paperwork, read on for a style of resume that can conceal your alma mater's name, and thus your disability.

## Accreditation and Licenses

Record any certification and professional licensure you possess that may be required for the kind of work you do or want to do. If you're a certified public accountant, registered nurse, or real estate broker, show your credentials here. Include the title, issuing agency, and date of issuance of your accreditation or license.

## Military Service

The gulf war victory has spiffed up the image of military personnel. If you have an honorable discharge from the armed forces or are currently a reservist, briefly mention it in your resume. If military service is a major part of your background, it will play a more major part in your resume. In either case, stress factors from your military history relevant to the work you're seeking.

Richard Crowder, Jr. of Clarksville, Tennessee, discloses a "100 percent service-connected" disability of paraplegia. Some employers, unfamiliar with how their private health insurance companies cover existing disabilities, may find comfort knowing that you have medical coverage through the Department of Veterans Affairs. That comfort level may keep them reading your resume. If you don't disclose your disability in the resume, VA benefits can be brought up later.

## Volunteer Experience

Record work-related unpaid experience. Even if it isn't job related, if it shows enthusiasm, energy, and a high level of interest, list it. Employers like these characteristics.

Include dates you volunteered, organization names, supervisors' names, and job titles. Emphasize accomplishments, skills learned, and major responsibilities and duties.

Here's another category, like employment experience, that lends itself well to disclosure of your disability. Remember, use positive statements about accomplishments. A volunteer with the American Cancer Society may be able to state this accomplishment: *As peer counselor, helped thirty-two cancer victors return to gainful employment.*

## Professional Affiliations and Organization Memberships

List professional and other memberships that show enthusiasm, energy, and a high level of interest. Remember, these are the traits employers like.

You may want to disclose your disability through membership in an organization. Nancy Griffin of Indianapolis does not specifically disclose that she is an amputee. Instead, she lists her current positions as board president of the Indianapolis Resource Center for Independent Living, consumer committee representative for the Indiana Governor's Planning Council for People with Disabilities, and board volunteer for the National Council on Independent Living, among others. Each of these say a lot about Griffin's enthusiasm, energy, and high level of interest.

Record names of organizations, positions held, committees you were on, and dates of membership.

## Special Abilities and Projects

List special abilities and projects related to work. What are job-related special abilities? A few examples: fluent in Spanish, keyboard 100 words-per-minute, expert in WordPerfect 5.1, can rebuild vehicle engines.

If you want to disclose your disability, here's another opening. Include a special ability related to your disability. Jennifer Lee Robertson lists "fluent in sign language" to disclose her hearing loss.

What are job-related special projects? They're projects completed as part of employment, volunteer, or organizational experiences that hold special job significance. Suppose you're applying for a job as an administrative assistant to a globe-trotting executive. If you headed the planning and budgeting committee for the local high school senior trip to Washington, D.C., the executive may be duly impressed.

# Personal Data

Some employment experts strongly urge job seekers to leave personal data out of resumes in an attempt to have all applicants screened without regard to age, race, religion, sex, national origin, or disability. These idealists say that since civil rights laws make it illegal for employers to ask for this information or to base their decisions on it, you shouldn't include it.

Realists say you should include this optional category *when it's to your advantage to do so.* Carefully chosen personal information can give the employer an image of you as an active, enthusiastic, interesting person.

The decision of what personal information, if any, to include in your resume is your call. Review the pros and cons of including the personal data that follow. Keep in mind that landing the job is your goal.

## Sex

If your name leaves doubt as to your sex, clarify it for the employer. Why? Look at it this way: Most names are male- or female-sounding by nature. If your name was Robert or Mary, employers would automatically know your gender. It may work against you if you're a man named Cary and the employer gets an image of a woman. An employer may have difficulty reimaging you as a man. The same is true if you're a woman named Shaun.

It works to your advantage to give employers an accurate composite of you—it's that first image that burns in the memory.

## Date of Birth or Age

If you are young, think about giving your age or employers may infer you're older than you are. Consider excluding your age if you're over forty. Unfortunately, the high cost of insurance and pension benefits sometimes makes employers consider age when hiring.

## Height and Weight

Your height and weight may be valuable information in the entertainment field. Otherwise, omit it.

## Marital Status

You may want to include your marital status if you think it will have a positive bearing on your job search. How do you know? In most cases you probably won't, but perhaps there are occasions where you have first-hand information about a specific opening at a specific company.

Litigation Law Firm A may seek young associates who are single. Its partners think that because single employees don't have to worry about the home front, they are better able to put in the all-nighters new litigation associates frequently suffer. The partners at Litigation Law Firm B may prefer wedded associates on the theory that married people are more stable and better able to fit in at the firm's social occasions with corporate clients.

Right or wrong, these practices do occur. If you know of an employer's attitudes concerning employees' marital status and you don't want to work for someone who holds such prejudices, don't apply. But stay focused on your goal—getting the job you want.

### Number of Children

If you're applying at a childcare center and have no paid or unpaid work-related experience, list the number of children you have. You may want to include their ages to show you have experience with small fry, but don't go overboard by listing their names and birth dates.

In most other circumstances it's best to omit a reference to children. Remember, only volunteer to the employer information that—from the employer's perspective—will help qualify you for the job.

### State of Health

Health may seem to be an obvious spot to disclose your disability, but it may, in fact, be the worst place.

Health is a positive word meaning fitness, strength, and vigor. Even so, when most people think of health they think in terms of what's wrong with someone, not what's right. If you choose to disclose in your resume, you want to tell the employer "I'm a person who happens to have a disability," not "I'm a sick person." No matter how positively you disclose under the category "Health," employers may subconsciously associate your disability with illness.

### Citizenship

If your citizenship status is unclear, you may want to mention it.

### Hobbies

If your hobbies are work related, if they show a diversity of interest, or if they in some way increase your chances of getting an interview, by all means, list them.

Suppose you know that the hiring manager at the company where you're applying is a shutterbug. If your hobby is photography, incorporate it in your resume. Suppose your research shows a company has an extracurricular team sport—volleyball or bowling, for example—and you participate in that sport. Insert the information: You automatically gain points as a team player in the job screener's eyes.

If you choose to disclose your disability, this is an appropriate place to do it. Don Brandon of Anchorage, Alaska, discloses his paraplegia in his resume, listing wheelchair road racing, alpine skiing, and wheelchair basketball as hobbies. Considering his hobbies, do you think many employers question Brandon's ability to be mobile in the workplace?

**Travel Experience**

Travel shows a diversity of interest.

If in work or in play you've traveled the world, or your own little corner of it, you've made a positive statement about your mobility. You may use this category to disclose or use it as part of a disclosure of your disability. Alternatively, you may choose not to disclose in your resume but disclose later, at which time the employer may have a positive recall of your mobility from your travel statement.

**Availability for Employment**

Don't include an availability date in your resume. If you indicate you can start immediately, it means you're out of a job. If you're not going to be available for two weeks or a month, you have a better chance of an employer holding a position open for you after you meet in an interview.

**Geographical Employment Preference**

If you're applying to a nationwide company, you may want to include your geographical preferences.

**Willingness to Relocate**

If you're willing to relocate, say so.

When it's time to design and edit your standout resume(s), take out your personal data work sheet and decide whether or not to include this category. If you vote for inclusion, present the items you select in a positive manner that enhances your prospect of getting an interview.

# References

Generally, references should not be included with resumes. Here are two good reasons. First, it's more paperwork for job screeners to read, and you want them to give as much time as possible to your resume and cover letter. Second, people you name as references may become irritated by too many employer calls.

*Space-saving tip:* Omit category entirely. "References available upon request" is unnecessary; employers presume you'll make them available when they ask.

Two exceptions to this send-no-references advice exist. First, when you're specifically instructed to do so in a recruitment ad or by the person requesting the resume. Second, when you have extraordinary references—for example, famous people, important political figures, or individuals of stature in your area of competence.

Get permission *now* from a group of people you wish to use as business and education references. Ask if they prefer your prospective employers to contact them at their places of business or their residences.

How do you choose your references? Carefully. You must choose people who know you, like you, and have a desire to help you succeed. You must choose people who can sell you using good oral and written skills. And you must choose people who have successful professional lives. References may be supervisors, your boss's boss, co-workers, subordinates, members of associations, vocational rehabilitation counselors, teachers, and friends. As you research each position and employer, you will select from among these references those who are best matched to sell you and your abilities for the job for which you're applying.

You've recorded the information you'll use in writing your resume. Now it's time to choose a resume style.

## RESUMES ARE LIKE CLOTHES: DIFFERENT STYLES LOOK GOOD ON DIFFERENT PEOPLE

Part of designing your resume to match your chosen occupation is selecting information to include. Another part is deciding how to "clothe" that information.

*Just as you choose a style of clothing that's flattering to your physique, you should choose a style of resume that's flattering to your skills, education, and previous experience.*

Styles—whether clothes or resumes—should boast your strengths and minimize your faults. Would you buy a style of clothing that accentuates what you consider to be a less-than-perfect part of your body? Of course not. Then why choose a style of resume that red flags the extended time gap between your last two jobs?

Dishonest? Hardly. Consider the other side of the issue. When was the last time you saw a company volunteer the following kinds of information in a recruitment ad?

- Secretary wanted for nagging boss.
- Bulldozer operator wanted: work more sporadic than industry standard.
- Customer service supervisor wanted for company that sells defective products.

Never do you see organizations blare their weaknesses in an ad, nor should you in your ad—your resume.

If you feel it's important for an employer to know something that may be negative and that isn't in your resume, mention it during the interview. Then you have a captive audience and adequate time to discuss it.

## Which Resume Style Flatters You?

You may have heard resumes called reverse chronological, analytic, creative, targeted, functional, resume letter, achievement, summary, combination, marketing letter, hybrid, amplified, historical, synoptic, skills, qualifications brief, or something else. These terms define styles of resumes.

Here you'll look at three basic styles, most others being variations of these:

1) Reverse Chronological

2) Functional

3) Combination

## Style 1: Reverse Chronological Resume

A reverse chronological resume lists jobs you've had. Your most recent job is listed first, your job before that is listed second, and so on. Each job has employment dates, job duties, and achievements.

**Advantages**

- Highlights steady employment and school record
- Points out well-known or prestigious employers
- Preferred by many employers because it is straightforward
- Easiest to prepare

**Disadvantages**

- May not provide enough evidence of skills
- Accentuates problems in job hopping and any gaps in employment
- Only emphasizes experience in similar positions—detrimental if career changer; often weak for first-time job hunter

- Gives dates, allowing employer to estimate age—detrimental if age is a consideration

```
            Take Time Now
             to Study the
  Reverse Chronological Resume Sample
```

## Style 2: Functional Resume

A functional resume groups key skills into categories that tell an employer what you can do for the organization—for example, supervision of children, selling, data management, repairing. In their purest form, functional resumes omit dates, schools, and employers.

### Advantages

- Stresses selected skills and achievements
- Camouflages scant or spotty work experience or lack of promotions
- De-emphasizes poor or unrelated school record
- Downplays irrelevant jobs—especially advantageous for career changers
- Helps veterans relate military training to civilian jobs and displaced homemakers translate skills learned at home to workplace
- Focuses on future (what you can do) rather than on past (what you have done)

### Disadvantages

- Makes some employers suspicious of your past
- Turns some employers cold because they just don't like this indirect style
- Ignores employers you may want to highlight
- Disregards at what level listed skills are carried out, for how long, and whether you succeeded
- Difficult to interpret and employers may want to see more information

# KAREN S. HILL, R.N.
111 West 54th Street
Kansas City, KS 66202
(913) 362-1434

**OBJECTIVE:**    **HEAD NURSE**

**SUMMARY:**    Registered nurse with 12 years' progressive charge
responsibility experience, including 8 years as oncology
head nurse at a large metropolitan hospital

**EXPERIENCE:**
**1982–1992**    **LOS ANGELES CITY HOSPITAL**
**Head nurse – Oncology floor** (1984 to 1992)
**Charge nurse – Oncology floor** (1982 to 1984)
*Received Distinguished Professional Service Award (1983, 1988, 1990)*
• Headed nursing staff caring for 90-bed cancer floor
• Supervised and scheduled staff of 20 nurses
• Developed and instructed in-service training courses on
post-operative cancer care, support and medications
• Directed patient care, frequently involving critical
situations
• Counseled patients in pre- and post-operative
medications and treatments

**1980–1982**    **LOS ANGELES BAYSIDE CLINIC**
**Staff nurse**
• Performed charge nurse responsibilities during
weekend shifts
• Provided general health care services to very busy clinic
of more than 30,000 patients annually

**VOLUNTEER:**
**1988–1992**    **LOS ANGELES CANCER CENTER**
**Peer counselor**
• Led weekly group sessions of cancer victors returning to
work
• Counseled one-on-one more than 100 newly diagnosed
cancer patients

**LICENSE &**    **Registered Nurse licensed in Kansas and California**
**EDUCATION:**    **Certified in CPR and Advanced Life Support**

**UNIVERSITY OF CALIFORNIA, LOS ANGELES**
**M.S. in Nursing** – 1980 *magna cum laude*
*Awarded teaching assistantships, research assistantships and
scholarships*

**UNIVERSITY OF KANSAS MEDICAL CENTER**
**B.S. in Nursing** – 1977 *summa cum laude*
*Awarded Certificate of Merit for Outstanding Contribution*

REVERSE CHRONOLOGICAL RESUME

```
┌─────────────────────────────┐
│        Take Time Now        │
│         to Study the        │
│  Functional Resume Sample   │
└─────────────────────────────┘
```

## Style 3: Combination Resume

A combination resume blends your personal best from both reverse chronological and functional resumes.

### Advantages

- Allows you to stress education, experience, or skills and accomplishments
- Satisfies employer's desire to know names and dates of schools and employers

### Disadvantage

- Requires extra care in planning and layout

```
┌─────────────────────────────┐
│        Take Time Now        │
│         to Study the        │
│  Combination Resume Sample  │
└─────────────────────────────┘
```

## More Sample Resumes

For a better understanding of how different styles are suited to different people and different job hunts, check out these three resume writing guides:

*The Guide To Basic Resume Writing* by the Job and Career Information Services Committee of the Adult Lifelong Learning Section of the Public Library Association, American Library Association, offers a concise look at creating a resume. The book includes sample resumes for such job seeker categories as worker with little training or skills, first-time job seeker, career changer, older worker, and worker moving into management.

*The Resume Solution: How To Write (And Use) a Resume That Gets Results* by David Swanson includes notes about the person behind each sample resume. The notes help readers understand why each resume was done in the way it was.

*Resumes That Knock 'Em Dead* by Martin John Yate gives over 100 examples of real resumes that got real jobs for real people. The

# R. KEITH JORDAN
4355 South Highland Road
Dallas, TX 75235
(214) 352-3100

### RECEPTIONIST

More than two years of reception experience in busy offices

### RECEPTION SKILLS
- Well-groomed, stylish dresser
- Cheerful, friendly greeter
- Pleasant telephone voice
- Punctual – *Was **never** late and missed only 2 days of work in 2-1/2 years*

### EQUIPMENT SKILLS
- Efficient on 30-line telephone system
- WordPerfect 5.1 (using IBM personal computer) – accurately keyboard 70 words per minute
- DacEasy Accounting 4.2 (using PC) – data entry and client statement generation
- Skilled with transcription equipment
- Accurate on 10-key adding machine
- Operate fax

### GOOD WORKER SKILLS
- Learn quickly
- Self-motivated
- Honest, dependable, reliable
- Pride in doing a good job
- Follow instructions
- Get along with supervisors and co-workers
- Meet deadlines
- Well organized

### RECEPTION EXPERIENCE
- Large, national stock brokerage (1-1/2 years)
  *My supervisor said she had "had more compliments from both clients and employees on [my] job performance than for any previous receptionist"*
- Small, family-operated accounting firm (1 year)

### EDUCATION
- Studying nights toward A.A. degree
  *3.9 GPA in business courses*
  *Top grade in keyboarding class*
- WordPerfect 5.1 training
  *My instructor said I "grasped the computer program concepts faster than any prior student"*

FUNCTIONAL RESUME

# MARILYN MORALES

**65 Tinning Street**          San Francisco, CA 94107          **(415) 545-3379**

---

## COMPUTER SYSTEMS ANALYST

Strong background of more than 10 years as programmer/analyst developing, testing and documenting software on minicomputers and mainframe computers

---

## COMPUTER SKILLS

**LANGUAGES &**
**OPERATING SYSTEMS:**  ASSEMBLER, BASIC, C, COBOL, FORTRAN, MS-DOS, PASCAL

**HARDWARE:**  Apple, Compaq, DEC, Hewlett Packard, IBM, PRIME

---

## WORK HIGHLIGHTS

- *Redesigned computer system with minimal equipment cost, resulting in a faster, more efficient program with total processing output increased 500%*
- *Directed staff of 10 in the conversion of a manual inventory system to a computerized system*
- *Designed, programmed, tested and documented a report generating program that tracked distribution of more than 1 million parts*
- *Trained and cross-trained 75 employees on all phases of company's computer system*
- *Chosen as team leader because of strong oral and written communication skills*

---

## EXPERIENCE

Concord Pharmaceuticals                                         San Francisco, CA
**Senior systems analyst**                                      **1989 to Present**
**Systems analyst**                                             **1987 to 1989**
Conduct programming and research projects for manufacturer of pharmaceuticals

Willis Computer Laboratories                                    San Francisco, CA
**Programmer**                                                  **1981 to 1987**
Developed, debugged, and documented software for company's customer billing system ($16M manufacturer of hardware and software with 4 divisions and 300 employees)

---

## EDUCATION

University of California, Berkeley
**B.S. Computer Science**                                       **1981**
Held part-time jobs and paid all college tuition and expenses

---

## PROFESSIONAL AFFILIATIONS

Association of Computer Professionals
**Officer (president, vice president and treasurer)**
**of local chapter**                                            **1989 to Present**

COMBINATION RESUME

examples include such high-demand occupations as computer operator, electrician, food service salesperson, legal secretary, and software engineer.

## Choose Your Style

Let's review the advantages of the three styles of resumes discussed in this chapter. Reverse chronological resumes show off a strong school and work history. Functional resumes spotlight what you can do rather than charting a time line of what you have done and where you have done it. Combination resumes blend the best of reverse chronological and functional in a style created especially for you.

If you're an older first-time job hunter or a career changer, you may have special reason to consider a functional or combination resume. If your disability occurred later in life and caused an interruption in your work record, you may also want to consider a functional or combination resume. These two styles are particularly advantageous in cases in which past experience is best explained in a one-on-one interview rather than on paper.

As a general benchmark, the combination resume is the style that most benefits job seekers who have disabilities. This is because members of the disability community often have gaps in their work histories. But new graduates may do as well or better with a *thoughtfully constructed* reverse chronological style.

No matter what style you choose, design it to fit you.

## DID SOMEONE SAY "CURRICULUM VITAE?"

A curriculum vitae—also called a vita—is not a resume, nor is it a style of resume. But a curriculum vitae, by itself or in conjunction with a resume, may be used as a job hunt tool in some arenas.

At one time, formal curricula vitae were used only when applying to academic institutions. Although their use is more widespread today, resumes and curricula vitae are not interchangeable job hunt documents. What are their differences?

A **resume** is a job hunt document carefully designed to reveal your qualifications for a specific type of position. It focuses attention on an individual's strongest qualifications. It often is one to two pages in length.

A **curriculum vitae** is a formal, comprehensive biographical statement, which includes an individual's publications and honors. One of its uses is by applicants seeking academic jobs and professional-level health care and research positions. It may also be used in applying for social services and other types of positions. A curriculum vitae often is three to fifteen pages in length.

If you're applying to an organization that requests a curriculum vitae, get specifics on items to be covered.

## RESUME DO'S AND DON'TS

Let's review. You've gathered data by category on work sheets. You've reviewed sample resumes. You've decided which style looks best for you. Now look at key tips on writing an interview-winning resume.

## Resume Do's

- **Do prepare the draft of your resume yourself.** You may not be able to do the final writing or the final production. But by organizing your thoughts in resume form, you reinforce the information in your mind that you'll use at an interview. It is acceptable to get professional resume writers to tune up your document, but be aware that many professionals turn out a mass-production product that savvy recruiters can spot a mile away. A well thought out, honest, sincere effort beats a slick, professionally printed canned copy every time.

- **Do lead with your most qualifying experience.** Education generally follows work experience on a resume, unless the applicant is a new graduate, has scant work history, or the applicant is applying for a position relating to teaching. Then education takes the lead.

- **Do consider a consolidated experience category.** Many people with disabilities will draw upon volunteer rather than paid work experience to show evidence of job qualifications. Others will have spotty work histories. This certainly is understandable. But why put blinking lights around a less than ideal work history? Instead, consider combining all work-related history under the heading of "Related Experience" (rather than "Work Experience"). This includes paid and volunteer jobs whether full- or part-time, internships, summer jobs, and after school jobs—everything. Even when employers discount volunteer experience, as often happens to women who are returning to the job market, they have to admire your resourcefulness in the approach.

- **Do include other names you've been known by.** For a variety of reasons, many people will have more than one name during their lifetime. If your legal name is different now than it was at the time of a listed degree or employment, enter the name just after the appropriate entry so the information can be verified.

- **Do use action words.** Action words add life to your resume. *Achieved, designed, expanded, interpreted, improved, mastered, simplified,* and *won* hold a lot of punch.

- **Do use grouping of thoughts.** Because you're not using full sentences, you can drop the "I" beginning from every sentence. "I coordinated..." becomes *Coordinated...* Dropping the "I" puts emphasis on the action verb and keeps you from sounding like a braggart.

- **Do emphasize accomplishments.** Now is not the time to be humble. Emphasize specific accomplishments and results over duties and responsibilities.

- **Do use concrete examples that can be measured.** Be specific, using "measured" examples. "I'm good with children" is nonspecific and sounds braggy. *Supervised six preschoolers* gives strength to your achievement. Here are more examples:

Numbers
- *Missed one day of work in two years.*
- *Answered 150 telephone calls on a typical day.*

Percentages
- *Increased productivity 20 percent by assigning flex hours to staff.*
- *Reduced this year's Christmas inventory shortages by 15 percent over last year's.*

Amounts
- *Saved my employer $250 a month by devising new method of inventory control.*
- *Increased response to direct mail sales by $17,000 annually.*

Supreme Statements
- *Was the only candy striper ever allowed to work on the pediatrics ward of Trinity Lutheran Hospital.*
- *My employer said I was the most accurate bookkeeper he had ever hired.*

- **Do avoid anything negative.** If employers might consider it negative, cut it. This could include disclosure, which has been comprehensively discussed earlier. It could include indications that you don't finish what you start, such as "Attended Ajax College." The remedy is to spell out what you gained by attending Ajax College and, if true, indicate your intention to continue studying for your degree by night. It could include volunteering that you are a single parent with two toddlers.

In brief, before leaving an item in your resume, put yourself in the employer's head and ask if a statement raises a question about the applicant's appropriateness for the job.

- **Do keep the length at one or two pages.** While there are cases when longer resumes are acceptable, in today's hurried world most readers doze off after one or two pages.

- **Do be generous with white space.** Use wide margins and space between sections. Employers try to remain objective when looking at resumes, but human nature guides them toward those that are easiest to read. Resumes with lots of white space are easiest to read.

  To prove the point, pick up a newspaper. Notice how many paragraphs are only one sentence in length. Why? Because, in the interests of readability, a cardinal rule in newswriting is to keep paragraphs brief. Short paragraphs put more paragraphs on the page. More paragraphs mean more paragraph indents and more possibilities of short last lines. More white space, more readable copy.

- **Do use bullets, bold type, capital letters, and underlining.** Special type guides the eye and breaks up material—as long as it isn't overdone. Columns and short lines are the easiest to read. Screeners read more of those resumes that are easy to read.

- **Do check consistency in capitalization and punctuation.** Uniformly capitalize, but don't capitalize words that aren't proper nouns. You don't have to put periods at the end of lines or phrases, but if you do it, do it consistently.

- **Do check continuity of history.** Be conscious of the time flow in education and experience. Make sure it progresses from last to first.

- **Do review your resume item by item.** If you're in doubt about whether to include something, ask yourself if it adds anything to your objective of being hired for the job. Then ask yourself if it adds anything to what you can do for the employer. If it doesn't do either, cut it.

- **Do have at least two other people review it.** Consider business people you know through work, family, or church. Solicit their professional opinion. Ask them for specific criticism and suggestions.

After editing and editing and editing, rewriting your resume one more time is probably the last thing you want to do. But if incorporating reviewers' suggestions into another rewrite leads to more job interviews and eventually a job, isn't it worth the additional effort?

- **Do proofread.** Even a single spelling, grammar, punctuation, or typographical error can make a negative impression. Alterations, use of white corrective fluid, or black marks from poor-quality photocopying look bad as well. When employers have so many applicants to choose from, why would they choose someone who presents him- or herself poorly? Employers may think a sloppy resume reflects the potential quality of its writer's on-job performance.

- **Do proofread again.**

- **Do have at least two other people proofread it.** Don't ask just anyone to proofread your resume; find people whose eyes fly to errors. The two people who proofread your resume may or may not be the pair who reviewed it.

- **Do send your references a copy of your resume.** Clue references on what you want employers to know about you by giving them a copy of your resume. Highlight key portions you want emphasized. Having your resume gives them a ready reminder of details when employers call. Your references will appreciate the courtesy.

- **Do use good paper.** Buy the best paper you can afford. Use standard size (8½" x 11"), twenty- to twenty-four-pound weight with some cotton fiber. Use white or off-white, never gray or pastel mauve—the employer may dislike the color. Another reason to avoid colors is that some produce dirty-looking photocopies. If an employer shares your resume with other organization members, you want all copies to make a crisp first impression, not a muddy one.

- **Do consider printing options.** "Original" resumes prepared individually on electronic typewriters, word processors, or computers with letter-quality or laser printers are the most impressive. They also allow a resume to be revised easily and targeted for a specific job opening at a specific organization.

If original resumes are not possible, a first-class photocopy shop can copy your original master onto your quality resume paper. Some commercial copy shops now have super photocopy equipment that costs many thousands of dollars. The quality of the commercial copiers' crisp, clean, and sharp reproduction is dramatically superior to that of ordinary copiers. Prices are reasonable. Look into it.

## Resume Don'ts

- **Don't exaggerate.** Don't overstate your qualifications. You must be able to do the job if you get it. Avoid claiming "complete responsibility" for anything. Some screeners turn off when an applicant takes credit for what they feel must be a team effort.

- **Don't use the word "RESUME" in heading.** It's a waste of precious space.

- **Don't make handwritten corrections to old resumes.** Update your resume. Scribbled changes not only look messy, they make an employer think you've been job hunting for a long time and that nobody wants to hire you.

- **Don't date your resume.** The reason is the same as the one above.

- **Don't put a title in front of your name.** Never put "Mr.," "Ms.," "Miss," or "Mrs." before your name in a resume. It looks out of place.

- **Don't use nicknames.** Nicknames—such as Elizabeth "Betsy" Knotts or William "Red" Hall—don't belong in resumes. Neither do initials. "R.J." Conners should apply using his given name of Robert J. Conners.

- **Don't use unusual abbreviations or obscure acronyms.** Unfamiliar abbreviations and acronyms are puzzling. On first mention, organization names and terms used in particular professions should be spelled out. Acronyms or abbreviations are acceptable on second mention. Use New York Stock Exchange on first reference, NYSE on second. Use United Mine Workers of America on first reference, Mine Workers union on second.

  Commonly known academic degrees—such as M.D. (Doctor of Medicine) or M.B.A. (Master of Business Administration)—can be abbreviated. Lesser known degrees—such as M.S.Env.E. (Master of Science in Environmental Engineering) or D.A.I.S. (Doctor of Arts in Information Systems)—are better spelled out.

- **Don't include months.** Months are unnecessary in historical dates. They can work against you by red flagging minor time gaps and short-term jobs.

- **Don't include religion, race, national origin, or political affiliation.** Don't include these items unless you're applying to an organization where this information may be considered advantageous, such as a bookkeeper at a church.
- **Don't include salary requirements.** Salaries are negotiable. Until an interview, you don't know what's being offered and the employer only has a paper picture of you—hardly enough information upon which either of you can base a salary.
- **Don't include salaries for previous jobs.** Salary histories rarely work to your advantage.
- **Don't include a reason for leaving your last job.** The reason for leaving your last job is a matter to be discussed, if you choose to, in an interview.

## LAY OUT YOUR STANDOUT RESUME

Now that you're armed with an arsenal of information, you're ready to lay out your standout resume.

Constantly keep in mind that your resume may have but thirty seconds to impress a screener. The appearance of your resume is uniquely important because it is often your first contact with an employer and, as such, is your first opportunity to make a good impression.

The first several versions of your resume will be drafts. You decide which headings to use and what to call them. You choose entries from your work sheets and massage the material into a great advertisement. You edit, edit, edit.

Put your resume aside, then come back to it in a day or two. Reread it, checking to see if it clearly answers these employer questions:

- Who are you?
- What job do you want?
- What do you know?
- What can you do?
- What have you done?

If your resume doesn't answer these basic employer questions, edit until it does. Then it's time to make the final cuts.

## SNIP, SNIP, SNIP!

One of the hardest things when composing a resume is coming up with information to put in it. Once we've gone through the process of writing down all the wonderful things we've accomplished in our lives, it's even harder—but necessary—to leave most of them on the cutting room floor.

Think of a movie production. Many scenes—or parts of scenes—that are filmed never make it to the big screen. Why? Because editors know that great scenes stand out best when presented in a fast-flowing pattern without the distraction of unnecessary mediocre scenes.

Cut anything from your final resume that either doesn't add something to your objective of being hired for this job or that doesn't suggest what you can do for the employer. Cut, cut, cut. Then cut some more until it is one or two pages long. Remember, mediocre resumes that aren't edited until they stand out have a good chance of hitting the job screener's cutting room floor.

Resumes are just half of your job hunt advertisement. Cover letters are the other half.

## ANATOMY OF A COVER LETTER

Put as much care into creating a standout cover letter as you did into creating a standout resume. After all, it is the first part of your first impression.

Your cover letter's job is to grab the attention of screeners immediately and to match your credentials to three major responsibilities of the job. Isn't this restating qualifications already in your resume? Yes. Won't this make the screener read repetitious information? Yes. But stating the match up front will save the screener time searching through your resume. And when the screener turns to your resume and comes across your qualifications again, it will reinforce how right you are for the job. *This* information bears repeating and rereading.

Cover letters, like resumes, have primary parts. In addition to your address, the date, the address of the person or organization you're applying to, and a closing, a cover letter has a body. The body of a standout cover letter is three paragraphs.

### First Paragraph

In the first paragraph, you *explain the reason you're writing the letter, what you want, and how you came to contact the person or organization.* Are you responding to an advertisement or writing at the suggestion of a third-party referral? The very best letter opens with the name of a mutual friend or associate of the employer: *John*

*Mayberry suggested I send you my resume. . . .*Use verbs like *fascinated, delighted,* and *intrigued* to convey enthusiasm.

## Second Paragraph

Here's where you put sizzle in the sell. *Briefly highlight a few accomplishments that match three major responsibilities of the position or needs of the organization.* Choose your strongest points to impress the employer most.

## Third Paragraph

Indicate a resume is enclosed. *Request an interview.* Tell the reader you will call to follow up. This will help you end-run the gatekeeper—a secretary or assistant, for example—when you telephone because you can truthfully say the person is expecting your call.

Two sample cover letters are included to get you going: one is unsolicited, the other is responding to an ad. Besides addressing a different reason for writing, each gives a different example of an option for follow up.

---

> Take Time Now
> to Study the
> **Sample Cover Letters**

---

## COVER LETTER DO'S AND DON'TS

Like resumes, cover letters also have do's and don'ts. Follow these guidelines when preparing yours.

## Cover Letter Do's

- **Do make each letter an original.** Duplicated letters with fill-ins are obvious. Don't use them. Electronic typewriters, word processors, or computers with letter-quality printers produce the most impressive cover letters. If you don't have access to one of these, type your letter. If you don't have a typewriter, pay someone who does.

- **Do follow instructions in recruitment ads.** If you're responding to a recruitment ad, follow instructions given in the ad. If it asks you to send a copy of your references with your resume, do it.

2734 Hornblend Street
San Diego, CA 92107
(619) 236-4512

July 26, 1992

Richard K. Circuit, Esq.
Circuit, McKellogg, Kinney & Ross
1205 Prospect Street, Suite 400
La Jolla, CA 92037

Dear Mr. Circuit:

Our mutual friend Bill Johnson recommended I contact you regarding the possibility of an opening for a senior associate attorney. I am excited by the prospect of interviewing at your prestigious firm.

Bill explained to me the expansion you're contemplating. He also relayed your experience requirements for the anticipated opening. My <u>five years of civil litigation experience</u> (three years at Wahl, Road & Westinghouse specializing in real estate and two years at Miller & Thomas specializing in contract law) exceeds your requirements. My ability to <u>successfully lead a real estate litigation team</u>—such as the one you may be assembling—is proven with the $1.4 million award to my client in WILSON v. BOYLE. Further, I know that Circuit, McKellogg, Kinney & Ross takes pride in hiring top law students: I ranked in the <u>top 5 percent of my graduating class</u> at the University of San Diego School of Law and was <u>editor of the law review.</u>

A copy of my resume is enclosed. I will call you later this week to see when we can meet.

Sincerely,

Diane S. Rausch

UNSOLICITED COVER LETTER

510 Adams Avenue
Newark, NJ 07102
(201) 523-4390

July 26, 1992

Ms. Caroline Dobson, Manager
Broadway Theatre Productions, Inc.
2496 Broadway
New York, NY 10013

Dear Ms. Dobson:

Your ad in the <u>New York Times</u> seeking a carpenter to work on theater productions greatly interests me. I've recently moved to the New York area and am anxious to continue in theater work.

My professional qualifications listed below are a perfect match for your stated requirements.

| <u>Experience You Require</u> | <u>My Qualifications</u> |
| --- | --- |
| Carpentry, 5 yrs | More than 15 years' experience as a licensed carpenter, including 10 as a general contractor. |
| Theater, 2 yrs | Five years at San Diego's Old Globe Theatre and 2 years at San Diego Repertory Theatre (productions included <u>Skin of Our Teeth</u>, <u>Antony and Cleopatra</u>, <u>Kiss Me Kate</u>, <u>Comedy of Errors</u>, and <u>Phantom of the Opera</u>). |
| Supervisory, 2 yrs | Lead carpenter at the Old Globe and stage manager at the San Diego Rep. General contractor supervising 2 to 15 employees and subcontractors. |

My skills and experience are more fully outlined in the enclosed resume. I will call you on Thursday to see when we can arrange an interview.

Sincerely,


Michael O'Meinz

COVER LETTER RESPONDING TO AN AD

You'll have to make your own decision about requests for salary histories. Some experts argue that you must include one if the ad asks for it. Others are emphatic about not mailing it because it may price you out of the market (too much or too little) and that it is information you will want to discuss face to face. If you decide to withhold it, state in the letter that you will be glad to discuss your salary record in an interview.

- **Do include your telephone number in the heading.** Make it as easy as possible for the employer to contact you. List your telephone number directly under your address.

- **Do date your cover letter.**

- **Do time your letter's arrival.** Plan your package's arrival to avoid arriving on the screener's desk on Monday, the heaviest mail day, or Friday, the wrap-up day. Be prompt when responding to ads, but don't fret if your package arrives a day or two after the first wave of responses. It may actually get more attention then.

- **Do use industry jargon when possible.** Here's where you lay on your knowledge of the career field—but don't overdo it.

- **Do make every word count.**

- **Do keep the letter to one page.**

- **Do pay attention to layout.** Make sure your letter looks balanced on the page. Is it too high or too low on the page? Are the margins too wide or too narrow?

- **Do proofread.**

- **Do proofread again.**

- **Do have someone else proofread it.**

- **Do use coordinated or matching paper.** Use paper that relates to your resume for a polished sales look. You may use the same size paper or Monarch size (7¼" x 10½"). Remember, this is your advertisement for an interview.

- **Do keep a copy of every cover letter.**

- **Do make envelopes count.** Purchase business envelopes (size 9 or 10) that match your cover letters.

   *Tip:* If you want your paperwork to stand out from the stacks of business-size envelopes and large manila envelopes job screeners receive, mail your resumes and cover letters in large *white* envelopes (9" x 12"). The large size keeps your paperwork sharper looking with no mailing folds. The white color matches your paperwork.

- **Do sign your letter and enclose your resume.** An unsigned letter or forgotten resume conveys carelessness.

## Cover Letter Don'ts

- **Don't put your name in the heading.** The correct place for your typed name is below your signature, not in the heading with your address.
- **Don't use "Dear Sir."** In the job hunt world, "sirs" live in wastebaskets. Use names. If you are making direct application or networking, call for the name and title of the person who would supervise or interview you. If you are responding to a recruitment ad, the name will be in the ad. An exception is the ad that only gives a box number. In that case, you have no choice other than to write *Dear Employer.* Never address an unknown person as "Dear Sir" or "Dear Madam."
- **Don't refer to yourself by a nickname.** When you meet face to face you can tell the interviewer the name you prefer.
- **Don't be cutesy.** Businesslike demeanor wins interviews over the gimmicky, novel, or unconventional—unless you're applying for an advertising position.
- **Don't overuse "I."** Use the first-person pronoun sparingly. Try not to start paragraphs with "I."
- **Don't used abbreviations or acronyms.** Period.
- **Don't tell all in the letter.** A strong cover letter entices the reader but saves your best for the interview.
- **Don't include your photograph.** Photographs give employers a chance to discriminate. So unless you're applying for a position where the employer can legally ask for yours, it's not advisable to send one.
- **Don't forget to follow up.** If you give a specific day that you will follow up, calendar it and be sure to call.

Each time your write a cover letter, review it carefully. Ask yourself if the letter answers these employer questions:

- Why are you writing?
- What do you want?
- Why are your qualifications of interest to our organization?
- How do you plan to follow up?

If it doesn't, rewrite until it does.

When your standout resumes and cover letters show a job match that sizzles, employers' interests will be piqued.

# 10

# Finding job leads

You're all dressed up and now you're ready to find a place to go. You've written a standout resume, perhaps in several versions, an exercise that has ordered your thinking about your skills and qualifications. You've drafted a standout cover letter shell that you'll *customize employer by employer,* this shows that you're a serious contender for employment and that your qualifications are a good match for the job's specifications.

In today's competitive job market, it's more important than ever to effectively organize and target your job search. Successful job seekers who hear those magic words, "You're hired," know the fastest way to win the job they want is to:

- Devote more time daily to searching
- Use multiple methods of finding job leads and contact more employers
- Line up more interviews

It is the successful job seekers with whom you're competing. They won't be working part time to land the position they want—and possibly the position you want. The "pro" job seekers are dialing the telephone and pounding the pavement forty to eighty hours a week.

Every applicant must search harder than ever when times are tough because more people are competing to fill fewer job openings. The Americans with Disabilities Act may help get your foot in the application process door, but *you* must convince the prospective employer that you are a perfect match for the job—more perfect than all the other people applying for the same position. *Remember, ADA holds the promise of* **equal** *employment opportunities, but it does not require preferential hiring to job seekers with disabilities.*

Think of job searching as hiring yourself to find the job you want. So no sleeping in, no goofing off. Get to work early, stay late, and find as many job leads and set up as many interviews as you possibly can.

## JOB LEADS, JOB LEADS, JOB LEADS

In finding job leads, as in resume writing, there are no absolutes. From time to time, you'll read pronouncements by "experts" who say there's only *one* way to job hunt—networking, for instance—and that everything else—such as responding to newspaper recruitment ads—is a waste of time. Don't believe them. There really are no absolutes in job search. Anyone who says otherwise lacks an in-depth and sophisticated understanding of job finding.

This is not to say that some methods may not work better for certain individuals than for others. A number of studies have been done on effective job-hunt channels but none are definitive. One, a recent large national study by "The Fordyce Letter," an employment industry newsletter, reports on the hiring methods used by employers when filling positions paying $25,000 a year and up. Among human resource specialists surveyed, walk-ins, in-house files, and recruitment ads took top honors. Unsolicited mailed-in resumes, job fairs, and database services ranked lowest.

The Fordyce survey shows *employers' most regularly used methods of hiring.* Your mission is to discover and pursue *your most effective methods of finding job leads*—the ones that produce the most good leads for you. Concentrate on these methods but not to the total neglect of the others. You never know when a less-used method will score one good lead—the lead you've been waiting for.

For a clearer picture of the various methods of finding job leads, let's break the possibilities down into three categories:

1) **Personal contacts and contacts of personal contacts and their contacts**

2) **Direct approach**

3) **Job market services (such as employment agencies and recruitment ads)**

Most studies agree that as many as two-thirds of the nation's jobs are found using category one and two—personal contacts and the direct approach. But, for people with disabilities, category three is compelling because quite a few of its services revolve around intermediaries who can open employment doors for you.

Here are effective ways to find job leads. As you read, place a check mark next to those with which you feel most comfortable and with which you are most likely to stick until your campaign ends with victory.

## Category 1: Personal Contacts and Contacts of Personal Contacts and Their Contacts

Many job hunters identify personal contacts as the richest source of finding job leads. And many employers prefer to hire applicants who have been referred by someone they know.

| "The Fordyce Letter" Employer Hiring Methods Study | |
| --- | --- |
| **Hiring Method** | **Percent** |
| Walk-ins | 99% |
| In-house files | 98% |
| Recruitment ads | 91% |
| Employee referrals | 56% |
| Private employment agencies | 24% |
| Public employment services | 18% |
| Executive search firms | 5% |
| Database services | 3% |
| Job fairs | 1% |
| Unsolicited mailed-in resumes | 1% |

Note: Percentages do not total 100%; employers checked most regularly used methods

Based on "Employer Practices and Attitudes Survey," "The Fordyce Letter." December 1991.

It is commonly believed that a vast percentage of jobs—as much as 80 percent—are filled without ever coming to public attention through job market services. By using personal contacts, you will be tapping the "hidden job market" that many people believe hoards a majority of the best positions.

"Personal contacts are especially important for people with disabilities," says Nancy Griffin, consumer options consultant for the Indiana Association of Rehabilitation Facilities in Indianapolis. "When someone who knows you and recognizes your abilities and experience refers you to a prospective employer, the *disability* gets set aside and the *person* is what matters. Working from referrals is better than going in an employer's door cold and having to deal with all the issues raised because of your disability," says Griffin, who is an amputee. "You go in with the employer presold on your talent."

Personal contacts basically come in two flavors: *Third-party referrers* and *referral chains.*

### Third-Party Referrers

Third-party referrers are, for most people with disabilities, probably the method of choice for job finding. Suppose you've made friends with your physician. A little sleeve tugging may convince the busy doctor to make a few calls on your behalf to other patients who are employers. Can you imagine an employer turning down his or her own doctor's simple request to meet with you? Third-party referrers can be thought of as the fairy godmothers and godfathers of job seekers. Interviews arranged by influential third parties are the crown jewels of job search to any job seeker, but they are even more precious to job seekers with disabilities. Why?

As mentioned in Chapter 2, a legal mandate against disability employment discrimination doesn't mean that—poof! bias is history. It does mean that when a personal contact presents an employer with a qualified applicant who happens to have a disability, the applicant is virtually guaranteed an interview. Five hypothetical employer scenarios explain why this is so, using their histories of and attitudes toward hiring workers with disabilities.

*Experienced and Welcoming.* Company A has hired individuals with disabilities in the past and has found them to be first-rate employees. When a personal contact refers an applicant with a disability, Company A calendars an interview on the spot.

*Experienced and Negative.* Company B has hired a few individuals with disabilities and has had nothing but bad experiences. Company B has a case of BC syndrome (Brown Cow syndrome):

because it has seen one cow that's brown, it assumes all cows are brown. Although Company B assumes anyone it hires who has a disability will result in a troublesome employment, when a personal contact refers an applicant with a disability and sings that person's praises, Company B agrees—primarily because of ADA—to try one more time and schedules an interview.

*Inexperienced but Willing.* Company C has never hired an individual with a disability because no one with a known disability has ever applied. Aware of ADA and the inevitable response of many individuals with disabilities to join the work force, Company C welcomes the opportunity to increase its pool of qualified applicants and potential employees. Company C tells the personal contact to have the applicant send in a resume and call to set up an interview.

*Inexperienced and Wary.* Company D has never hired an individual with a disability because it has been afraid of the unknowns of employing a worker with a disability. Company D has been warned by its attorneys of the stiff penalties and legal entanglements associated with burying its executive head in the sand and pleading ignorance of ADA. Company D realizes that the day will come when it must interview and possibly hire a qualified applicant with a disability or face the consequences.

When a personal contact refers an applicant with a disability, Company D jumps at the chance to interview someone who is recommended. Company D asks the personal contact questions—*and gets reassuring answers*—about the applicant's disability. (Company D knows that it legally cannot ask the applicant these questions.)

*Inexperienced and Unknowing.* Company E is a smallish firm whose management has been so busy surviving in the marketplace that the firm's decision makers are unaware of ADA and its workplace-changing implications. Your third-party referrer, who does know about it because you told the referrer, can explain that the new legislation is in effect and what it means to Company E. If Company E is in a hiring mode (for jobs for which you qualify) and refuses to even interview you, it does so at its own risk.

From your perspective, it matters little whether your personal contact refers you to an employer who is experienced and welcoming, experienced and negative, inexperienced but willing, inexperienced and wary, or inexperienced and unknowing. What matters is that you now have the opportunity to sell yourself in an interview.

When making the contact, your referrer can handle the disability disclosure question for you, assuring prospective employers that you are willing and able to do the job. Functioning, in effect, as your agents, third-party referrers can praise you to the skies—which will be more believable than you tooting your own horn. You are riding into interviews on the credibility coattails of third-party referrers. Bless them!

### Referral Chains

Referral chains—buzz worded "networking"—are the next best thing to third-party referrers. Referral chains have been around a long time but leaped into national prominence in the 1970s with publication of Tom Jackson's book *The Hidden Job Market*. In a nutshell, referral chains use people links to hopscotch from unemployment to employment. You start with people you know and ask them to refer you to people they know. The process continues ad infinitum until you find a job. Using referral chains is merely making and using contacts in ever-widening circles.

"The value of networking is that it's not just the first person you contact who may help," explains Nancy Griffin, "the contacts just keep going. It's not a conversation with one person, it's a conversation with all the people they talk to, and all the people *they* talk to, and so on and so on."

Begin today by making a list of people you know who may be a link to a job opportunity. Title it "Networking List 1: Personal Contacts." Consider people who can:

- Offer you a job
- Refer you to someone who can arrange an interview
- Tell you about a job opening
- Give you the name of someone who can do any of the above

Include on your contact list the following groups of people under which you list specific individuals:

- Family
- Friends
- Neighbors
- Employers and former employers
- Co-workers and former co-workers
- Teachers and former teachers
- Classmates and former classmates
- Members of my church or synagogue
- Members of my professional organizations

- Members of my health/sports clubs
- Members of my social clubs
- Friends of my parents and other family members
- My friends' parents and other family members
- Doctors, dentists, physical therapists, counselors, and staffs
- Bank officers and staff
- Insurance representatives, attorneys, stockbrokers, and staffs
- Librarians
- Mail carriers and police officers
- Beauticians, manicurists, massage therapists
- Taxi and busdrivers
- Retailers
- People who turn me down for a job

This sampling of personal contacts gives you an idea of the magnitude of networking opportunities waiting to be tapped as you go about everyday life. Ann Baber and Lynne Wayman's book, *Great Connections: Small Talk and Networking for Businesspeople,* helps you turn small talk into profitable networking whether in one-on-one chance meetings or at large organized gatherings. *Network Your Way To Job and Career Success: Your Complete Guide To Creating New Opportunities,* by Ronald L. Krannich, Ph.D., and Caryl Rae Krannich, Ph.D., gives practical guidance on how to develop, expand, and use networks for finding jobs and advancing careers.

Whether you network in person or pick up the telephone and call contacts, here are three questions to help track down job leads:

- *Do you know an employer who may have a position open in my line of work?*
- *Would you be willing to call this person and make an introduction?* —or— *May I tell this person that you recommended I call?*
- *Do you know anyone else who knows an employer that may have an opening?*

Your personal contacts list will continue to grow as each lead branches off into other leads. Faithfully get in touch with each and every one of them. It's important to keep accurate records.

Begin a second list titled "Networking List 2: Potential Employers" for employer leads you'll discover while talking with the people on your first list. Make telephone calls to the potential employers on this list to set up interviews. When you make calls on a referral basis, you are making "warm calls." This is in contrast to "cold calls" in which you call strangers without using a third party's coattails.

Keep your calls brief by planning ahead what you're going to say. You may have sixty seconds or less to line up an interview. Clearly state:

- Who you are
- Who referred you
- The type of position you seek
- What you want—an interview or another reference

Ask for an interview in a way that makes it extremely difficult for the target employer to reject you out of hand, as this example illustrates.

*My name is—. Richard Johnson, my former teacher, asked me to call you. I attended ABC School of Technology and graduated in the top 10 percent of my class. Mr. Johnson thinks we should meet. I'm interested in a position as a robot repairer. If you can see me, when would be a convenient time for us to get together? Would Wednesday afternoon or Friday morning be better for you?*

Sometimes you'll get interviews, sometimes you won't. When you fail to make a connection, take a deep breath and keep building your referral chain.

*I'm sorry to hear that. I was looking forward to meeting with you. Thanks for your time. Oh, by the way, can you think of other people I should be talking to? It would be a big help to me if you could make a couple of suggestions.* (After hearing names and telephone numbers.) *Is it okay with you if I mention to these referrals that you gave me their names?*

Another primary method of networking is meeting people in large groups, particularly those found at professional meetings, conferences, and trade shows. If you don't know which local meetings to attend, read meeting calendars in newspaper business sections and locate organizations in *The Encyclopedia of Associations*, Gale Research.

At the meetings, exchange business cards. If you're unemployed, your own business card should have your name and contact information; handwrite on the front of the card the type of position you seek.

But the mere exchange of business cards does not a contact make. Volunteer for committees that lend visibility. Without being a bore, do talk about the fact that you're job hunting.

If you can afford to attend a regional or national conference, you may net forty to fifty potentially rewarding contacts quickly, says networking expert Dr. Mel Schnapper, president of Successful Job Hunting, a career consulting firm in Chicago. Give each your card and resume.

"Job hunting at a conference is a 6:30 A.M. to midnight job. You are gathering referrals that can lead to future interviews. Back home, immediately write letters, recalling conversations. Then 'bullet' your accomplishments relevant to the employer you're targeting. Call the people later and ask if they've read your resume. Chances are they haven't. Repeat your strengths, and ask who they know who would hire someone with your qualifications," Dr. Schnapper advises.

Referral chains work best when you're still employed or not under pressure to find a job immediately. Once you learn effective techniques, you can network your way to dozens of prospective job leads each week.

## Category 2: Direct Approach

It can be argued that using a referral to warm-call an employer who has not advertised a job opening is a direct approach. But an even more direct approach is what sales people call "cold calling." It means looking for work by going unreferred from one employer to another.

Consider the three basic methods of initiating direct contact:

- Walking into the employment site unannounced
- Writing for an interview
- Telephoning for an interview

The first method is unsuitable for professional or managerial positions, but may work fine for blue collar and office support employment. A secretary, for instance, may start at the top of a tall office building and work down, applying at each firm until a job is found.

The second method, sending an unsolicited resume with a cover letter, may work, but don't count on it. Even when you feel you're better at writing than talking, improve your odds by telephoning after sending the letter. Because your letter says you will call to set an interview time, you truthfully can answer *Yes* when a secretary (read "gatekeeper" to the boss) asks if your call is expected.

Telephoning, the third method, is probably the most effective way to set up unreferred interviews, providing you have good verbal skills and self-confidence. To compile a telemarketing list for cold calling, start with the Yellow Pages. Add employer names from commercial job bank books that list employers in a given city, plus employer lists found in library business directories (see Chapter 11 on researching employers). You will cold call employer after employer.

Think of two targets of cold calling: a human resources
department specialist and the hiring decision maker (the department manager who would be your boss). The human resources
specialist screens applicants to make sure they have the necessary
qualifications, while the department manager selects those who
will be hired. Suppose you are seeking a job in a broad career
field—such as office support—that can be done in many departments of a company. You would make straightforward calls to the
human resources office and ask for the employment manager. But
if you seek a position in a particular department of an organization,
the hiring manager would be your target.

You may not have great difficulty getting through to a human
resources department specialist (if not the employment manager).
But cutting through the barriers to decision makers is a practiced
art. First you must find out the name from the employer's
switchboard. If asked why you want to know, say you wish to send
correspondence to that department head and need the correct
name spelling, exact title, and address. The next day call back and,
without hesitation, ask for the person.

After identifying the hiring manager, you have two more
decisions to make before initiating your cold call.

1) Should you:
   a) be straightforward in asking for a job?
   b) ask for advice, hoping to get referrals as a result of the
      interview?

2) Are your chances for an interview strengthened by:
   a) immediate disclosure of your disability?
   b) delayed or no disclosure?

In the following example, which begins with getting past the
gatekeeper, we'll assume you are going to ask for advice and
immediately disclose your disability. Suppose you seek a position in
the marketing department. You get the marketing secretary's
name from the main switchboard.

|  |  |
|---|---|
| You to<br>Marketing secretary: | *Ms. Williams, this is —. May I speak to<br>Mr. Hano.* |
| Williams: | *May I tell him what this is about?* |
| You: | *Certainly, Ms. Williams. I am<br>contemplating a career change and as a<br>skilled individual who is covered by the<br>Americans with Disabilities Act, I<br>would appreciate the opportunity to find* |

> *out from Mr. Hano any thoughts or*
> *ideas to improve my job search. Don't*
> *misunderstand, Ms. Williams, I am not*
> *expecting Mr. Hano to offer me a job.*
> *But I do need to get into the loop, and I*
> *believe a few minutes spent with Mr.*
> *Hano would be invaluable in getting my*
> *search off to a strong start. I would only*
> *need a few minutes of his time, and it*
> *would mean a lot to me.* (**If told to**
> **send a resume.**) *That's a fine idea, and*
> *I certainly will do it. But if his schedule*
> *permits, I would value your help in*
> *setting up a time to talk to him as well.*

In this example, you are targeting (by finding out the hiring manager's name), paying the secretary the compliment of honesty, and making the secretary an ally by asking for help, as well as using your ADA coverage as a positive reason for calling. *Admittedly, the advance disclosure of your disability will work against you some of the time. But you'll encounter enough people of good will to make it worth the gamble.*

*Important:* When you do get an interview with a hiring manager on the basis of asking for advice, don't make a liar out of yourself. Don't ask for a job. Ask for advice and referrals. It's much easier to reach other people saying "Jack Hano" suggested you call than it is to call cold. A few of these "warm" referrals and you're off and running on your referral chain.

In another example, you ask for a job and do not disclose your disability.

> You to Human
> Resource Specialist:
>
> *Hello. My name is—, and I'm looking*
> *for a position in marketing research. Are*
> *you hiring now or do you plan to do so in*
> *the foreseeable future?* (**If answer is**
> **negative.**) *Can you suggest any of your*
> *colleagues who are in a hiring mode?*
> *Many thanks.*

Suppose you are cold telemarketing from a roster of a professional association to which you belong. Your message can be even briefer.

> You to Member:
>
> *Hello. I'm —, a fellow member of XYZ*
> *Association. I'm interested in a position*
> *in marketing research. In my search,*
> *who should I be talking to?*

When cold telemarketing, plan your script. Read it over and over—*aloud*. It becomes indelible in your memory. Hear yourself on an audiotape. Does your voice convey the warmth, persuasion, and confidence you hope to project? When you make your calls, use an old salesperson's trick—prop a mirror up where you can see yourself, and make sure you're smiling to keep a lilt in your voice.

If telemarketing—whether warm or cold calling—becomes one of your primary methods of finding job leads, spend adequate time learning sophisticated techniques and getting more tips on how to script your pursuit. A number of job hunt guides contain this information, such as the discussion "Dialing for Dollars" in J. Michael Farr's *The Very Quick Job Search: Get a Good Job in Less Time.*

Cold calling is very difficult work, and some people would rather dig ditches than do it. You're often rudely treated like a pesky intruder. The rejection rate is a killer, even to strong egos. That's one reason why you may want to consider immediate disclosure of your disability—people may be nicer to you. (It is good strategy to use any fact or characteristic, including your disability, that supports your objective of getting hired.)

The reason to attempt cold telemarketing is that, handled properly, it can be very effective. It's good time management to do intense cold calling in the morning and interview in the afternoon. This allows you to line up interviews for that same afternoon.

Remember, there are no absolutes in job search—only a wealth of ideas that work for some people some of the time. Personal contacts and the direct approach are traditional. Some people embellish these categories with creative spunk.

Early in her career, *New York Times* columnist Anna Quindlen applied for a reporter's job at another paper. She was hired after sending the editor a mock threatening note that read: HIRE ANNA QUINDLEN OR YOU SLEEP WITH THE FISHES.

Others have taken the direct approach to the moon. Far-out approaches have included sending carrier pigeons with interview requests tied to their legs, hiring a plane to trail a banner saying "Hire John Smith," and driving a taxi with a back-seat sign advising passengers that the driver is an unemployed advertising copywriter.

As entertaining as they are to read about, many exotic direct approach ideas fall flat. In *Working Woman* magazine, Joanne Davis, president of the New York advertising agency Omon, describes remembering tons of outlandish resumes, most of which she says were terrible. "One person sent me a shoe—an ugly, cheap, plastic shoe—with a note that began, 'Now that I have my foot in the door...." Even creative people usually prefer substance over stunts.

## Category 3: Job Market Services

Although the first two categories—personal contacts and the direct approach—represent two-thirds of job placements, category three may lead to the job you want. Below are a multitude of broadly defined job market services—some you may be familiar with, some not—waiting to serve you. Many offer job seekers free assistance, but some charge the applicant or employer a fee.

### School Placement Services

Two- or four-year colleges, universities, and vocational-technical schools typically operate placement offices to assist graduating students in finding employment. Even if you graduated some time ago, reconnect with the placement office to see if any jobs in the current openings file interest you. The placement office may serve job seeking graduates of any vintage.

### Public Libraries

The next chapter notes the role America's public libraries play in researching employers and providing job search guides. But did you know that some public libraries offer extensive employment services, which may include data banks of job openings? A number of larger libraries have established programs to enhance the use of the facilities by patrons with disabilities. In San Diego, for instance, the I Can Center is filled with resources of many types (not limited to jobs) for those with vision and hearing impairments.

### Committees on Employment of People with Disabilities

You can find job leads through the President's Committee on Employment of People with Disabilities and the related governors' and mayors' committees. These organizations exist to promote the employment opportunities of people with disabilities. Tell them you're ready to go to work and want assistance in finding job leads. Ask for a list of the committee's member employers—you can use it to make direct approaches.

### State Vocational Rehabilitation Agencies

State vocational rehabilitation agencies (called by different terms in various states) are great sources of just about every kind of employment service you can name. Here are a few that may be offered in your state: job training, transportation, equipment, job accommodation devices, support service assistants, supported employment services (if you need a coach on your work site to help you learn and keep your job), job seeking skill training, placement in a job, follow-up on the job, and initial stock and supplies for small businesses.

Sound great? It can be. But in their superb award-winning book, *Take Charge: A Strategic Guide for Blind Job Seekers*, Rami Rabby and Diane Croft warn of becoming too dependent on agencies serving people with disabilities. They say doing so can be detrimental by making the job seeker appear to the work world as one lacking in self-sufficiency and independence. Even if hired, these workers may be excluded from positions with power. Rabby, who is blind, and Croft put it this way:

> There is a difference between "taking advantage of" and "relinquishing control to" your state rehabilitation agency. . . . Conditioned by years of training, we have stood on the sidelines, little more than passive observers of our own fate, paralyzed by the notion that since the agency is there to "help us," it would be inappropriate for us to complain. Or to help ourselves.

> Too many years of chronic unemployment should have taught us that such a strategy is unproductive and guaranteed to keep us in a second-class status, both in the workplace and in society—a society that judges you by what work you do and how much you earn.

> Too many rehabilitation counselors have fallen into the same pit, unable to distinguish between "help" that relieves a client of responsibility and "help" that encourages, even forces, the client to do more for himself. The former strategy makes life easier in the short run but fails abysmally in the long run.

JC Penney Company Management Employment Manager Thomas Potraza of Dallas carries this thought one step further: "Job applicants benefit at the interview by having played the major role in authoring their own resume. Because they've gone through the process of organizing their thoughts for the resume, they are more prepared and more comfortable discussing their skills and qualifications at the interview."

The advice to rely on yourself applies to every service provider you encounter, not only with state vocational rehabilitation agency assistance. Here is the essential question to ask yourself: *Is the agency counselor helping me prepare my job search materials, or is the counselor preparing them for me?* If the latter, you risk not being mentally well prepared to do your best in interviews.

## Independent Living Centers

Independent living centers are a terrific source of employment leads. Operated on the local level, services vary from center to center, but many aid in preparing resumes and finding job openings. Some provide free job clubs where job seekers meet on a regular basis and support one another throughout the job hunt process. Contact the National Council on Independent Living for referral to the center located nearest you and information on services offered.

### Associations Serving the Disability Community

Hundreds of associations serving the disability community exist nationwide, with new ones forming continuously. Many that exist primarily as advocacy groups and rehabilitation service providers are combining these missions with job services. Some groups—such as the International Center for the Disabled, the Association for Mental Retardation (ARC), and the International Association of Jewish Vocational Services (services not based on religious affiliation)—have made employment guidance and the securing of competitive employment a primary goal at local, state, and national levels.

The sole mission of other organizations is to increase competitive employment opportunities for people with disabilities—such as Mainstream and Just One Break. Several disability-specific organizations offer comprehensive placement services—such as Job Opportunities for the Blind (JOB), a joint project of the National Federation of the Blind and the U.S. Department of Labor, and the National Center on Employment of the Deaf, a project of the U.S. Department of Education at Rochester Institute of Technology.

Still other organizations actively *recruit employers* interested in hiring people with disabilities. Examples are Projects with Industry, a series of programs of the Rehabilitation Services Administration of the U.S. Department of Education, and the Disability 2000-CEO Council of the National Organization on Disability.

Many associations have job banks, magazines, and newsletters. Many hold conventions, an excellent means for job seekers to ferret out job leads.

Refer to the appendixes of this book for associations that may interest you. Contact Direct Link for the Disabled for additional groups.

### Recruitment Ads

Recruitment ads—also commonly referred to as employment ads, help-wanted ads, and job ads—offer immediate openings, but the competition can be breathtaking. Some advertised job openings draw as many as 1000 replies. Still, recruitment ads should not be overlooked—today's ad may be tomorrow morning's job (it happens).

Where do you find recruitment ads? Large daily newspapers, small weekly newspapers, and local business journals print thousands of ads for job openings. Trade journals and newsletters—published by private firms, trade associations, and professional societies—cover most job fields and typically include recruitment ads.

Look for two types of ads for jobs: *in-column* and *display ad.* In-column ads are simpler and usually set in a lightface type; they appear in classified help-wanted advertising sections. Display ads are larger and more elaborate, enabling advertisers to use eye-catching borders, various typefaces, artwork, and company insignia. Display ads may appear in classified help-wanted sections or in other advertising sections—such as "Professional Opportunities" or "Career Opportunities"—or on news pages—such as business or sports.

Start your search by learning how to read and understand recruitment ads. They may include any or all of the following basic elements:

- Job title
- Job responsibilities
- Salary and benefits
- Qualifications
- Employer's name
- Contact person
- Address
- Telephone number

Sometimes you'll find an anonymous ad that lists only a box number and no defining employer information—called a "blind ad" in the industry. Employers sometimes choose to remain anonymous for a variety of valid reasons. One reason is to keep mobs of strangers from tying up their telephone lines and camping out on their doorsteps. Another is so they won't feel obligated to write tons of rejection letters. Still another is that to keep business running smoothly, it's often necessary to locate a replacement before terminating an existing employee.

Blind ads may be worth pursuing if the job looks favorable. Because fewer people respond, competition is generally less, increasing your chances of getting the interview. If you're afraid of inadvertently responding to your current employer's blind ad, send a "blind reply." Write a letter for a friend or relative to sign that stresses how your qualifications match the job requirements. In the letter, suggest the employer contact you through the third party, who will reveal your identity.

Here are some of the most important rules for finding job leads using recruitment ads:

- **Study ads until you understand their special language.** Advertising space is expensive so employers make a little say a lot. For example, "EOE" means equal opportunity employer, "Exp. pref." is experience preferred, and "F/T" is full time.

- **Scan the entire jobs section—the position you want may not be listed under the occupation title you expect.** You may find secretarial positions under "S" for secretary, "A" for administrative secretary, and "E" for executive secretary.

- **Answer ads your qualifications match—***and ads your qualifications come close to matching.* Although in competitive markets employers search for the perfect match, they may not find the perfect match and be flexible with job requirements.

- **Steer clear of ads that sound too good to be true.** An ad that "guarantees" you'll be independently wealthy after purchasing a start-up kit for "only $99.95" is a scam.

- **Call the employer listed in the ad and get the name of the decision maker in charge of hiring for the position.** When you send your resume, along with a customized cover letter, don't mention the ad. Your letter may seem like a happy coincidence and get more attention than it would buried in a stack of ad replies.

- **If you're stonewalled trying to get the decision maker's name, write to someone in a higher position, such as the company president.** Information is more likely to be sent down than up the ranks.

- **If you can't locate a telephone number for the employer, send your paperwork to the person or department—the human resources department, for example—given in the ad.** This time mention the specifics of the ad you're answering.

- **Follow instructions given in the ad.** If you're ask to send references along with your resume and you don't, you may be out of the running.

- **A question that continually rattles ad respondents is how to handle the request for a salary history.** For many reasons, your best answer is *Will discuss at interview,* but this evasion may cause your resume to be tossed. Jack Chapman's excellent *How to Make $1000 a Minute Negotiating Your Salaries and Raises* goes into the detail you should know to really understand the pay issue.

- **In your cover letter tell the employer you will call within a week to follow up and schedule an interview.** Do it.

- **Keep a copy of every cover letter (and resume, if other than your standard) you send to employers together with recruitment ads.** Organizing your job search materials—such as in a three-ring binder—makes information easy to locate when you call the employer or when the employer calls you.

- **Call every week or ten days.** It's a fine line between being a pest and being persistent, but it's worth the risk.

Beyond the basics, creatively responding to recruitment ads sometimes cinches the interview. A timing strategy that has worked for some people is to wait two or three days until after the first tonnage of resumes arrive, then hand-deliver yours in a large envelope. Many weary job screeners welcome one nicely packaged resume when faced with a mountain of unknowns.

### Public Employment Service Offices

Smart job seekers don't pass up any information or assistance, especially when it's free. Supported by tax dollars, the nation's 2000 public employment service offices—sometimes called the Job Service and the state employment service—offer free assistance to job seekers in locating job openings.

Services are available to any citizen or legal resident of the United States. Specialized services are provided to such groups as veterans (who by law get priority in services and placements), women, youth, older workers, and rural residents and workers. People with disabilities are guaranteed service by law, although budget cuts have eliminated the requirement for disability-specific counselors.

Plan to stop by the public employment service office at least once a week to check out the *Job Bank*, a nationwide computerized listing of position openings that is updated daily. Although a majority of the jobs listed are for unskilled and semiskilled positions, higher paid technical, professional, and managerial jobs are listed as well. This is a source of job leads you shouldn't pass up until you've examined it more closely.

The *Job Bank* includes private industry as well as government agency positions, and more jobs in more occupations are listed with public employment service offices than with any other single source. Why? Because by federal law, any private employer that has a federal contract must list all job vacancies with the public employment service office. This spells extra-good news for job seekers with disabilities—remember that employers receiving federal contracts in excess of $2,500 are prohibited from disability employment discrimination under Section 503 of the Rehabilitation Act (see Chapter 2).

In addition to helping you locate job leads, public employment service office staff can arrange interviews for you. And if you haven't decided what kind of work you want to do, many offices provide testing and career counseling.

Just as some offices are more active than others, some counselors may be more responsive to your needs than others. If you're not satisfied with the assistance you're receiving, request a change of counselors.

Check the state government section of your telephone directory for the public employment office nearest you.

### Private Employment Agencies

For-profit placement firms—commonly called employment agencies—do for a fee what tax-supported public employment services do for free. They match job seekers with job openings.

Who pays the fee? In the majority of cases the employer pays a fee to the placement firm when a referred applicant is hired. *Fees can be hefty, so be certain your contract states you will only be sent on interviews where the employer has agreed to pick up the entire agency fee.* An exception may be if the fee is split 50-50 between you and the employer and, in writing, the employer agrees to reimburse you after one year on the job.

Employment consultants, who work on commission, are in the business of finding people for jobs, not jobs for people. Like all commissioned sales people, they prefer to represent the hot goods that move fast. Job seekers with in-demand skills or credentials have always been hot items. Today—because of ADA—you may a hot ticket. Because placement firms prescreen applicants (removing much of the awkwardness employers may feel turning away unqualified applicants with disabilities), employment consultant referrals are often sought by fair-minded employers.

The other side of the coin is not pretty. Some less-than-ethical employers use placements firms to sidestep the law. In effect, they retain agencies to screen *out* applicants with disabilities while maintaining that they offer equal employment opportunities to all. But, in general, trust that most employers using placements firms are acting in good faith.

If you're lucky enough to find an agency that you feel will properly present you, find out if the firm is a member of your state's employment agency association or of the National Association of Personnel Consultants. If it is, it agrees to abide by specific business ethics.

**Temporary Help Agencies**

Temporary help agencies originally came into being to supply workers—such as clerical staff and laborers—to employers for short-term job assignments. Agency roles in the job market have expanded: short-term job placements include accountants, construction workers, lawyers, foreign language translators, nurses, and executives. Some employers maintain long-term temporary staff to allow flexibility in work force size and save on employee benefits.

Temporary agencies shouldn't be overlooked even if your goal is to leap immediately into full-time employment; a number of employers use them as a primary method of hiring. Temporary assignments allow workers and employers the luxury of exploring more permanent relationships without the risks involved in a direct hire. If after a time, the worker and the position say "match," no problem. The temporary agency charges a placement fee—in the industry called a conversion fee. (Again, be certain your contract states the fee is fully employer paid.)

An advantage of signing up with a temporary agency or agencies is that if you need money to pay the rent, work is immediate and you have control over work assignments.

**Executive Search Firms**

Executive search firms are the exclusive agents of employers. Hired under contract, executive recruiters—sometimes called headhunters—search for candidates with established track records in their respective fields to fill middle- and senior-level positions.

Executive recruiters pursue desirable candidates (typically employed), interview them, and check their references. Recruiters prepare written reports on finalist candidates for review prior to interviews by client employers.

Unless you've got an impressive track record, you're probably wasting precious time contacting executive recruiters.

**Database Services**

Here today, gone tonight. Turnover in database services is supersonic. Database services, or job banks, have been around for years. Although originally maintained manually, today most are computerized. The work and expense of keeping databases current, along with insufficient job applicant and employer entries, are the drawbacks and the ultimate death of many services. Database services that are successful are worth checking out. Some offer free services, some offer services for a modest fee, and some offer both, depending on who the job seeker is.

Peterson's *Connexion* is a first-rate computer database matching job seekers—such as college students, separating service members, and victims of corporate downsizing—with employers across the nation. *Career Placement Registry,* which claims to be the largest computerized information network in the world with more than 100,000 subscriber organizations, provides matching services to job seekers ranging from graduating seniors to experienced professionals.

For computer buffs who want to job hunt using personal computers, *Adnet Online* Employment Advertising Network is *free* to *Prodigy* members (employers pay a fee). Updated twice weekly, you can search job ads by corporation, career field and occupation, or geographic location. You can also get profiles and company news of member organizations—whether currently advertising or not. Finally, you can enter your own resume into the database.

## Job Fairs

Many people with disabilities have been steered toward job fairs—sometimes called career days or recruiting conferences—as a method of finding job leads. For good reason. At a job fair you can see and talk to more employers in one room than you would be able to reach in hours, if not days, of direct approach. Your time is maximized, and the cost of mailing hundreds of resumes is saved.

Jobs fairs are typically specialized—such as for nurses or for the disability community—and they allow you to target your search. Fairs are organized by professional associations, private employment agencies, professional organizers, and employers in industries suffering labor shortages.

Find out the rules of interviewing *before* you attend. Call the organizer and ask these questions: *Is there a registration fee? What fees, if any, must I pay if I am hired as a result of the job fair? How many employers are attending? Who are they? How many candidates are expected? Can I schedule interviews before the fair opens?* Even if you don't land a position, job fairs can be a networker's paradise.

### Professional, Trade, and Industrial Associations

Aligning yourself with professional, trade, and industrial associations has multi-faceted benefits in searching for job leads. Many associations have annual meetings, conventions, and trade shows with placement services at these events. If you find the registration fee too stiff for your budget, work the exhibit hall (which may be open to the public).

Some associations offer placement services. Other have more informal employment committees to help members find jobs. Some have newsletters that publish job openings or situations wanted. Most associations produce membership directories you can use for networking.

How do you locate professional, trade, and industrial associations? In *The Encyclopedia of Associations*, Gale Research. Widely available in major libraries, you'll find organizations with special interests in just about everything you can imagine—such as the Model T Ford Club International, New York Academy of Sciences, and Wild Blueberry Association of North America. *The Directory of Conventions*, *Successful Meetings* magazine, offers convention information.

### Church Job Clubs

Some churches sponsor job clubs, open to members and the community. Use the Yellow Pages and dial until you locate several in your area.

### Private Industry Councils

Private industry councils receive federal, state, and local government funds to match workers to companies needing trained personnel for which a shortage exists. Retraining programs are usually involved. One of the councils' objectives is finding employment for people with disabilities.

### TV Recruitment Shows

Cable TV is jumping on the job market services wagon with recruitment shows. Local stations run job exchange telethons when unemployment rates soar.

### Volunteer

Volunteer activities can lead to paid jobs.

*Caution:* Only volunteer where your heart is. Volunteers typically wear their hearts on their sleeves and if yours isn't, your motives will be as transparent as cellophane. And don't be afraid to ask to be hired when a job opening occurs.

## SUMMING UP JOB LEAD METHODS

Reread the methods outlined above for finding job leads. This time—since you have an overall view of the methods available—put an "X" next to those you think will be your personal best. If any methods have check marks from your first pass and "X's" from your second pass, make those your first targets.

After a week searching for job leads, evaluate how productive the methods you chose have been. Once out in the job jungle foraging for leads, you may want to read through this chapter's methods of finding job leads one more time. You may see new possibilities in methods you didn't see before. You may also want to check out *Jeff Allen's Best: Get the Interview*, by Jeffrey G. Allen, the nation's leading placement attorney, for 100 techniques to organize your search.

## TOP TARGET EMPLOYERS

In researching employers, an important consideration is whether or not they have established policies relating to the recruitment of workers with disabilities. Is the employer:

- An affirmation action employer?
- A federal, state, or local government agency employer?
- A federal contractor?
- A federal grant recipient?
- An employer with a program to hire and support individuals with disabilities?

If so, your strategy in pursuing job leads may include disclosure of your disability in the early stages of the job hunt process (see Chapter 8). If not, you may need to dig deeper into the employer's practices relating to applicants with disabilities to plot the most productive course of action (see Chapter 11).

One of the richest mines of employment information for workers with disabilities is the marvelous, award-winning *CAREERS & the disABLED*, Equal Opportunity Publications. The magazine offers everything from ADA analysis articles to Zofcom Control System/TongueTouch Keypad equipment announcements. Each edition (spring, fall, and winter) lists an affirmative action career directory of employers committed to the recruitment of entry-level and professional people with disabilities. Editor James Schneider says the directory "alerts readers to where their resumes will be welcomed." *CAREERS & the disABLED* goes further by offering a resume service; job seekers can send their resumes to the magazine to be forwarded to specified employers.

"Individuals with disabilities, when seeking employment," says Gail Goetze, today a labor relations specialist at the Oklahoma City Air Logistics Center, Tinker Air Force Base, "may find the need to target those employers who have identified themselves as having a

mission for the recruitment, selection, advancements, and retention of qualified individuals with disabilities." Goetze, who has a
form of muscular dystrophy, did just that when he sent his resume
to every advertiser in *CAREERS & the disABLED* and to the
magazine's resume service.

Employers that openly recruit workers with disabilities—such as
at job fairs, at association convention exhibits, and through job
advertisements—should be top-target employers. Even though
these employers send the message that they want your resume,
*research them first to determine the **best time** to disclose your disability.*

## THE NUMBERS GAME

Remember, absolutes in finding job leads are a myth—well,
almost. The numbers game is an exception:

- Devote *more* time daily to searching
- Use *multiple* methods of finding job leads and contact *more*
  employers
- Line up *more* interviews

The more time you spend searching, the more methods you use
and the more people you contact, and the more interviews you line
up, the faster your chances of getting the job you want.

As Benjamin Disraeli said:

*The secret of success is constancy to purpose.*

# 11

# Researching employers

Employer research can power the plan that you make to fit work into your life. Your research goal is twofold.

First, you want to identify employers that have the welcome mat out for people with disabilities, or at least employers that will not resort to devious methods to slam the door in your face, law or no law. The data uncovered in this phase of research can be described as being on your agenda. *It matters to you.*

Second, employer research provides the ammunition you need to ace a job interview. The preinterview data you collect for this purpose is on the employer's agenda. *It appeals to the employer's interests.*

## YOUR AGENDA: SIZING UP EMPLOYERS

Pick up a copy of today's newspaper or turn on a television news show, and the chances are good that you'll find companies and industries making headlines. Some stories describe organizational successes, but others recount a litany of problems: Sales are slow. Prices are dropping. Mergers, buyouts, and takeovers are restructuring the world of business. Government investigations of alleged wrongdoings are ongoing. Products are being recalled. Hundreds of thousands of workers are being laid off. Work formerly done in the United States is being exported to low-wage countries. Entire manufacturing industries are no more.

These news stories remind us that tomorrow's work market only faintly echoes yesteryear's. That's why it will pay you to wield sharply honed investigative shovels in digging up target employers.

Unless you must have a job right now, this very minute, aim for employment in a work culture that is compatible with your values and lifestyle preferences, as well as one for which there appears to be some stability. Even though, in many instances, you will be unable to obtain a truly helpful depth of information for your agenda until you receive a job offer, it is well worth the effort to obtain as much advance information as possible.

As you go about collecting information on your agenda, it is very important to do so with judgment. Kathleen A. Jennings, president of ET Search Inc., a La Jolla, California, executive recruiting firm for tax specialists, explains. "Never call an employer with whom you might want to interview and ask: How do you feel about hiring someone my age? Do you give drug or psychological tests? How generous are your health insurance benefits because I may need them?" Jennings recommends that you use less blatant methods to find out which, from your view, are the most attractive employers and the particulars of what they offer employees.

A variety of subtle methods to uncover the personnel philosophies of specific employers are identified later in this chapter. But first, here are questions that suggest research topics to help site your favorite employment targets.

1) Does the employer have a history of hiring and providing job accommodations for employees with disabilities? Modifying equipment? Providing or allowing supported employment? Restructuring jobs?

2) Is the employer's location convenient? Where is the main office? Facilities? Are they accessible? Is the commuting time feasible?

3) What are the employer's policies about time schedules? What hours is the organization open? Are the hours flexible? Are alternative work schedules available—part time, job sharing, flextime, time-limited projects, telecommuting? Does the employer hire freelance workers or outside consultants?

4) Does the employer have a reputation for paying market-rate salaries?

5) Does the employer have a reputation for offering a full employee benefits package? Vacation? Sick leave? Dental plan? Eye-care plan? Life insurance? Disability? Childcare program? Bonus compensation program? Profit sharing? Employee stock purchase? Product discounts? Retirement plan? In health insurance, do plans have pre-existing conditions clauses? Who pays premiums?

6) Does the employer provide on-job training? Encourage employees to further education or training and, if so, are tuition and books reimbursed?

7) Does the employer have a reputation for promoting from within the organization? If the business is family owned, are family members promoted before other employees?

8) Is the organization in a growth or a shrinking industry?

**Interpreting Your Responses:**

1) "Yes" answers to these questions mean the employer welcomes applicants with disabilities.

2) Analyze the practicality of getting to the job and mobility once there.

3) If you want an alternative work schedule, you'll need to do considerable sleuthing to turn up opportunities—they're tough to find. It's much easier to move from full-time employment to an alterative work schedule once the employer gets to know you and your work than to begin as an alternative employee.

4) If an organization has not paid the going rates in the past, do not expect it to do so in the future.

5) Benefits are vital in today's economy. The human resources office may have a written statement available describing vacations, sick leave, cause for dismissal, and so forth. Health insurance is prohibitively expensive for many employers. If you are covered by another policy—for instance, a spouse's— it may be to your advantage to let the employer know you are willing to waive your health insurance coverage. Or perhaps you can trade off other benefits for health insurance if the employer offers a "cafeteria" approach to benefits.

6) Depending on your occupation, on-job training may or may not be important. But in every case, new hires need the help of an experienced worker to move smoothly into the organizational structure.

7) You may grow resentful if the employer refuses to promote from the ranks or gives preference to family members.

8) Being in a growth industry offers brighter prospects than being in a shrinking industry, but even a shrinking industry may offer good opportunities over your working lifetime.

Need more ideas? Turn to your **Equal-to-the-Task Composite** in Chapter 4 and review your work values and personal values for additional questions that matter to you.

## THE EMPLOYER'S AGENDA: SIZING YOU UP

Top salespeople know a secret. They find out what the buyer wants and needs and persuade the buyer that their offerings match those wants and needs. The secret can work for you, too.

- By researching the employer's organization before each interview, you will be able to show how your qualifications fit hand-in-glove with the job's requirements.

- You will be able to explain why you are the best candidate for the job.

- You will be able to convince the employer that your disability will not hold you back from being perfect for the job.

"Researching an employer before the job interview is absolutely essential," says Lauralyn Jones, senior employment administrator at SmithKline Beecham Pharmaceuticals in Philadelphia, one of the world's leading pharmaceutical companies. "This is particularly true in a competitive job market—which is what we're faced with."

Jones stresses that informed job seekers show initiative that interviewers won't miss. "We were involved in a merger in 1989 and have been in the newspaper about once a month since. I find it frustrating and hard to accept when applicants say they couldn't find anything on the company," Jones says. "Do you know some applicants still get our name wrong?"

How intensive must your preinterview research be? It varies. You'll have to do a more sophisticated version if you are seeking a professional or managerial job than if you are qualified for employment at a lower level of responsibility.

Whether you invest only a telephone call to the organization's switchboard or do hours of research, "doing your homework" before an interview helps you relax and shine. Because you have taken the time to prepare, you will come across as one who really does care about work. This quality holds enormous attraction for employers. As Eva June, a principal in Walling and June, an executive search firm in Alexandria, Virginia, says, "I've never met an employer who refused to hire a candidate because the candidate cared too much about work."

Review the following preinterview questions, and see which ones you'll need to bone up on for the job you seek.

1) What does the employer do? What products does the organization make, or what services does it offer? What market does it serve?

2) What category is the employer in? Profit-making company? Nonprofit firm (college, association, foundation)? Federal government agency? State or local agency? Federal contractor? Federal grant recipient?

3) How many employees does the employer have? Fifteen or more? Twenty-five or more? One thousand or more?

4) What seems to be the organization's biggest problems? Do you have skills that would be useful in solving those problems?

5) Does the employer have new products that suggest impressive growth and subsequent opportunities for your input?

6) What are the precise duties, skills required, and outcomes expected of the position in question?

7) What's going on in the employer's industry? What advantages do the firm's products or services have over those offered by competitors? What's the firm's market share for the product, and is that market share growing? How much of its sales are in exports?

8) What is the organization's financial outlook? In an era of mergers and restructurings, is it likely to be substantially altered in the foreseeable future? Does the employer have a history of major layoffs?

**Interpreting Your Responses:**

1) If you don't know the reason the employer exists, you appear disinterested, lazy, or not aware.

2) In general, you may find large corporations, nonprofit organizations, and government agencies more welcoming than mid-sized or small private companies. This is, of course, a sweeping generalization to which there are many exceptions. Employers who are federal contractors or beneficiaries of federal funds are likely to be receptive to applications from people with disabilities for reasons discussed in earlier chapters.

3) The size of the employer's work force relates to when the Americans with Disabilities Act becomes effective, and for employers with more than 1000 employees, the likelihood of having a program to recruit individuals with disabilities.

4-6) This data is the foundation for showing how your qualifications are a wonderful pairing with the job's specifications. (But don't fall into the trap of being a know-it-all or trying to solve gigantic problems in a thirty-minute interview; merely comment that your skills in computer programming, for instance, equip you to work on the problem of quality control in information processing.)

7) Virtually every for-profit company is trying hard to look good when compared to its competitors. If you're applying to a firm that makes computer software, for example, take time to read a critic's review of that software's advantages over others.

8) New hires are made even in organizations where massive layoffs occur. To avoid negative publicity, hiring often is done quietly through headhunters. Sometimes rehiring former employees creates problems among those who were not brought back, and legal challenges result. Should you find yourself interviewing in such a situation, you can comment: *Maybe an outsider is the solution to this touchy situation. I think I would be a good person to fill the position. Not only am I qualified and a proven team builder, but I'm a noncontroversial choice with the added benefit of qualifying under ADA.*

## HOW TO RESEARCH EMPLOYERS

Now that you know which questions to ask, how do you find the answers? Try these resources and techniques.

**Ask Around**

Ask your relatives, friends, and acquaintances. Reputable employers usually have a good reputation in the community. Try to find people who have worked for the employer in the past. Just keep asking. Mike knows Suzie who knows Jim who knows. . . . Since they have little to lose, former employees can honestly answer many questions on your list.

**Talk with Current Employees**

Employee satisfaction is a commodity you can't measure by reading company brochures and annual reports. It is best gauged by talking directly with employees. If an employer treats workers well, they'll make no secret of it.

Employees can tell you if workers with disabilities are regarded with respect and offered equal opportunities for promotion and full participation in employment activities. Employees can supply other meaningful information, too. To illustrate, if you're thinking about a sales job, you'll want to know if management pays workers on time or exploits them by fiddling with commissions.

If you know an employee currently working for the employer, ask to discuss the employer with this person away from the work site. If you don't know any employees, you may want to informally chat with a worker outside the business location going to or coming from work.

*Caution:* The success of this approach is dependent on the type of job for which you're applying. For example, it would be appropriate to strike up a conversation with a food service worker before or after a work shift, but it is unlikely you'd get answers by nabbing a vice president of finance on the way to the company parking lot, at a bowling alley, or at a restaurant. For that level of contact, your chances are best at professional association meetings (described in Chapter 10).

### Contact Competitors, Suppliers, and Customers

Make contacts with direct competitors, major suppliers, and customers of the employer. These contacts can supply you with a wealth of information. No one, for instance, researches an employer harder than the employer's competition.

### Telephone the Employer

Many routine questions can be answered by telephoning the employer. Receptionists and switchboard operators, who are used to fielding questions from the public, can be good sources of information. Other staff accustomed to answering telephone inquiries are sales, marketing, customer service, public relations, and human relations and personnel departments.

The employer's hours, for instance, can be obtained from anyone who answers the phone. Questions regarding location assignments and starting pay for entry-level positions can be answered by the manager of a fast-food restaurant or by the human resource manager of a department store.

### Use Stockholder Resources

Annual corporate reports are often available in college and business libraries. Copies can also be obtained free of charge by writing to the corporate communications or corporate financial office of the company; get the address from a library reference directory of companies. Even if you don't know how to check the numbers, the chairman's letter may discuss current problems and major developments, reflect the personality of the chief executive (which is in turn reflected in the organization), and describe where the company presents itself as it would like to be seen. Annual reports may be candid or evasive. Never use them as your sole source of information on an employer.

In addition to annual reports, stock analyst reports are excellent sources for industry and market share information. Inquire at a stockbroker's office to see if analyst reports are available for companies in which you're interested. Investment and money management newsletters and magazines are additional information resources. Many large companies maintain stockholder relations departments whose mission is to provide information that makes it easy to invest in their organizations; corporate directories identify stockholder relations specialists.

## Obtain Job Descriptions

As mentioned in Chapter 2, reviewing a job description prepared specifically for the position you seek is a great way to determine a job match and prepare for an interview. Organizations large enough to have a director or manager of personnel or human resources may have prepared a job description before interviewing for a position.

The best time to get a job description is before the interview. This allows you to study it and match your skills and qualifications to those required for the job. It can help you separate marginal job functions from essential functions before you're in the interviewing seat. This valuable knowledge allows you to prepare to ask for and suggest possible job accommodations, if needed. What's more, you can prepare to explain how you would accomplish each function of the position should the employer ask you.

The trick is getting the job descriptions. Sometimes they're posted at the employer's work site or at public employment offices, libraries, schools, and community centers. With a telephone call to the employer's human resources department, you may be able to obtain the job description you need—but don't be surprised if you're told it's an internal document not available to the public.

If that happens, you can refer to job description reference books in a library. Another approach is to use a government job description for the occupation; many occupations in the civilian job market are duplicated in the government job market.

If all else fails, you can devise your own job description from various sources—career books, magazine articles, and information from friends. Even a job description you create has the value of focusing your attention on matching your qualifications with the job's requirements, preparing you to separate marginal from essential job functions, and anticipating any accommodations you may need.

If you strike out getting a job description before the interview, it's still valuable to request the document during the interview. Use it to focus the interviewer on the job match and thwart attempts to disqualify you using "essential functions" as a dodge.

### Call Committees on Employment of People with Disabilities

Call the President's Committee on Employment of People with Disabilities and the related governor's and mayor's committees. Ask if employers you're researching are members. If they are, it's likely that they recruit employees with disabilities.

### Read Industry Trade Magazines

Industry trade magazines offer valuable insight into employers. You can, for instance, find a wealth of information about advertising firms of all sizes in *Advertising Age*. Visit a major library to find similar magazines covering all types of businesses. How do you know which is the right trade journal? Ask people in the field what they read. A librarian can help you locate the periodicals in *Ulrich's International Periodicals Directory*, R.R. Bowker Company. For specific articles, check *Business Periodicals Index*, H.W. Wilson Company.

### Scour Daily Newspapers

Daily newspapers in the cities where the target employers are active are a good source of data. Don't overlook the area's weekly business journal.

### Study Consumer Magazines' "Best Companies" Surveys

Lists of best companies to work for—based on a variety of criteria—are compiled annually by magazines. *Fortune* and *Money* publish extensive listings on top employers.

### Utilize Library References and Directories

Your assault on employer research should include familiarizing yourself with the business reference section of a public library. A librarian can help you locate resources given in this chapter and recommend others.

For large, publicly held corporations, look at such standard references as *Standard & Poor's Bond Guide*, Standard & Poor's Corporation. Find the company's bond rating. If it's BBB+ or above, it's judged to be a financially sound company. If it's rated CCC or below, the company is carrying too much debt, which may lead to layoffs or other problems.

*Standard & Poor's Register of Corporations, Directors, and Executives*, Standard & Poor's Corporation, offers a bounty of information for the corporate job seeker. *Ward's Business Directory of U.S. Private and Public Companies*, Gale Research, lists number of employees, revenues, and general company information. *Hoover's Handbook: Profiles of Over 500 Major Corporations*, edited by Gary Hoover and Alta Campbell, offers one-page listings that detail a corporation's history, management, products, and performance. *Thomas Register of American Manufacturers*, Thomas Publishing Company, discloses the nation's manufacturers and what they make. Many other directories are published listing U.S. employers.

A number of books are specific to job hunting, such as *How To Get a Job in Southern California*, by Thomas M. Camden and Jonathan Palmer, *Government Job Finder*, by Daniel Lauber, and *Peterson's Job Opportunities for Engineering, Science, and Computer Graduates*, Peterson's Guides. Employers hiring new graduates are listed in *College Placement Annual*, College Placement Council.

*The Career Guide: Dun's Employment Opportunities Directory*, Dun's Marketing Services, may be a top choice for job seekers with disabilities since it focuses on U.S. companies with more than 1000 employees. The guide lists contact people, addresses, hiring practices, benefits, and career-development programs on thousands of companies. *The Hidden Job Market: A Job Seeker's Guide to America's 2,000 Little-Known but Fastest-Growing High-Tech Companies*, compiled by Corporate Technology Information Services from their database of 35,000 technology manufacturers and developers, goes beyond identifying company contacts and the number of employees. Other easy-to-find information (companies are organized by state and area code) include the number of employees added in the past year, percentage growth, year founded, and annual sales.

A reference guide that shouldn't be overlooked is *Professional Careers Sourcebook: An Information Guide for Career Planning*, edited by Kathleen M. Savage and Charity Anne Dorgan. If you've targeted a career requiring education or training beyond high school, this book has compiled a lot of research for you. Each of the more than 100 occupations listed begins with a synopsis, salary information, and employment outlook, followed by an extensive resource list specific to the occupation.

Of particular interest to job seekers is an excellent bimonthly newsletter, *Corporate Jobs Outlooks!* Published by corporate research expert Jack W. Plunkett, each issue gives readers easy methods for comparing salaries, benefits, employee training, advancement opportunities, and financial stability. And each year Plunkett analyzes job prospects at 100 of the nation's leading employers and includes a cumulative index and hot ideas section for job seekers. It is widely available at colleges and libraries.

### Check College Career Planning and Placement Offices

College and university career planning and placement offices often have employer files of many national corporations. Some also have information about local employers. Ask a campus career counselor at your alma mater for grapevine insights that won't appear in employer files.

**Call Chambers of Commerce**

Call your state and local chambers of commerce and request a directory of businesses.

# EMPLOYER SIZE: LARGE OR SMALL?

Organization size is a research component you may want to take extra time to think about in attempting to satisfy your preferred work values. Merely because an employer is a certain size does not guarantee characteristics and practices will mirror those of other employers in the same size category. But, in general, advantages based on employer size—large or small—do exist.

See if any of the following are major employment factors to you. As you read, place a check mark next to those you find important so you can concentrate on them. While researching employers, ask yourself if you're more likely to satisfy your preferred values at a larger or smaller employer.

### LARGE EMPLOYER

- More likely to have an established policy or program for hiring job seekers with disabilities
- Starting pay often higher
- Pay often remains higher
- Superior employment benefits package
- Greater financial and people resources may allow more chance of securing reasonable job accommodations
- More extensive formal training programs
- Outside training more likely to be permitted or encouraged
- Co-workers doing similar jobs can be used as resources to help solve problems as they arise
- More job levels for promotions
- Gain detailed experience in one or a few functions
- Larger size permits lateral department transfers; diverse operations permit functional and geographic transfers
- More scientific promotion policies; less danger of relatives being favored as in a family-owned business
- Greater expenditures on research to ensure progress

- Less danger of being merged with larger employer because of financial difficulties, competition of new products, or uneconomical size
- More slowly affected by minor changes in business fortunes

## SMALL EMPLOYER

- Pay may match larger companies at higher levels even though generally lower starting
- Little need for geographical relocation, upsetting family life and friendships
- Policies and procedures more flexible
- More willing to hire older, experienced workers
- Learn business from the ground up
- Often get wider experience; valuable if you are interested in going into business yourself
- Work is often more varied and not as routine
- Individual may be able to give more direction to work of organization and more readily see results of his or her efforts
- Chance for responsibility can be high from start
- Individual initiative may be more encouraged
- Quicker assumption of responsibility and more immediate assignment to a specific job
- Person of ability may stand out sooner and more prominently, meaning titles and promotions often come faster and competition may be less
- High personal recognition
- Easier identification with goals of employer; more apt to be known by top management
- Chance to influence management and policy at lower levels except where owner/board prefers high control
- Well positioned to benefit from growth of the organization
- May offer eventual ownership possibilities

Some people begin their first job with a specific size employer and stay with that basic size their entire career. Others experiment and intentionally change employer size when they change jobs, testing the advantages of size. If you let work and personal values lead, you may find yourself naturally steered toward a larger or smaller employer.

On balance, an ideal pathway is to begin at a large organization, mainly to obtain topflight on-job training and to establish credentials, and then consider moving to a smaller employer where you may exercise more control over your life. It is difficult to start at a small company and move into a giant corporation after the first few years in the job market.

## SELECTING THE RIGHT EMPLOYERS TO PURSUE

"Best" employers depend on who you are and what you're looking for in employment. The only best employer list on which to base decisions is your own—the one you personally research and compile from all the information you gather.

To successfully research an employer, understand the importance of your fact-finding mission, but don't stall your job search with busy work. Recognize when it's time to move from the relatively stress-free comfort of research to the interview phase.

If you're not able to answer all the questions on your list before interview time, add unanswered research questions to your list of interview questions. If the questions address critical factors that may have far-reaching implications for your career, don't accept a job offer until you've gotten satisfactory answers. If you take shortcuts and accept a position with important questions unresolved, you may find yourself later leaving the job—and your resume will tell the tale to the next prospective employer.

Unless you need money to pay the rent, don't settle for anything less than a good job match.

## HOW ONE WOMAN RESEARCHED HER WAY INTO A JOB

In her book, *300 New Ways To Get a Better Job,* Dallas career counselor Eleanor Baldwin recounts how one woman, whom she calls Maria Adams, combined reference guides and ingenuity into a job hunting scenario with a most impressive finish.

After combing corporate reference guides to identify employers she wanted to work for, Adams called stockholder relations representatives at selected companies. To each, she said she was calling to learn about the company, not that she was seeking employment. Being a friendly person, Adams built rapport and obtained the name of the decision maker in the company department in which she wanted to work.

Armed with research, Adams wrote cover letters with resumes and convinced the stockholder relations representatives to hand deliver them to decision makers. After following up with a telephone call to the decision makers, Adams was able to arrange six interviews that produced three job offers.

Although Adams' results were spectacular—and perhaps not to be duplicated—her experience echoes the theme of this chapter: Researching employers can make all the difference between employment and unemployment.

# 12

# Interviewing: a chance to show how valuable you are

The great cellist Gregor Piatigorsky, like many world-class performers, got butterflies from stage fright. But once on the concert platform, he radiated self-assurance.

"Forget about modesty," he once advised a pupil. Timidity has no place in performances. "Be a show-off. There has never been written a modest symphony, a humble rhapsody. You must be able to say, with great feeling, 'I hate you' or 'I love you.' Once you are able to say that, you will find you can play the cello."

Piatigorsky's wisdom relates directly to job interviews in two ways:

First, the interview is a theatrical event. It is not a random slice of real life but a rehearsable, foreseeable, and manageable event in which you can set the stage to strongly influence the outcome.

The advice to merely "Be yourself" is self-defeating counsel. Believe this, and you will still be looking for work as the century turns. The correct advice is *Be your best self.* Your best self means understanding that there is nothing natural in squeezing a lifetime of intelligent thoughts, valuable experiences, and related work history into a thirty- or forty-five-minute talk between strangers. During an interview, you are on stage—doing your act.

Second, throughout the interview you must present the image of an attractive job candidate through every means available to you: selective presentation of your background, effective answers and strategic questions, and the unspoken statements made by body communication.

When Piatigorsky advised being a show-off, he meant it in a gentle sense. He certainly was not suggesting being an overbearing know-it-all. He meant confidently performing the best of your repertoire to capture the audience, rather than giving a meek, tentative performance that leaves the audience unmoved.

The "great feeling" the cellist refers to is another way of saying "Be passionate about the employment you seek and communicate that passion in the interview."

In this usage, passion means enthusiastic attitude, commitment, fire in the belly. You care! Employers read passion as profit—and employers hire and promote employees whom they think will make or save their organizations money.

## IF YOU FAIL THE INTERVIEW
## YOU WILL NOT BE HIRED

At this stage of your job search, the interview is everything. It is the single most important determinant of whether or not you will receive a job offer. Think of it as a pass/fail half hour. That's why you've got to work hard to present an Academy Award performance.

From the perspective of a job seeker with a disability, your interviewing challenge is simple to diagram.

```
┌─────────────────────────────────────────────┐
│   ENABLE-YOURSELF INTERVIEWING SKILLS        │
│        "Yes, I can do the job!"              │
┌───┴─────────────────────────────────────────┴───┐
│                                                  │
│   SUPERB GENERAL INTERVIEWING SKILLS             │
│                                                  │
└──────────────────────────────────────────────────┘
```

All job seekers in a competitive market must master the bottom layer: *Superb General Interviewing Skills.*

You and all job seekers with disabilities must master not only the bottom layer of the diagram but the top layer as well: *Enable-Yourself Interviewing Skills* that reinforce your assertion of being able to do the job. By every action and statement, overt and subtle, you must assure the interviewer that not only are you the best candidate for the position, but also that your functional limitation will not stand in the way of the job getting done to the employer's satisfaction.

Yes, even with the Americans with Disabilities Act, it's an unavoidable challenge.

This chapter concentrates on the top layer of the diagram: *Enable-Yourself Interviewing Skills.* That's what's special about this book.

Of the content in the diagram's bottom layer—*Superb General Interviewing Skills*—only the most important, difference-making concepts are presented in this chapter. To share with you everything you need to know about the broad topic of interviewing would take another book. That's why you should read at least one, preferably several, of these five books:

*Jeff Allen's Best: Win the Job* and *The Complete Q&A Job Interview Book,* both by Jeffrey G. Allen.

*Knock 'Em Dead with Great Answers to Tough Interview Questions,* by Martin Yate.

*The Five-Minute Interview,* by Richard Beatty.

*Power Interviews: Job-Winning Tactics from Fortune 500 Recruiters,* by Dr. Neil Yeager and Lee Hough.

## INTERVIEW DO'S AND DON'TS

Interviews, like resumes and cover letters, have do's and don'ts. Follow these fundamental guidelines to help you shine on interview day.

## Interview Do's

- Do a dry-run trip before interview day. Be sure you know how to get to the building and whether or not it is accessible. If you have a mobility impairment, it's good strategy not to ask the person setting up the interview for directions; you want to demonstrate you're self-reliant. Call back later and anonymously get the information. (If you're interviewing out of town, call Travelin' Talk Network to put you in touch with contact people in your destination city.)

- Do check your appearance. Clothes neat and clean? Hair combed? Clean shaven? Not too much makeup? Fingernails clean? Shoes shined?

- Do arrive alone—leave family and friends at home. If you are blind, leave your driver at the building door. Show you are independent and mobile. Guide dogs, of course, are appropriate.

- Do arrive early, so you're comfortable and relaxed. But don't go into the reception area to be announced until five minutes before your scheduled interview.
- Do remove all outer clothing (coat and hat) in the reception area.
- Do accept mobility assistance once you arrive if you're blind. Most interviewers send their secretaries—or come themselves—to escort applicants from the reception room to their inner offices. Let the escort know exactly what you want to do—such as *May I take your arm* or *I will follow behind you*. If the interviewer doesn't send an escort, ask for someone to accompany you. (Although it's always important to demonstrate your independence and traveling ability, you don't want to risk getting rattled by a totally new setting; it is more important to remain composed and confident for the interviewer.)
- Do smile warmly, make direct eye contact (look squarely at the nose), and give the interviewer a firm, but gentle handshake. As you shake hands, say *Hello, Ms. Jones. I'm——. It's a pleasure meeting you*. If you sense the interviewer doesn't know whether or not to shake your hand—such as if you have cerebral palsy or wear a hook—extend it without hesitation. Why? Because doing so normalizes the situation. If your hand is refused, simply withdraw it discretely. If you're not able to shake hands, smile warmly and make direct eye contact as you introduce yourself.
- Do stand until you're invited to sit. When you do, show high energy by not slouching. If you use a wheelchair, don't be embarrassed or apologize if the interviewer must move a chair to make room for your wheelchair. Simply say, *Thank you.*
- Do bring an extra original copy of the resume you sent the prospective employer. Have it ready to present if asked.
- Do take employment tests with grace if asked to do so. The interviewer's demeanor may tell you whether or not the test is given to every applicant for the position, or whether you're being asked to take it because you have a disability. See Chapter 2.
- Do find positive things to say about your current or last employer. (Conversely, never says anything negative, even when encouraged to. You left your last job not because the employer is terrible, but because you seek greater opportunity, challenge, or pay.)

- Do be positive about everything. This is particularly important to job seekers with disabilities. Uninformed employers may have bought into a sterotypical myth that all people with disabilities are sour complainers.
- Do have a list of references ready to give the interviewer if requested.

## Interview Don'ts

- Don't assume you'll get the job because the employer fears ADA sanctions.
- Don't apologize for your disability or dwell on it.
- Don't argue. Even if discriminatory questions are asked, be diplomatic, polite, and tactful.
- Don't chew gum.
- Don't smoke—under any circumstances.
- Don't wear dark glasses—unless you do so because of a visual impairment. Even prescriptioned glasses that are tinted may cause you to miss valuable eye contact or to appear "shady" with something to hide.
- Don't wear strong perfumes or colognes.
- Don't experiment with a new hairstyle on interview day.
- Don't address an interviewer by first name.
- Don't crack your knuckles or play with your pen, hair, or eyeglasses. Nervous habits distract interviewers.
- Don't gaze out the window or at pictures around the room.
- Don't read any documents on the interviewer's desk or pick up anything in the office.
- Don't try to control the interview.
- Don't apologize for any lack of experience. Keep stressing your positive traits—such as being a quick learner and loyal employee.
- Don't tell the interviewer how many resumes you've sent out or how many interviews you've been on. It will appear that no one wants you.
- Don't tell the employer how badly you need the job. Sympathy doesn't translate to employment.
- Don't look at your watch during the interview. Doing so interferes with rapport.
- Don't lie. Even if you're not caught in it, you'll worry that you will be.

## CARDINAL CONCEPTS FOR TOP SCORES IN INTERVIEWS

True or false? The applicant with the best technical qualifications is most likely to find employment. The statement is false. The applicant with the best job hunting skills is most likely to find employment.

No matter how technically spectacular you are, if you don't know how to line up interviews and how to close the sale, you won't be hired. But when you do, you'll know how to win jobs for which you may not be a 100 percent perfect match. These key concepts show you what really works.

## Screening vs. Selection Interviews

In employer organizations large enough to have a human resources or personnel department, expect two types of interviews: *screening* and *selection.*

**Screening interviews** are conducted to screen out unqualified applicants. Screening interviewers—human resources specialists—usually are experienced at the task and conduct the interview in a highly professional manner. Screeners do not make hiring decisions, but pass on qualified candidates to hiring managers, usually department heads who will supervise the employee being hired.

In a screening interview, your objective is not to make waves. Answer the questions and don't volunteer unsolicited information. Don't try to dazzle the interviewer with your sparkling personality because you risk saying something that may go against the grain of the screener's personal beliefs. It's an unnecessary risk because the screener isn't going to make the judgment call.

**Selection interviews** are conducted to hire applicants. Selection interviewers—hiring managers—meet with prescreened applicants to make hiring decisions. They may consult with human resources specialists, but it is hiring managers who make selections.

In a selection interview, display your personality and interview "full out." If you and the person to whom you would report are incompatible, you'll save yourself grief if you discover it now, rather than be an unhappy camper for a year until you can find another job. Never forget: Your boss controls your raises, promotions, assignments, continued employment, and references. That makes it worth the risk to reveal your personality and mindset. Volunteer facts that support your contention of being a strong match for the position.

Don't be surprised if you are called back for several interviews. You may be asked to interview with a panel of people, an increasingly common practice today. The checking and double-checking reflect employers' fears of making a costly hiring mistake. They do it with everybody, not just job seekers with disabilities.

In organizations too small to have a human resources department, the screener and the selector often are the same person. In some cases, the hiring manager's subordinate or secretary may do the screening, referring only a short list of candidates to the decision maker.

## Practice Interviewing

To perform well, wise job seekers rehearse. Practice interviewing is like rehearsing your lines for a play. Once you've memorized them, "run" your lines with other people. Cast family and friends to play the part of interviewer. Think of two types of practice interviewing: *rehearsals* and *dress rehearsals.*

Hold **rehearsals** to become comfortable with your responses to anticipated interview questions. You can rehearse sitting across the kitchen table or driving to the library. Speak your lines aloud to embed them in your memory.

Once you feel good about the language and the flow, hold **dress rehearsals**. Dress rehearsals are intended to make you feel comfortable with your interviewing image. Again, you'll need an "interviewer" to feed you questions, and this time you'll need a video camcorder with a tripod. *There's no substitute for this important job-seeking strategy,* so borrow or rent a camcorder if you don't own one.

Have your "interviewer" sit close to the camcorder. Pretend the camcorder is the interviewer. Talk directly into the lens—the interviewer's eyes. What you see on the video tape is exactly how the interviewer would be seeing you.

During dress rehearsals you're practicing body language and learning what your nonverbal movements, mannerisms, and gestures tell the interviewer about you. Camcorders capture your every head scratch and knuckle crack. When you first watch yourself in living color, you'll notice distracting behaviors you've never noticed before.

If you find distracting behaviors that are related to your disability, do what you can to minimize them. For example, if you stutter, take three deep breaths from your toes all the way through your body. Exhale slowly. This may help relax you before the interview begins.

Most annoying behaviors are merely bad habits. Do you jingle change in your pocket, for instance, or tug at your jacket sleeve? Either makes you look nervous and short on self-confidence. Watch for leg swinging and nail biting. Watch for tapping and fooling with your hair or a pen. Watch for rocking from side to side.

Do you cross your arms, bow your head, and lean so far back in your chair that you look like you want to take a nap? Uncross your arms, raise your head, and lean slightly forward to convey interest. Do darting eyes make you seem shifty? Don't forget to smile.

During the dress rehearsal you can improve voice and language control. Do you talk too fast or too slow? Do you stumble over your words? Is your language riddled with ya knows and uh, uhs? Studying your dress rehearsal video—*and taping again and again and again*—can help you become more polished.

Another advantage camcorders bring to dress rehearsals is allowing you to check out your appearance through the employer's eyes. Does that new outfit, hair style, or makeup make you look more like you're ready for Mardi Gras than a serious job interview? Videotaping your dress rehearsal can help you put these things in focus.

It may take dozens of dress rehearsals before you feel comfortable with your interviewing image. Practice, practice, practice, practice, practice—think of it like going for an Olympic gold. Like an Olympian, think of this: If you're not practicing, some other contender is.

## Anticipate Timing of the Disclosure of Your Disability

Remember, the litmus test for whether or not to disclose your disability—and if so, when—should be:

*Does disclosure of my disability at this time and in this way support my objective of getting hired?*

## Research, Review Before Each Interview

If you have not already researched the company and the position, do so before each interview. Analyze the job description (real or mock) and, point by point, review your qualifications for the position. Write down the match between the job's requirements and you. It's important to speak aloud your customized matching answers based on specific research. The writing and the audio exercises help input the information into your memory banks to pull out at the interview. Knowing that you are prepared will calm your nervousness, allowing you to be a star at the interview.

## Dress the Part

Most organizations have an image that is reflected even in the way their employees dress. Subtly convince the interviewer that you fit that image by dressing the part and looking as though you belong.

If your goal is to work at an upscale stock brokerage, for instance, wear a traditional dark suit with a white shirt like others in the establishment. If you want to work in an art gallery, wear a trendy colorful creation that reflects your artistic flair. If you want to work for a modeling agency, then and only then might a miniskirt be appropriate.

Dress for the part you want to win. If you're not sure what the part calls for, scout it out. Watch people coming and going to work at the organization you've targeted. Always dress a bit better for the interview.

*The image you present in the first few minutes of contact with the interviewer is paramount in determining whether you'll be hired.* Dress and grooming play a major role in what psychologists call the "halo effect"—if you excel in one area, it's assumed you excel in others. Give interviewers every reason to believe you excel.

"If you are interviewed for an office position, you must dress the part whether you're disabled or not," says Walt Shinault, a financial consultant at Merrill Lynch in Jackson, Mississippi. "It may seem obvious, but one of my friends who has a disability went on an interview wearing jeans—needless to say, he didn't get the job." Shinault, who severed his spinal cord in a freak accident while practicing a college cheerleading stunt, says "Being in a wheelchair is no excuse to dress unprofessionally."

In selecting appropriate clothing that works with your disability, bear in mind these considerations.

**Does the clothing minimize my disability?** Many people with disabilities find they have problems with proportion, size, and shape. By learning the same clever use of color, line, and fabric that designers incorporate—such as vertical lines to make you look taller and thinner—you can make the body appear to be a different shape than it actually is.

If you have scoliosis, a sideways curvature of the spine, for example, diagonal lines that run opposite the curvature will visually lift a low shoulder and balance the scoliosis. If you use a wheelchair for mobility, clean, uncluttered lines show best on your seated figure. If you have had a laryngectomy, neckwear that accessorizes and blends with each outfit makes the stoma, a surgically created neck opening, disappear.

**Is the clothing comfortable?** If you use a wheelchair, off-the-rack-suits can be altered to alleviate the pouchy effect in the seat area and the lapel and shoulder roll of the jacket. If you have cerebral palsy, an absorbent fabric helps relieve the discomfort associated with dribbling that otherwise keeps your clothing constantly damp.

**Is the clothing durable and does it work with the devices I use to get around?** Braces, artificial limbs, crutches, and wheelchairs can be tough on clothing. Look for fabric strength in areas that must take heavy wear.

Check out Nellie Thornton's *Fashion for Disabled People,* showing with words and illustrations the importance of fashion, understanding problems, and finding solutions. E&J Avenues markets a line of clothing specifically designed for people who use wheelchairs. Laryngectomee Fashions sells fashioned stoma covers. The National Odd Shoe Exchange matches right-foot amputees with left-foot amputees to swap unneeded shoes. (See appendix B3 for more information on these resources.)

## Understand the Value of Your Initial Feedback Questions

Although your research has prepared you to speak of how your qualifications match the job's requirements, verify your knowledge early in the interview and then ride that information to the winner's circle. As soon as you can, ask:

- *How do you see the scope of this job?*
- *What qualifications would your ideal candidate have?*

Take notes. Throughout the interview, frame your qualifications in the terms the interviewer used and feed them back at every opportunity. In brief, the strategy is to confirm your understanding of what the employer wants and then convince the employer that that's what you're selling.

## Understand Which Questions to Ask When

Few job candidates understand that the timing of when you ask what can earn you or cost you interview points. Questions you ask fall into two categories:

1) The Employer's Agenda—those that sell you

2) Your Agenda—those that answer your personal questions

(Reread "Your Agenda" and "The Employer's Agenda" in Chapter 11.)

When the interviewer asks early on, "Do you have any questions about the job?" it's not the time to find out what's in it for you. This is your chance to sell yourself and convince the interviewer that you're the right person to hire.

Use **The Employer's Agenda questions** *before* **the offer** as a sophisticated selling tool to position yourself as serious, focused, and committed to work. Interviewers expect job candidates who are interested in the position to have questions, and work-related questions never turn interviewers off. Don't worry about spending as much as ten minutes asking work-focused, task-focused, and function-focused "selling" questions.

Your initial feedback questions sell you, so if you haven't had an opportunity to ask them yet, this is the perfect time.

Here are other selected interview questions on The Employer's Agenda that you may want to ask:

- *Can you describe a typical day? What are the precise duties and responsibilities and outcomes expected of the position?*
- *What type of training would I receive, if any? From whom?*
- *To whom would I report? What positions would report to me, if any?*
- *How does this position relate to the department, and how does the department relate to the organization as a whole?*
- *Are there continuing education opportunities that would improve the productivity of the person holding this position?*
- *Was the last person who held this position promoted? What is the potential for promotion? What would be a normal career path from this position?*
- *Where is the organization headed? Do you expect a change in structure?*

*After* **(or** *near***) a job offer**, the employer will be happy to answer **Your Agenda questions**. Prior to that, interviewers aren't really concerned about your needs. They're busy trying to decide if they're interested in you. They resent spending time discussing things such as insurance, vacation, and lunch hours this early in the game—and they wonder about your priorities.

## Understand Basic Salary Negotiating Techniques

The rules of thumb:

- Try to delay talking salary until after the offer
- When you do get to figures, use ranges (aim near the top of the range) to give yourself flexibility

- Try to get the employer to name the figures first

If asked prematurely to name your price, say you are confident that compensation will present no difficulty once the scope of the job is firmed up. Add that you're sure the employer will be fair, paying the market rate. This approach requires that you research the market rate. A simple method is to check such library references as Gale Research's *American Salaries and Wages Survey*. In round figures, add 5 percent per year to salaries from the base year in which the pay data was gathered for a ball-park handle on what the job is worth today.

If pressed, you can say: *The salary I had with my other job was based on different work and responsibilities. Concentrating on this position, what is the salary range you have in mind?* or *With my qualifications for this specific position, what compensation level do you see as appropriate?* The strategy is to indicate that your old salary and job (maybe as a volunteer) belonged in a different world. If you name the figure first, you may underprice or overprice yourself.

One of the best-kept secrets in the working world is the value of developing skills in salary negotiation. Discover negotiating principles and practice them in rehearsal sessions until it's easy for you. Your best chance to move up and increase your pay is when you change jobs, not when you come up for a performance review. If you need motivation, remember that learning how to talk money can be worth additional thousands of dollars per year. Even in bureaucracies, you may be able to negotiate your way to a job title that pays a higher salary.

To learn the finer points of salary negotiation, read *Salary Success: Know What You're Worth and Get It*, by Ronald L. Krannich, Ph.D., and Caryl Rae Krannich, Ph.D., and *How to Make $1000 a Minute Negotiating Your Salaries and Raises*, by Jack Chapman.

## Focus Sharply on What You Want to Do

Employers are not interested in the applicant who is willing to "do anything" when they can hire someone who is specialized by experience, training, or interest. In a medical analogy, it's like choosing a general practitioner to do bone surgery when you could have an orthopedic surgeon.

## Anticipate Typical General Questions

Certain questions are almost guaranteed to turn up in interviews. Think through your answers in advance and practice until you can deliver them on "automatic pilot." Here are a few of the most frequently asked questions, although the phrasing will vary.

**Tell me about yourself.** Memorize a one-minute response that includes your name, geographic origins, the name of the person who referred you (if any), your experience and areas of expertise, your schooling, one or two major achievements, and your objective and how it fits the job. In this example, an accounting graduate who has been out of college for almost a year without being able to find a permanent job interviews for an accounting position that specified the applicant must be computer skilled.

*My name is—. I grew up in Kansas City, Missouri. Jeff Harrow suggested I come by and talk with you. I have well-developed skills in accounting and computers. Since graduation from Kansas State University, I have worked as an accountant at several well-regarded companies as a temporary employee—experiences that have broadened my perspective of the business world. On one job, I was complimented for my work in interpreting financial statements for clients. On another, I helped in the automating of the accounting system, which also was one of my emphasis areas in college. I am seeking to find an entry-level position in accounting, and my research suggests this is an ideal place. My accounting and computer skills appear to be well matched to the position's requirements.*

The one-minute background statement will or will not include a mention of your disability, depending upon your disclosure strategy. If you've previously disclosed, think of a light, charming, seemingly off-the-cuff way to put the interviewer at ease. A job seeker who uses a wheelchair, for example, might include something like this:

*When a motorcycle accident in college changed my way of getting around, it really came home to me that I think with my brain, not with my legs.* In this casual comment, you've introduced the topic of your disability (which releases the tension of "when and how will it come up?") and told the interviewer it's okay to talk about it. You've also made three important points about your disability: 1) you're experienced in dealing with it, 2) you have the ability to get around, and 3) you remind the interviewer that the focus should be on your thinking ability, not on your physical disability.

The true questions behind the "Tell me about yourself" request are these: Are you our kind of person? Will you fit into our company culture? Are you a good person to work with?

Suppose your disability is visible. No matter. It is shared values and similar viewpoints that determine if you are like the group of employees you hope to join. Remember, it's human nature to like people who are like ourselves.

**Why do you want to work here?** Base your answer on the preinterview research you conducted on the employer. The primary reasons should relate to the fit of your skills with the job or that the employer enjoys a good reputation. Even if mobility is an obvious problem for you, do not base the primary reason on location—that the work site is near your home.

**Is there anything that would prevent you from performing the job duties?** Experienced interviewers ask this of everyone, not only those they perceive to have a disability. Your answer: *No, not as I understand them.* This may mean you must do the job differently than others, and if so, you will explain. The substance of your explanation is discussed more fully earlier, in Chapter 2 on ADA (essential functions of the job and reasonable accommodation) and Chapter 5 on making the job fit you (job accommodations and functional limitations).

**What are your greatest strengths?** This question opens a golden opportunity to bowl over your interviewer with information that supports your objective of being offered the position in discussion.

Review the self-analysis you did in Chapter 4 to prod your memory. Choose three outstanding abilities to discuss.

How can you use this opportunity as yet another way to infuse *Enable-Yourself Interviewing Skills* into the conversation? Suppose you've recovered from a heart attack that kept you out of work as a magazine editor for nine months, leaving a gap in your resume. Your answer in part might be: *I have always had the ability to meet deadlines. My recent heart episode taught me the value of working smart as well as working hard. It taught me to look for more efficient ways to get the task done. For instance, now I would move up writers' deadlines by two weeks to allow for late deliveries to me.*

*Tip:* Whenever you feel that your statement may seem like you're bragging, attribute it to another person: *My teacher said that I was one of the fastest-learning students he'd ever had.* If your teacher never said any such thing, don't lie. But you can call your teacher and ask: *Would you agree that I'm one of the fastest-learning students you ever taught?*

**What is your greatest weakness?** One woman handled this one with quiet humor: "Chocolate," she said. The standard advice is to avoid a real weakness ("I am a bumbler at budgeting") and instead pick a strength-in-disguise (*I become impatient when others on the team don't finish their work on time*).

The "greatest weakness" question is fraught with danger for job seekers with disabilities who, unless they've been counseled against it, often identify the disability as the soft spot. Even if your disability is as challenging as the inability to use your hands, resist any temptation to flag it as a weakness. This is the wrong place in the interview to focus on a functional limitation that may not advance your candidacy.

If the interviewer prods—which is legal under ADA—asking, for instance, how it is that your deafness won't impair your ability to be a truckdriver ("How can you hear emergency vehicle sirens?"), be ready with a positive message. *The state department of motor vehicles does not consider deafness a restriction, and it only issues commercial driver's licenses to those it considers to be safe drivers. My hearing loss doesn't affect my driving reflexes. As a matter of fact, it has been a plus because it has inspired me to take in and process more visual information, thus developing an increased visual awareness.*

**Are you unemployed now?** If you are unemployed, a simple "yes" here will not suffice. You must prevent the interviewer from jumping to negative conclusions.

*If you were employed and left voluntarily,* your basic answer is that in fairness to your previous employer, you didn't feel you could conduct an adequate job search for the best match.

*If you were laid off,* the thrust of your answer is that the events of recent years have thrown the job market into chaos and that you are re-establishing your successful career.

*If you were fired for cause,* it was a learning experience and you have learned the lesson. Or there were extenuating circumstances (which had better be believable).

*If you have never held a job,* focus on how hard you work, how quickly you learn, and how enthusiastic you are about doing this job.

If you have disclosed your disability, you can add that you are seeking an enlightened management who believes in fair employment practices based on ability. Then ask: *Have I found that fairness here?*

**Why should I hire you instead of other equally qualified candidates?** The essential answer is structured like this:

Set the stage by summarizing the interviewer's description of the job. Go point by point. For each requirement, mention your related skills or accomplishments.

Next, by asking the following questions employers will assume you will be an appreciative and loyal employee. *How often have you had to train someone for this position? How often do you find that your direct reports are on unofficial coffee breaks or chatting on personal telephone calls?*

You may want to bring up your disability here when it gives you an edge by saving the employer money. Suppose training is required, for example. If you can get on-job training through an agency serving the disability community, mention it to the employer (see Chapter 5 on making the job fit you).

Now close with a recap of the benefits you offer, and itemize your qualifications. *I hope I've convinced you that I have the qualifications you seek. I'm skilled in using computers, can meet productivity goals, can innovate, and can lead others. I'm a team player, and this job will have a high priority in my life.*

## Anticipate Typical General Objections

Be ready for objections by anticipating your answers in advance. These are common roadblocks.

**Your experience isn't exactly what we need.** Respond by saying that while you don't have exactly 100 percent of the experience, you will compensate for that by giving 110 percent effort. This works only when the competition is no better matched than you.

**Sorry, but you lack a college degree, and this job requires one.** This objection is very difficult to overcome in a competitive market. Your best answer is to say you are currently enrolled in a degree program and expect to finish on such and such a date. But at the same time, stress that your qualifications are above average as indicated by your previous experiences as the only nongraduate at your job level. If you have no experience, you haven't got a prayer on this one.

**You're overqualified.** It may be true. If you can convince the employer that you will not leave at the first hint of a better job or that you will not grow restless and dissatisfied, you'll have a shot at the job. Overqualified applicants—with and without disabilities—are more likely to be hired in a competitive job market. To weed through an excess of applicants, a common screening technique is to bring up education and experience requirements. The theory is, why take a sergeant when you can get a lieutenant for the same money?

When the "overqualified" objection is a smoke screen for age discrimination, focus your response on the benefits of mature judgment, noting that age is an asset in bottom-line driven companies. Potential is good, but skills and experience are money in the bank. Even in a youth-oriented culture, a wise head is a good anchor. A thought-provoking question is: *I see you hire many young people. Do you think it would be beneficial for them to have a co-worker with roots and seasoned judgment?*

## How to Manage the Disability Factor

Since ADA does not require employers to become experts on disabilities, once your disability is disclosed many will have questions—some spoken, some unspoken.

The law says that prior to making an offer of employment, employer questions about your disability must relate to *essential functions* of the job and determining whether you are qualified to perform them. This means *with or without reasonable accommodation.*

If an employer inquires about your disability other than to understand how you would perform a task, ask yourself: Is the employer asking out of genuine interest in me? If so, forgive ADA employer restrictions on questions about the nature and severity of your disability. Consider a brief discussion addressing specific employer concerns before refocusing on the job match. It may go a long way toward landing you a job offer.

"If I sense any hesitancy or unspoken concerns in interviews," says Sharon Haddy, principal at Norco Elementary School in Norco, California, "I may say something such as: 'If I were you, I know I would have some questions about whether I can handle students, and I have no qualms about discussing it.'" Haddy, who uses a wheelchair as a result of poliomyelitis, advises you to invite questions.

*When interviewers have concerns about your disability and they don't ask questions about them, you won't get the job.*

## Anticipate Typical Disability-Related Questions and Objections (Verbalized and Nonverbalized)

Make lemonade out of the lemons employers toss your way. Practice out loud positive responses to typical employer questions and objections related to your disability until they flow comfortably and convincingly. Plan how to handle tactfully those you can't turn into positives.

**Dispelling Myths About Workers with Disabilities** will give you a start on disarming employers using powerful statistics. As an example, suppose an interviewer says, "Our organization runs a tight ship. Every employee must work to 100 percent productivity." Translation: Workers with disabilities are less productive so I can't hire you.

Your *Enable-Yourself Interviewing Skills* response would be something like this: *I agree that the success of an organization rests on the productivity of its employees. Did you know that more than three-fourths of*

*(continued on page 232)*

# Dispelling Myths about Workers with Disabilities

Here are common myths—and the realities—to help interviewers separate fact from fiction when comparing you with candidates without disabilities. The ability to dispel disability myths and promote facts is an essential *Enable-Yourself Interviewing Skill.*

| | |
|---|---|
| Myth: | *Workers with disabilities cost more to employ.* |
| Fact: | More than three-fourths of managers surveyed say the costs of employing both workers with and workers without disabilities are about the same.[1] |

| | |
|---|---|
| Myth: | *Workers with disabilities require costly job accommodations.* |
| Fact: | Employers surveyed say more than three-fourths of job accommodations for workers with disabilities cost less than $500; half cost nothing.[2] |
| Fact: | Employers surveyed say the cost of accommodations virtually never drives the cost of employment above the average range of costs for all employees.[1] |

| | |
|---|---|
| Myth: | *Workers with disabilities don't fit in with co-workers.* |
| Fact: | Almost all employers surveyed reject the argument that workers with disabilities don't fit in with most workers without disabilities.[1] |
| Fact: | Two-thirds of the public surveyed say most of their co-workers would have no problems working alongside individuals with disabilities.[3] |
| Fact: | Two-thirds of the public surveyed supports policies that would increase the number of people with disabilities working with them. |

| | |
|---|---|
| Myth: | *Workers with disabilities are a greater safety risk to themselves and co-workers.* |
| Fact: | Nearly half of employers surveyed agreed that workers with disabilities have *fewer* accidents on the job than workers without disabilities. (The survey did not report how many employers say workers with disabilities have an *equal* number of accidents on the job.)[1] |

*(continued)*

| | |
|---|---|
| Myth: | *Workers with disabilities are less productive.* |
| Fact: | Three-fourths of department heads/line managers surveyed rate workers with disabilities as equally or more productive than workers without disabilities.[1] |
| Fact: | More than three-fourths of the public feels workers with disabilities are equally or more productive than the average worker.[3] |

| | |
|---|---|
| Myth: | *Workers with disabilities are harder to supervise.* |
| Fact: | More than three-fourths of department heads/line managers surveyed who have supervised workers with disabilities say they are no more difficult to supervise than workers without disabilities.[1] |

| | |
|---|---|
| Myth: | *Workers with disabilities miss more work.* |
| Fact: | More than three-fourths of department heads/line managers surveyed rate workers with disabilities as being equally or more punctual and having equal or better attendance records than workers without disabilities.[1] |

| | |
|---|---|
| Myth: | *Workers with disabilities aren't reliable.* |
| Fact: | More than three-fourths of department heads/line managers surveyed rate workers with disabilities as equally or more reliable than workers without disabilities.[1] |

| | |
|---|---|
| Myth: | *Workers with disabilities do not want to work.* |
| Fact: | Two-thirds of working-age Americans with disabilities surveyed are not employed; of those, two-thirds want to work.[4] |
| Fact: | More than three-fourths of department heads/line managers surveyed rate workers with disabilities as equally or more willing to work hard compared with workers without disabilities.[1] |

| | |
|---|---|
| Myth: | *Bringing more workers with disabilities into the work force will take jobs from people without disabilities who need them.* |
| Fact: | People with disabilities, need jobs too. Costs to be self supporting exceed government allowances. Only a small portion of the public surveyed think bringing more people with disabilities into the work force will threaten to take jobs from people without disabilities; conversely, more than three-fourths thinks it will be a boost to the nation by taking people off welfare and putting them to work.[3] |

*(continued)*

| Myth: | *The public does not support the Americans with Disabilities Act.* |
|-------|----------------------------------|
| Fact: | Almost all of the public surveyed support the ADA provision banning job discrimination based on disability.[3] |
| Fact: | More than three-fourths of the public surveyed support affirmative action programs for people with disabilities similar to those many employers and colleges have for women and minorities.[3] |
| Fact: | More than three-fourths of the public support the provision that says that employers with more than fifteen employees must make reasonable accommodations for workers with disabilities.[3] |

[1] Louis Harris and Associates Survey for the International Center for the Disabled, *The ICD Survey II: Employing Disabled Americans*
[2] Berkeley Planning Associates Survey for the U.S. Department of Labor's Employment Standards Administration, *A Study of Accommodations Provided to Handicapped Employees by Federal Contractors*
[3] Louis Harris and Associates Survey for the National Organization on Disability, *Public Attitudes Toward People with Disabilities*
[4] Louis Harris and Associates Survey for the International Center for the Disabled, *The ICD Survey of Disabled Americans: Bringing Disabled Americans into the Mainstream*

*line managers surveyed recently say workers with disabilities are equally or more productive than their co-workers?*

If you can truthfully say it, an alternative would be: *I agree that the success of an organization rests on the productivity of its employees. That's why I was pleased when my last supervisor specifically mentioned my high level of productivity in my performance review.*

Here are some other typical questions and objections employers may raise—or think. Plan ahead how you will respond.

**Will my insurance rates go up if I hire you?** This may be the number one concern of employers in today's market of skyrocketing insurance premiums. Unless you're interviewing at a large organization with a policy of hiring people with disabilities (where the interviewer will know the facts), calm this fear before leaving the interview.

"Health insurance, life insurance, and workers' compensation insurance companies do not raise insurance rates merely because workers with disabilities are added to group policies," says Richard Gulley, chief executive officer of Robert F. Driver Company, the largest insurance brokerage in San Diego.

"At renewal time, most insurance companies rerate group policies based on the sex and age of participating employees and dependents of the organization," Gulley says. "The experience factor—the number and dollar amount of claims—also influences rates, but it is usually spread over a large pool of employees from *many* organizations. If the pool is of sufficient size, one individual's disability is unlikely to affect the premiums of the employer."

When discussing insurance and disabilities, remember: claims affect insurance, not disabilities. If you fear an employer will falsely assume you will have greater than average medical claims because of your disability, speak up. *I know rising medical insurance premiums is on everyone's minds today. I want you to know that my disability requires no greater medical care than any of my friends or co-workers who don't have disabilities.*

When an employer changes insurance carriers, the claim history of participating employees of the organization may be reviewed. If the medical history of one person causes a small business to be shut out of coverage, the solution may be a high-risk pool. "Over half the states currently have high-risk pools for *individuals* who are denied coverage because of their health," says Gulley.

Employers may see dollar signs when they hear "high risk." To calm their fears you may want to say: *If the company ever changes insurance carriers and my medical history places me in a "high-risk" category, I would have no problem being enrolled as an individual in the state's high-risk pool. And I would be happy to pay the difference, if any, between the premiums for my coverage and those of any other employee on your group plan.* (If an employer asks you to pay the difference—or forces you into a high-risk pool—discrimination may be at work. But nothing says *you* can't ask the employer.)

Some states without high-risk pools have Blue Cross and Blue Shield high-risk plans. Call your state insurance department for more information.

**How would you be able to get out of the building in case of an emergency—such as a fire?** The employer is not only worried about your safety here, but also worried about the organization's liability in case something were to happen to you. Make the employer comfortable on this issue. Explain the buddy system—three employees who volunteer to assist you in exiting the building safely. The employer knows that in a fire, for example, the elevators will be off limits. If you work above ground level and use a wheelchair, describe exactly how your "buddies" would carry you down the stairs.

**How will you get to work?** If you sense it's an issue, answer it—in a positive way—before it's asked. *Since I would be driving my van to work every day, if anyone ever needs a ride to outside meetings, I would be happy to drive them.* With this statement you've said you have transportation to and from work, you are mobile and independent should you need to leave the office during the workday, and you're a team player.

If you use public transportation, you might say: *I was happy to see that the bus stop is so convenient to the office. It's also nice that it runs so frequently and so late — I prefer not to take a cab when I work late.* Here you've said you've planned ahead and know the bus route and schedule, that sometimes you expect to work late, and that you will take a cab if you need to.

**What if I hire you and you don't work out? Will I have a difficult time firing you?** This may be in many interviewer minds, although few, if any, will speak it. Here's where you pick one of the statistics on the **Dispelling Myths About Workers with Disabilities** list and put your own twist on it. Cite a statistic, state a positive personal fact, and then briefly follow with a comment that if you don't perform to the employer's satisfaction you would expect to be let go.

*Nearly half of the department managers surveyed recently rate their workers with disabilities as being more punctual and having a better attendance record than co-workers. I've found that to be true in my case. As a matter of fact, I only missed three days of work in the two years I was at XYZ Company. I'm sure I would have no problem complying with your company's attendance policies, but if I failed to do so I would expect to be released.*

**This position deals with highly sensitive information. If you're hired, your reader (or interpreter) will have access to confidential material.** This objection may come up if you're seeking a position that deals with confidential information and you're blind and use a reader or you're deaf or without speech and use an interpreter (regardless of who's footing the bill for the support service assistant). Here's your response: *I understand your concern for confidentiality since I rely on readers to handle many of my business and personal matters. Just as you must check histories and rely on your judgment about hiring trustworthy employees to handle confidential information, I must select trustworthy readers to handle any confidential information with which they assist me.*

**I know you've said you can do the job, but in light of your disability I'm having a hard time really understanding how you would do it. Would you mind showing me?** If you have a severe disability, many employers who *want* to believe you can perform on the job may find it impossible to envision how. Even though this question is legal, many interviewers who are thinking it will not ask it. You have a platinum opportunity to calm employer fears by using a one-two-three strategy: *persuade by personal example, persuade by another person's example,* and *persuade by an employer's experience.*

*Persuading by personal example* is the strategy that won Mike Stearn his data systems analyst position with the Los Angeles County Municipal Courts. Stearn, who is blind, says, "I found that the best way to communicate was through my 'dog and pony' show. I demonstrated for employers exactly what I could do. I brought my equipment with me, and I brought computer programs I had written." If practical, Stearn advises, take devices with you to the interview to show the potential employer how you would perform the job.

*Persuading by another person's example* is the second step of the one-two-three strategy. After showing the interviewer how you would perform the job—or after explaining the technique if taking your devices with you is impractical—offer the names and telephone numbers of two or three successfully employed people with similar disabilities whom the employer may contact for more information. Whether or not the employer ever makes the calls, you've scored points by demonstrating that other people with similar disabilities are productive workers.

*Persuading by an employer's experience* is the final step of the one-two-three strategy. Give the interviewer the names and telephone numbers of two or three employers who employ people with similar disabilities. Your potential employers are more likely to ask other employers than to ask you the frank questions that will disarm their fears. And many will more likely believe the other employers' answers over yours.

Where do you find the "persuaders" for steps two and three of this strategy? They may be people you already know or they may be people to whom the Job Accommodation Network or another agency serving the disability community refers you. If you're operating from a referral, contact the persuaders, explain your goal, and get their permission to give their names and numbers to potential employers.

**I don't know anything about making accommodations for a disability such as yours. I wouldn't know where to start.** Make lemonade immediately. *Start with me! I'm an expert at dealing with my disability, and I'm certain we'll have no problem addressing an accommodation for this position. If we need help, the Job Accommodation Network — which operates over a toll-free telephone line — can probably have a solution within twenty-four hours. Many other service organizations also offer free advice and counseling — and some even offer financial assistance. I'm confident accommodation will not be a problem.* Continue this conversation by selling the employer with money talk (discussed later in this chapter).

# Style Yourself as a Hot Candidate

Employers don't hire people because they feel sorry for them. They hire people who are competent to accomplish a specific, definable purpose.

**Style yourself as such a person in small as well as in large matters.** For instance, careers author Jeff Allen suggests that unless you are engaged in spellbinding conversation, try to leave after forty-five minutes. The interviewer may be feeling locked in but hesitant to appear impolite in ending the meeting. Just say you have another appointment (even if it's with your mother). Employers are like anybody else—they always want the hot candidates that others are considering. Allen offers two additional tips to position yourself as a hot candidate.

**Avoid meal interviews.** In his book, *Jeff Allen's Best: Win the Job,* Allen says there's no way to predict an interviewer's personal preferences in eating and drinking habits. "I'm not talking about obvious errors like using your knife as a spoon or as a slingshot. (I know it works well, but it must be cleaned with your shirt before you use it for a shoehorn.)" Allen reports that one candidate was ruled out just because he salted his food!

**Complete a job application in advance, if possible.** Allen suggests calling the human resources receptionist to request a copy of the application in advance. "Arriving with it neatly typed saves time, makes a good impression, and guides you through the interview like a road map," Allen explains.

Here's a variation on this tip, one that is especially pertinent for job seekers with visual impairments. (It may be appropriate for job seekers with fingering limitations as well.) Obtain a "stock" application form at any office supply store. Get help in filling it out in advance. When you arrive and are asked to fill out an application, ask if your prefilled-out form is an acceptable substitute. (This shows you understand the principles of alternate methods of doing a job.) If your form is not acceptable, inquire whether you may take the application home to complete. If the employer denies your request, an employee may be available to act as a reader.

Why isn't it wise to ask for a reader right away? Even though you may be entitled to a reader under ADA, requesting one may make you lose footing as a hot candidate. Many employers, unaccustomed to how self-sufficient an employee who is blind can truly be, falsely may assume that you'll need a full-time reader or constant help from co-workers.

*Caution:* If you come across an application form that asks something like this: "Do you have any physical conditions that may limit your ability to perform the job applied for?" *Stop!* Reread the wording carefully. If you're sure you can do the job, answer *No*. If you can't truthfully answer *No*, write *Will discuss in interview*. This isn't the place to disclose your disability.

## People Are Hired Because They Are Liked

The hedge on this statement is that all other things are equal, which they never are. But between two fairly equally qualified candidates, the one most liked will be hired. That's why you want to be liked from Minute One. Learn to break the ice with non-threatening small talk when you first meet the interviewer. Say: *Your offices are very attractive. Were they redecorated recently?* or *I noticed the receptionist is using a computer. Are you on a network?* or *That's a handsome trophy. Do you play tennis often?*

Try to express interest in something that interests the interviewer, making a connection. The psychology is to convert the pronouns "you" and "I" to "we." Remember, we like people who are like us.

## Be Alert to the Interviewer's Perspective

One reason people do poorly in interviews is self-absorption. They are so focused on how they're doing that they fail to pay attention to the interviewer's needs and motivations. Often they're nervous wrecks worrying about "me, me, me." It's like a public speaker who is so engrossed with his image that he fails to notice the audience is leaving in droves.

A job seeker with a disability should be particularly aware of any nervous behavior on the part of the interviewer. The interviewer may feel ill at ease talking to someone with a disability.

"Do you ever wonder why so many people don't feel comfortable in looking at or being near someone who has an obvious physical disability?" asks George Kuhrts, Southwest regional director of Canine Companions for Independence in Rancho Santa Fe, California. "It's not so much that they're threatened by the disabled persons and their problems. It's that they have trouble facing their own vulnerability, their own possibility of losing physical health and well-being."

If you wish the interviewer to concentrate on your *Enable-Yourself Interviewing Skills*, you must first put the interviewer at ease. One approach is to turn the tables: *Thank you for your kindness in making me feel more comfortable. I was a little nervous when I came in. Did I say a little nervous? It was more like a ten on the Richter scale.*

Another illustration: If you are blind, work words like "see" and "saw" into your conversation early so the interviewer will realize the language is okay to use. The interviewer will be more relaxed and not as preoccupied trying not to slip and say something that may offend you.

A variation of interviewer discomfort is when the interviewer feels uneasy with the entire situation, particularly if it involves a severe physical disability—such as a candidate who is armless and uses her feet to keyboard her own reports. In an unconscious strategy to deal with the discomfort, the interviewer derails the hiring conversation by continually telling the applicant how amazing she is. How wonderfully brave. How admirable. The strokes are warming, but they won't move the job seeker toward her objective of getting hired.

If this happens to you, graciously acknowledge the compliments, but firmly turn the conversation to showing how you are a perfect candidate for the job. *Thanks very much for your vote of confidence. I appreciate hearing it. I have worked very hard to become a qualified job candidate and, if I may, I'd like to describe some of my skills and abilities. As I understand it, this position calls for someone who has strong ability in sales. When I did volunteer fundraising for —.*

In another illustration of sensitivity to the interviewer, body language may tell you that you are boring the interviewer. What should you do about it? Ask for direction: *Would you rather hear more about my experience in X, or shall we move to my skills in Y?*

## Anticipate Unusual Developments

Unusual developments may present themselves on interview day. Think of as many as you can, and plan ahead how you'll handle them. Here are just a few to consider.

### Being Kept Waiting

If the wait is less than thirty minutes, relax. Don't display annoyance. Sometimes interviewers intentionally keep job candidates waiting and later have the receptionist report on candidates' demeanors. Like a candid camera test—How did the applicant react in a frustrating situation?

If thirty minutes passes and you're still waiting, shift into the "hot candidate" strategy. Tell the receptionist you have another appointment (even if it's again with your mother), and you will only be able to wait a few more minutes. The receptionist should notify the interviewer. You'll either be seen quickly or, if you're not seen within another fifteen minutes, ask to reschedule your interview. Not only do you want to avoid the image that you have nothing else to do but wait around, but by this time your energy level will be zapped.

Obviously, there will be times when this strategy may work against you—such as when the reception room is filled with candidates all waiting to interview *behind* you. If you leave then, you risk the chance that one of them will be hired on the spot and your hot candidate positioning will be pointless. The best strategy here is to ask the receptionist if you can use a private telephone to reschedule another appointment. Then make a call—even if it's to your own answering machine—because the receptionist may be watching the lights on the switchboard.

### Telephone Call Interrupting Your Interview

Some employers are fond of having a real or fabricated telephone call interrupt during interviews. This gives them a first-hand opportunity to study job candidates' responses to being interrupted, behavior while waiting, and ability to restart the interview. Gaze out the window or focus on a picture on the wall, giving the interviewer "privacy." If it seems to be a lengthy or confidential call, whisper or signal *Shall I wait outside?*

When the interviewer apologizes for the interruption, respond with: *No problem. Life is full of unexpected situations best dealt with at the moment. Now, concerning my design experience as it relates to the job you want done —.* Here you have told the employer you were not bothered by the interview interruption, you expect interruptions and deal with them as they come up, and you have the ability to refocus quickly at the point where you were interrupted.

### Uncomfortable Silence

Plan for it and you'll be better equipped to sit there and smile pleasantly. If you have new information to convey that will boast the job match, speak up. If not, don't indiscriminately babble. Purposeful silence is an interview tactic designed to unnerve you into blurting out information that can't be safely asked in a direct manner.

### Stress Interview

Stress interviewing is faddish—it comes and goes, although some interviewers swear by it. It may take on any level of intensity from "sell me this dictaphone" to seating you in a chair with uneven legs, to several interviewers aiming a series of rapid-fire questions at you. Realize that the purpose of stress interviews is to see how you function under stress, but some experts warn about investing your career years with an employer whose mind works this way. Evaluate the situation carefully.

"While a college student, I had an interview that was a nightmare with the head of personnel at a Fortune 500 company," says Jim Haidinyak, a development engineer for International Business Machines in Austin, Texas. "The interviewer said, 'It's obvious you have this disability [Haidinyak uses a wheelchair], and it seems to me a lot of people won't want to work with you. What do you think?' I said 'I don't think that's true,' and he came back with 'I think it is, and I think it will adversely affect your performance. What do you think about that?'"

At this point, Haidinyak could have lost his composure and blown the entire interview, but he didn't. "'Give me a second to think about it,' I told him. Then I calmly answered, 'You're asking impertinent questions that have nothing to do with the job, and I think it would be best if we consider this interview over.' The interviewer said, 'Don't get mad. I'm just trying to get your reaction.' 'You got it—As far as I'm concerned this interview is over,' I said and calmly left, not believing what had just happened and mentally writing off any possibility of getting that job."

Haidinyak's controlled but confident handling of the situation scored points for him. "I was called back for another interview. They said they were impressed with my people skills and the fact that I kept my composure," he says. "Although I had applied for a technical position, I was offered a management position." (Because it meant a relocation, Haidinyak declined.)

Today, because of ADA, a *hard-core* stress interview like Haidinyak's is unlikely, but get the message: Some employers will intentionally test to see how comfortable *you* are with your disability on the theory that if you aren't comfortable with it, you'll never make co-workers and supervisors comfortable with it.

Be watchful of other interviewers who, unintentionally, will stress you through bigotry or ignorance.

## Sell the Employer with Money Talk

Other than making money, nothing makes most employers happier than saving money. Use every opportunity you can to let the interviewer know that hiring you has a cost benefit to the organization.

### Sell the Employer with Job Accommodations

Put yourself in the employer's chair. You're interviewing an applicant with your disability. You're unfamiliar with the functional limitations of the disability—let alone that particular individual—and yet you know the law says you must make reasonable accommodations. Won't the cost of such accommodations be paramount in your mind, maybe to the point of distraction? With the employer's perspective in mind, now think timing.

If you need no job accommodations, if you plan to supply your own adaptive equipment, or if the accommodations you need are not costly, *discuss job accommodations early in the interview.* Yes, even if you don't need any—the employer may not know that, and it will put the cost fear to rest.

For some, needed job accommodations will be costly and will not be a selling point. If the accommodations you need are costly, you will need to balance the timing of the discussion with what the interviewer is thinking.

If you sense the interviewer is ready to make an offer, you may want to postpone the discussion. If you sense the interviewer is holding off making an offer until you discuss job accommodations, bring it up.

Remember, if you have a disability that requires a job accommodation, you must make employers aware of it before they have any legal obligation to provide it. Ask yourself this question before opening up the conversation:

*Does discussing my needed job accommodation at this time support my objective of getting hired?*

### Sell the Employer with IRS Tax Incentives

Carry a copy of the *Tax Information for Persons with Handicaps or Disabilities* pamphlet you previously had the IRS send you. When the timing seems right, say something like this: *Did you know the IRS has three business tax incentives to encourage employers to hire workers with disabilities? There's a deduction for the cost of making facilities and vehicles accessible. There's a tax credit to small businesses providing job accommodations. And there's a tax credit for employers who hire individuals with disabilities. I have a copy of an IRS pamphlet that explains these incentives if you'd like to see it.* If only one or two of the IRS incentives apply to your situation, modify this statement accordingly.

### Sell the Employer with Social Security Work Incentives

If you are currently out of work and looking for a job, employers may assume you will lose your government benefits when you begin working. Some will be reluctant to "try you" in a job because they don't want to be responsible for that loss.

Search for appropriate timing to mention the *Employment Opportunity for Disabled Americans Act of 1986*. You may decide to reassure the employer by saying something like this: *The law is quite complex, but basically Congress has made it easier for me to bring home a paycheck and not lose my Social Security benefits. I want you to know that my health care will not be your problem because I'll be able to keep my Medicare coverage.*

It may not be necessary to go into the finer points of all Social Security–related benefits—Social Security Disability Insurance, Supplemental Security Income, Trial Work Periods, Impairment-Related Work Expenses, or the Plan for Achieving Self-Support—but *you* should be aware of all your options. Some benefits vary by state, so well in advance of your job search, call the Social Security Administration to get details.

### Sell the Employer with Trade-Offs

This may be another way to turn the insurance negative into a positive. Suppose you have health care coverage through another source—such as your spouse's insurance, a private insurance plan, Medicare, Medicaid, the military, or the Department of Veterans Affairs. You may elect to waive the potential employer's coverage: *Although medical insurance is very important to me, I want you to know that I'd be happy to waive your coverage because I have coverage under my wife's plan.* (This strategy is especially effective with employers who self-insure employee health care costs.)

You may say that's a concession, not a trade-off. Wrong, it is a trade-off—health insurance you don't need for the job you want.

*Caution:* Although the example of a health insurance trade-off is a very effective negotiating tool, you must be comfortable with the fact that you could be signing away your right to ever join your employer's insurance plan. If your spouse later loses coverage, for example, you may find yourself without medical insurance.

## When All Else Fails, Offer an "Extended Assessment Period"

Suppose you've decided this is the job you want and you've given your best interview performance. Still it doesn't look like you're going to get the job. Try this strategy: Offer the employer an "extended assessment period" of one day.

*I'm really interested in this position and think I'm a match for the job. I appreciate your hesitation to make me an offer, so why don't we try an extended assessment period of one day? Although a single day won't let you assess my on-job skills, it will give you an opportunity to see how I function in the workplace.* And that's what the hesitation in making an offer may be—Can you function and fit in? An extended assessment period gives you the chance to prove you can.

Why shouldn't you offer your services "free of charge" for a longer period of perhaps several weeks? Because it's illegal. The Fair Labor Standards Act says working for free is against the law, except for nonprofit volunteer programs. Advice to the contrary is incorrect.

## Never Leave Empty Handed

Because you are alert to signals from the interviewer, you'll realize when the interview is over. Most likely the clue will be verbal—such as "I think that about covers what we need to know"—or physical—such as the interviewer standing up or looking at a watch. At this point, do your grand finale, find out what happens next, and leave the door open for calling back.

As you mount your third-act curtain call, remember to summarize your qualifications because people forget what they hear. And if you have a visible disability, no matter what you did to normalize the interview, the interviewer may not have soaked up what you were saying all along.

After your summary, ask: *Do you see any gaps between my qualifications and the requirements for the position you are attempting to fill?* Make written notes of any objections (to use in your follow-up letter), as well as attempt to overcome them on the spot.

Once again—believe it or not—restate the benefits you offer. Then express your interest in the position. *It looks like you had me in mind when you created (or advertised) this position. I'm really interested. Do you have any further questions at this time?*

Internalize and practice this finale formula:

1) Sell

2) Ask for objections

3) Listen and write

4) Try to overcome objections

5) Sell

If you don't leave with a job offer, try to leave with the ability to follow up gracefully. *What is the next step in the hiring process? Is it okay if I check back with you on Thursday?*

If the employer says "Yes," execute your super follow-up plan described in the next section.

If the employer says "No, we'll be in touch with you," switch objectives. Leave the interview with something for your time and investment by asking: *Do you know of others in the organization or in another company who might be interested in my qualifications?*

Suppose the interview was a dead end and the interviewer couldn't think of anyone to refer you to. Write anyway. A polite thank-you may still generate leads. *It was a pleasure talking with you today and although we agreed that my qualifications are apart from your needs at this time, I very much respect the work being done at your company, and I hope you'll keep my resume should a more appropriate opening occur. If you happen to hear of others who could use my talents, I will be grateful if you will let me know so I may contact them. Thanks, and I hope our paths will cross again soon.*

## FOLLOW UP THE INTERVIEW

References and what happens *after* the interview are the most overlooked and underestimated areas of the job-finding process. Jeff Allen hits this deficit hard in his excellent book *The Perfect Follow-Up Method To Get the Job.*

Most job seekers, Allen says, walk away saying to themselves either: "I really did well, now all I have to do is wait for them to say 'yes,' or "It's out of my hands, yes or no. I can't change their minds." Wrong!

You can design a system of actions, beginning with the initial interview, to affect what happens when employers compare candidates and decide who will receive the job offer.

As soon as you get home, write the interviewer a thank-you note. The most effective thank-you notes are really sales messages. *I want you to know that I am very interested in the position of machine repairer we discussed today. Based on the information you outlined in our talk, I am sure my skills can make significant savings in your project. I will check back with you Thursday to see how the search is progressing. In any event, thank you for the time and consideration you extended to me today. I enjoyed meeting you.*

Make it easy for wisely selected references to sing your praises. (You don't use the same set of references for every position, but selectively choose them for impact.) *Leave nothing to chance.* After each interview, provide your references with a "reference summary"—a brief capsule of your resume, plus key points you wish brought out that you learned during your initial interview. If, for instance, you find out from the interview that previous employees did not show up for work on time every day, note on your resume summary that timely attendance is one of your strong points and give examples. *The operating principle here is to let your references sell you to employers.*

Admittedly, this sophisticated effort is work, but it's exquisitely effective. It always carries more weight when somebody else says you are an outstanding candidate than when you say it yourself. That's one reason film stars have agents.

Now continue your super follow-up plan with a telephone call on Thursday (the day you arranged as you exited the interview) to check the employer's progress on filling the position. Your best reason for calling is to give the interviewer new information—such as you must decide whether or not to take another offer. But don't count on another offer conveniently arising. Nor should you run a bluff on a nonexistent offer; you may be told to take the phantom job.

If the position is still in a holding pattern, call again in a week. Still no progress? Call again the following week. It's better to be thought of as very persistent than not to be thought of at all.

## ACCEPT THE JOB

Just because you have a disability, don't assume you must gratefully grab any job offer that comes along. Obviously each situation is different; in a competitive job market you may agree to trade-offs you wouldn't dream of accepting when the market is thriving. It's always a good idea to express generous interest in a job offer and ask for a day or two to carefully think about it. If the offer appears to be acceptable, set a time within the next day or so to conclude the discussion.

As you reflect, you may realize you forgot to nail down a particular fringe benefit, job accommodation, or other understanding. Do it before accepting the offer because it is really very difficult to renegotiate a point after the fact.

Few people, other than top executives, are awarded employment contracts today. But do ask for an informal letter of understanding outlining the job title, starting day, pay, and benefits.

## IT'S SHOW BIZ ALL THE WAY

If the interview is a theatrical event, about now you may be thinking about opening day. How will you ever remember all your "lines" and "direction"? Admittedly, for many readers, the counsel in these pages is a new way of thinking. But, as educators say, there's a learning curve.

If you'll really dig in and reread and practice as often as you need, one day the pieces will click into place and you'll put it all together and become an accomplished job seeker. Like Gregor Piatigorsky, you may still get butterflies from stage fright. But once in the interview chair, you'll radiate self-assurance. A star is born.

# 13

## Postscript: positive thoughts pack power

So often when we read about people who have soared in success, we think, "Fine for the superstar. He or she has an edge. She can sing; I can't. He has a mega brain; I don't. She has artistic ability; I can't draw a straight line." And so on. The trap many of us fall into is thinking that career success is reserved for the gifted or the lucky few.

It's true that history books and the media tend to zero in on high-profile achievers—you'll even find a sampling of such people here. That's because famous people are inspirational. But—after reading this book—you know that celebrating accomplishments of big-timers with disabilities doesn't tell the whole story.

You know that today's career winners are both individuals with modest as well as high profiles. You know that thousands upon thousands of individuals with disabilities are racking up successes, and they are represented in virtually every career field. You know that success is rarely an accident.

Now it is time to begin in earnest to use all that you've learned in this book. You faithfully follow every suggested strategy, practice every recommended tactic.

And nothing happens. You're no further along than when you started. Few leads. Fewer interviews. Zero job offers. What's wrong?

Robert Swain, a New York outplacement counselor, says three variables shape the search.

| High-Profile Winners of the Past | | |
|---|---|---|
| **Name** | **Occupation** | **Disability** |
| Albert Einstein | Theoretical physicist | Dyslexia |
| John Milton | Greatest English poet after Shakespeare | Blindness |
| Marilyn Monroe | Actress, *The Misfits* | Stutter |
| Ludwig van Beethoven | Composer/pianist | Deafness |
| Napoleon I | Emperor of France, one of history's greatest military commanders | Epilepsy |
| Woodrow Wilson | U.S. President | Dyslexia |
| Franz Liszt | Pianist/composer | Mar Fan syndrome |
| Clara Barton | Founder of the American Red Cross | Stutter |
| George Patton | Five-star general of the Army | Learning disability |
| Sir Isaac Newton | Mathematician and physicist | Stutter |
| Homer | Ancient Greek poet | Blindness |
| George VI | British monarch | Stutter |
| Thomas Edison | Inventor | Dyslexia |
| Franklin Delano Roosevelt | U.S. President | Postpolio disability |
| Aristotle | Ancient Greek philosopher and scientist | Stutter |
| Helen Keller | Author and lecturer | Deafness and blindness |
| Lord Byron | Poet | Clubfoot |
| John F. Kennedy | U.S. President | Addison's disease |
| Sir Winston Churchill | Prime minister of Great Britain, one of the greatest orators of the 20th century | Stutter |
| William Butler Yeats | Poet and dramatist, one of the foremost literary figures of the 20th century | Dyslexia |

## High-Profile Winners of the Present

| Name | Occupation | Disability |
| --- | --- | --- |
| Carly Simon | Pop singer | Stutter |
| Jim Eisenreich | Kansas City Royals baseball player | Tourette syndrome |
| J. Robert Kerrey | U.S. Senator, Nebraska | Amputation |
| Ilana Mysior | Concert pianist | Mar Fan syndrome |
| Mitch Longley | Actor, NBC-TV's "Another World" | Paraplegia |
| Dr. Stephen Hawking | Renowned theoretical physicist | Amyotrophic lateral sclerosis (Lou Gehrig's disease) |
| James Earl Jones | Actor, *Field of Dreams* | Stutter |
| John Callahan | Cartoonist/author, *Don't Worry, He Won't Get Far on Foot* | Quadriplegia, alcoholism |
| Cher | Singer/actress, *Mermaids* | Dyslexia |
| Bree Walker | Evening news anchor on KCBS-TV, Los Angeles | Syndactilism (congenital deformity of hands/feet) |
| Peter Falk | Actor, ABC-TV's "Columbo" | Glass eye |
| Lewis Puller, Jr. | Author, *Fortunate Son* | Double amputation, alcoholism |
| Gordon Gund | Cleveland Cavaliers basketball team owner | Blindness |
| Marlee Matlin | Acress, NBC-TV's "Reasonable Doubts" | Deafness |
| Robert Dole | Senate Minority Leader, U.S. Senator, Kansas | Inability to use right arm |
| Stevie Wonder | Singer/songwriter | Blindness |
| Ronald Reagan | Former U.S. President | Hearing impairment |
| Katharine Hepburn | Actress, *On Golden Pond* | Parkinson's disease |
| Rolf Bernirsche | Former San Diego Charger/Dallas Cowboy football player, now financial executive | Crohn's disease |
| Helynn Hoffa | Author, *Yes You Can* | Postpolio disability |
| Chris Burke | Actor, ABC-TV's "Life Goes On" | Down syndrome |

1) Job market conditions constitute 20 percent of the effect on the hunt for employment. (A recession starves the job market, good times fatten it.)
2) Individual resources and experience count for 30 percent. (Your qualifications may be a mismatch for the work you seek. Or a mosaic of bad luck may combine to make your target group of employers rethink their hiring plans.)
3) The other 50 percent is your perspective and behavior (job seeking skills) while conducting your job search. This is the one thing you can control and change, says Swain.

Careers expert and author Phyllis Martin (*Martin's Magic Formula for Getting the Right Job*) confirms that the third point is dominant. Knowledge of the job-finding process and attitude is at the root of almost every hard-core unemployment case she has tracked among readers of her popular *Cincinnati Post* newspaper column.

"When job seekers know the right moves and are making them without results, it is the *implementation* of the strategies that need improvement. *Quality control in job seeking is as essential as quality control in any business endeavor*," Martin explains. "Job seekers may understand that they must reach a large number of prospective employers, but they may have an imperfect understanding of *how* to do it. Job seekers may read about interviewing techniques, but, without practicing to perfection those techniques, go through the motions with disappointing results."

When job search quality control is absent, Martin says job seekers may distort the message. "They complain, 'I've tried everything. What you recommend must not work.' They don't see that it is their execution of the strategy that needs improvement. *Correct implementation is everything.* Success is in the details."

## POSITIVE REFRAMING

Perspective is another key. Successful people believe in their own ability. If you're already pumped up and ready to take on the working world single handedly, three cheers! If you're not, increase your chances for success with a thought process called "positive reframing."

Positive reframing is fancy talk for changing beliefs that hold you back. It's the moving away from negative beliefs—powerlessness—and moving toward positive beliefs—empowerment. Shifting your negative beliefs to positive beliefs empowers you to approach job hunting with self-confidence.

To understand the power of reframing negative into positive beliefs, review the following examples.

NEGATIVE BELIEFS..................Reframed Into.................POSITIVE BELIEFS

| NEGATIVE BELIEFS | POSITIVE BELIEFS |
| --- | --- |
| The job market is in recession. There are no jobs. | What recession? Getting drowned in negative statistics only drags me down. I only need to find one job. |
| It's not what you know, it's who you know. I don't know anybody. | Everyone knows someone. My challenge is to figure out who I know and how to expand one connection into ten connections, into fifty connections, into 100 connections— and, if necessary, into 1000 connections. |
| I don't have the right know-how or degree. | I have compensatory skills and abilities to offer employers. My challenge is to position my skills and abilities to effectively present them to employers. (If there's really a mismatch, I will consider how to get the requisite education or training.) |
| The competition is overwhelming. | Nine out of ten people won't take the time to learn how to become a skilled job seeker. I will. This will give me an edge. |
| I don't have enough money to have resumes printed and drive around looking for a job. | I have a temporary budget problem that will be relieved after employment. I will review my expenses to see what can be cut back. If necessary, I will attempt to borrow funds for basic job-hunt expenses. |

What about disability-specific beliefs? Do you sometimes feel your disability makes you powerless in the job market? Here's another area of reframing opportunities. Consider the following examples.

NEGATIVE BELIEFS..................Reframed Into.................POSITIVE BELIEFS

| NEGATIVE BELIEFS | POSITIVE BELIEFS |
| --- | --- |
| Employers don't want to hire someone with a disability. | Employers want to hire *qualified* applicants. I'm qualified and will make a dedicated, hardworking employee that any employer will be happy to have on the payroll. |
| I can't compete with applicants who don't have disabilities. | ADA levels the playing field. I now have the best-time-in-history opportunity to sell myself in an interview. |
| Employers won't be willing to make the job accommodation I need. | Many employers will voluntarily make job accommodations for qualified applicants. Most employers are required by law to make *reasonable* accommodations. |

| Any employer who hires me will only do so because of ADA. I will be a token hire. | Once I'm on the job, I have the skills to prove to any employer that hiring me was the right decision. |
| Even if I get the job, co-workers will resent me and think I was given the job because of my disability. | A recent Louis Harris survey finds that four out of five Americans believe that workers with disabilities are equally or more productive than the average worker. The poll further finds that four out of five support affirmative action for people with disabilities. I will demonstrate to co-workers that I have earned my spot on the organization's team. |

You will feel more empowered once you reframe any negative beliefs you hold.


## REJECTION TRAINING

Another angle of the role played by perspective and behavior in the job search is the depression every human being feels from repeated rejection. Depression takes over and negatively impacts on your entire being. It's like being drenched in acid rain. You slink into interviews feeling like a soggy loser. You emanate negative vibrations that can be perceived a mile away.

How you choose to handle R&D—rejection and depression— will make all the difference in your hunt. It may help to know that it's very normal for virtually *all* job seekers to go through 100 "no's" to get to one good "yes."

There's little debate among hiring authorities that R&D can be lethal to a job search. Employers just don't hire people who drag low self-esteem behind them like tattered baggage. How can you refuse to allow yourself to be tarred by the black clouds of R&D? Rejection training is one answer.

First, recognize that rejection visits every living person. You're not the lone ranger. Rejection is simply the cost of doing business in a job search.

Second, make up your mind that whenever rejection parks its disgusting symptoms in your space, you will get angry, and then channel that anger into positive energy to continue your job search. Think back. Haven't you ever become really ticked off over something and found that anger fueled positive action?

To understand the level of energy you can draw on, relive the last time you were turned down for a job interview or received a "no" during an interview. At that moment, was your energy zapped—or were you outraged? If the latter, train yourself to turn that adrenaline flow into positive energy that will power your job search.

Another important power tool is the turning of rejections into job leads. *Always* ask the person who hands down the "no" for a referral to another employer. Many will feel bad about rejecting you and be eager to help.

No matter what, each day you must pick up your wounded spirit and greet a new dawn of hope as if it were your very first job-hunting day.

## BEATING THE BLUES

Psyching yourself up to search for a job forty to eighty hours a week may be the hardest work you'll ever do—especially when you keep hearing "no," "no," "no," "no." Here are tips to help you remain upbeat when your job search threatens to drag you down.

- Envision yourself as a winner. Just as athletes visualize themselves competing in and winning an event, visualize yourself in an interview and being offered the job you want.
- Get as much support from family and friends as you can. Hang out with upbeat people.
- Form a buddy job search team. The mechanics of how you structure such a team are unimportant—it is the team itself that has the power to boost your spirits, make you smile.
- Remind yourself there are more than 100 million jobs out there and you only need one of them.
- Remind yourself a rejection simply means you haven't found a job match yet. At least 95 percent of job search rejections are impersonal—so don't take them personally.
- Think of rejections as a learning experience and, without emotion, analyze and use them to improve your performance in your next interview.
- Remind yourself there are thousands of people with disabilities productively employed.
- Stop making excuses. Rise above self-pity.
- Get up every morning and dress for work; you are working whether or not you have appointments that day.
- Maintain your health and energy level by taking care of your body.
- Schedule leisure time to unwind. Balance is important to keep your stress level down.
- Laugh—whatever it takes, make yourself laugh at least one side-splitting laugh every day.

Do whatever it takes to rise above depression, advises San Diego attorney Theodore Pinnock, who also has a bachelor's degree in psychology and a master's degree in political science. The son of a Jamaican factory worker and a professional cook, Pinnock was the ninth of ten children in his family. Born with severe cerebral palsy, Pinnock uses a wheelchair for mobility and is an expert at overcoming rejection. Because of a speech impairment, he was misdiagnosed as being mentally retarded as a child and was institutionalized for more than seven years.

"I've faced discrimination because of disability and race all my life," says Pinnock. "But you can't just lie down and die. Laws don't change attitudes. Until we have a more positive outlook, not only on minorities and people with disabilities, but anyone with a different point of view—until they can be accepted into the mainstream—there will always be a problem," Pinnock believes.

If you don't intend to "just lie down and die," you'll see why rejection training to beat R&D is so important.

## YOUR MOVE

Sure, there'll be down days ahead during the intricate web of activities you must execute to find a good job. But remember, as an anonymous sage once said, "The lowest ebb is the turn of the tide."

As the tide rises, only you can seize control of your career vessel, trim the sails, and steer it to your harbor of choice. Others may crew your ship, but it's your watch, your command.

Historian Edward Gibbon knew it to be true:

*The winds and waves are always on the side of the ablest navigators.*

# PART IV

# Appendixes

The following lists of organizations are presented to ease the task of steering your career vessel. They can save you countless dollars and hours by identifying appropriate resources for your job hunt needs, supplying information on cost-effective job accommodations, and being on your support team throughout your job search.

For your convenience, voice, text telephone (TT), and fax telephone numbers are listed when this information is available. Text telephone identifies TDDs, TTYs, and other nonvoice devices.

We apologize for any changes in telephone numbers, locations, or organization titles you may come across. Each of the listed resources was verified at publication, but organizations spring up, fall down, and move around at a staggering rate.

If you find data that needs revision—or discover an organization that should be included—please share this information with me by dropping me a note at: Melanie Astaire Witt, P.O. Box 80864, San Diego, CA 92138.

# A

# Organizations, Associations, and Agencies

## A1: GENERAL ORGANIZATIONS AND ASSOCIATIONS

**Adventures in Movement for the Handicapped**
945 Danbury Rd.
Dayton, OH 45420
    Voice: 513-294-4611
    Fax: 513-294-3783

**Alcoholics Anonymous World Services**
General Services
P.O. Box 459
Grand Central Station
New York, NY 10163
    Voice: 212-686-1100

**Alexander Graham Bell Association for the Deaf**
3417 Volta Place NW
Washington, DC 20007
    Voice/TT: 202-337-5220
    Fax: 202-337-8314

**Alzheimer's Association**
919 North Michigan Ave. #1000
Chicago, IL 60611
    Voice: 800-272-3900
    Fax: 312-853-3660

**American Amputee Foundation**
P.O. Box 250218
Hillcrest Station
Little Rock, AR 72225
    Voice: 800-553-4483

**American Association of Kidney Patients**
111 South Parker St. #405
Tampa, FL 33606
    Voice: 800-749-2257
    Fax: 813-254-3270

**American Blind Lawyers Association**
c/o American Council of the Blind
(See below)

**American Cancer Society**
1599 Clifton Rd. NE
Atlanta, GA 30329
    Voice: 800-227-2345

**American Council on Alcoholism**
5024 Campbell Blvd. #H
Baltimore, MD 21236
    Voice: 410-931-9393
    Fax: 410-931-4585

**American Council of the Blind**
1155 15th St. NW #720
Washington, DC 20005
    Voice: 800-424-8666
    Fax: 202-467-5085

**American Deafness and Rehabilitation Association**
P.O. Box 251554
Little Rock, AR 72225
    Voice/TT: 501-663-7074
    Fax: 501-663-0336

**American Diabetes Association**
1660 Duke St.
Alexandria, VA 22314
  Voice: 800-232-3472
  Fax: 703-836-7439

**American Federation of Labor & Congress of Industrial Organizations**
815 16th St. NW
Washington, DC 20006
  Voice: 202-637-5000

**American Foundation for the Blind**
15 West 16th St.
New York, NY 10011
  Voice: 212-620-2000
  TT: 212-620-2158
  Fax: 212-727-7418

**American Heart Association**
7320 Greenville Ave.
Dallas, TX 75231
  Voice: 214-706-1179
  Fax: 214-706-1341

**American Kidney Fund**
6110 Executive Blvd. #1010
Rockville, MD 20852
  Voice: 800-638-8299
  Fax: 301-881-0898

**American Lung Association**
1740 Broadway
New York, NY 10019
  Voice: 212-315-8700
  Fax: 212-265-5642

**American Lupus Society**
3914 Del Amo Blvd. #922
Torrance, CA 90503
  Voice: 800-331-1802
  Fax: 310-542-9491

**American Occupational Therapy Association**
1383 Piccard Drive #301
Rockville, MD 20849
  Voice: 800-843-2682
  Fax: 301-948-5512

**American Paralysis Association**
500 Morris
Springfield, NJ 07081
  Voice: 800-225-0292

**American Parkinson's Disease Association**
60 Bay St. #401
Staten Island, NY 10301
  Voice: 800-223-2732
  Fax: 718-981-4399

**American Physical Therapy Association**
1111 North Fairfax St.
Alexandria, VA 22314
  Voice: 703-684-2782
  Fax: 703-706-3169

**American Society of Handicapped Physicians**
105 Morris Drive
Bastrop, LA 71220
  Voice: 318-281-4436

**American Speech-Language-Hearing Association**
10801 Rockville Pike
Rockville, MD 20852
  Voice/TT: 800-638-8255
  Fax: 301-571-0457

**American Tinnitus Association**
P.O. Box 5
Portland, OR 97207
  Voice: 503-248-9985

**Amyotrophic Lateral Sclerosis Association**
21021 Ventura Blvd. #321
Woodland Hills, CA 91364
  Voice: 800-782-4747
  Fax: 818-340-2060

**The Arc**
P.O. Box 300649
Arlington, TX 76010
  Voice: 817-261-6003
  TT: 817-277-0553
  Fax: 817-277-3491
(A national organization on mental retardation)

**Arthritis Foundation**
1314 Spring St. NW
Atlanta, GA 30309
  Voice: 800-283-7800
  Fax: 404-872-0457

**Associated Services for the Blind**
919 Walnut St.
Philadelphia, PA 19107
  Voice: 215-627-0600
  Fax: 215-922-0692

**Association for Education and Rehabilitation of the Blind and Visually Impaired**
206 North Washington St. #320
Alexandria, VA 22314
   Voice: 703-548-1884

**Association of Persons in Supported Employment**
5001 West Broad St. #34
Richmond, VA 23230
   Voice: 804-282-3655
   Fax: 804-282-2513

**Association for Mental Retardation (ARC)**
500 East Border #300
Arlington, TX 76010
   Voice: 817-261-6003
   Fax: 817-277-3491

**Autism Society of America**
8601 Georgia Ave. #503
Silver Spring, MD 20910
   Voice: 310-565-0433

**Berkeley Planning Associates**
440 Grand Ave. #500
Oakland, CA 94610
   Voice: 510-465-7884
   Fax: 510-465-7885

**Better Hearing Institute**
P.O. Box 1840
Washington, DC 20013
   Voice/TT: 800-327-9355
   Fax: 703-750-9302

**Billy Barty Foundation**
929 West Olive Ave. #C
Burbank, CA 91506
   Voice: 818-953-5410
   Fax: 818-953-7129

**Blinded American Veterans Foundation**
P.O. Box 65900
Washington, DC 20035
   Voice: 202-462-4430
   Fax: 202-265-0833

**Blinded Veterans Association**
477 H St. NW
Washington, DC 20001
   Voice: 800-669-7079

**Braille Institute of America**
741 North Vermont Ave.
Los Angeles, CA 90029
   Voice: 213-663-1111
   Fax: 213-666-5881

**Bureau of Services for Visually Impaired**
5533 Southwick Blvd. #101
Toledo, OH 43614
   Voice: 419-866-5811
   Fax: 419-866-1669

**Carroll Center for the Blind**
770 Centre St.
Newton, MA 02158
   Voice: 800-852-3131
   Fax: 617-969-6204

**Center for Developmental Disabilities**
Benson Building
University of South Carolina
Columbia, SC 29208
   Voice: 800-922-9234
   Fax: 803-777-6058

**CFIDS Association (Chronic Fatigue and Immune Dysfunction Syndrome)**
P.O. Box 220398
Charlotte, NC 28222
   Voice: 800-442-3437

**Charcot-Marie-Tooth Association**
600 Upland Ave.
Upland, PA 19015
   Voice/Fax: 215-499-7486

**Cleft Palate Association**
1218 Grandview Ave.
Pittsburgh, PA 15211
   Voice: 800-242-5338
   Fax: 412-481-0847

**Congress of Organizations of the Physically Disabled**
16630 Beverly Drive
Tinley Park, IL 60477
   Voice: 708-532-3566

**Council of Better Business Bureaus**
4200 Wilson Blvd. #800
Arlington, VA 22203
   Voice: 703-276-0100
   Fax: 703-525-8277

**Council of Citizens with Low Vision International**
1400 North Drake Rd. #218
Kalamazoo, MI 49006
   Voice: 616-381-9566

**Council for Exceptional Children**
1920 Association Drive
Reston, VA 22091
  Voice: 703-620-3660

**Cystic Fibrosis Foundation**
6931 Arlington Rd. #200
Bethesda, MD 20814
  Voice: 800-344-4823
  Fax: 301-951-6378

**Deafpride**
1350 Potomac Ave. SE
Washington, DC 20003
  Voice/TT: 202-675-6700
  Fax: 202-547-0547

**Direct Link for the Disabled**
P.O. Box 1036
Solvang, CA 93464
  Voice/TT/Fax: 805-688-1603

**Disability 2000-CEO Council**
c/o The National Organization
  on Disability
(See below)

**Disabled American Veterans**
P.O. Box 14301
Cincinnati, OH 45250
  Voice: 606-441-7300

**Dole Foundation for Employment of
People with Disabilities**
1819 H St. NW
Washington, DC 20006
  Voice/TT: 202-457-0318

**Dystonia Medical Research Foundation**
8383 Wilshire Blvd. #800
Beverly Hills, CA 90211
  Voice: 213-852-1630
  Fax: 213-852-4796

**Electronic Industries Foundation**
919 18th St.
9th Floor
Washington, DC 20006
  Voice: 202-955-5816
  TT: 202-955-5836

**Emphysema Anonymous**
P.O. Box 3224
Seminole, FL 34642
  Voice: 813-391-9977

**Epilepsy Foundation of America**
4351 Garden City Drive
Landover, MD 20785
  Voice: 800-332-1000
  TT: 301-459-3700
  Fax: 301-577-2684

**Federation of the Handicapped**
211 West 14th St.
New York, NY 10011
  Voice: 212-727-4200
  TT: 212-727-4324

**Foundation on Employment and Disability**
3820 Del Amo Blvd. #201
Torrance, CA 90503
  Voice: 310-214-3430
  Fax: 310-214-4153

**Foundation for Exceptional Children**
1920 Association Drive
Reston, VA 22091
  Voice: 703-620-1054

**Gazette International Networking Institute**
4502 Maryland Ave.
St. Louis, MO 63108
  Voice: 314-361-0475

**Glaucoma Foundation**
310 East Fourteenth St.
New York, NY 10003
  Voice: 212-260-1000

**Goodwill Industries of America**
9200 Wisconsin Ave.
Bethesda, MD 20814
  Voice: 301-530-6500
  Fax: 301-530-1516

**Guillain-Barre Syndrome Foundation
International**
P.O. Box 262
Wynnewood, PA 19096
  Voice: 215-667-0131

**Harold Russell Associates**
34 Old Town Rd.
Hyannis, MA 02601
  Voice: 508-775-1985

**Helen Keller National Center for Deaf-Blind Youths and Adults**
111 Middle Neck Rd.
Sands Point, NY 11050
Voice/TT: 516-944-8900
Fax: 516-944-7302

**Huntington's Disease Society of America**
140 West 22nd St.
New York, NY 10011
Voice: 800-345-4372
Fax: 212-243-2443

**IAM Cares (International Association of Machinists and Aerospace Workers Handicapped Youth)**
1300 Connecticut Ave. NW
Washington, DC 20036
Voice/TT: 202-857-5200

**Independent Visually Impaired Enterprises**
1155 15th St. NW #720
Washington, DC 20005
Voice: 202-467-5081
Fax: 202-467-5085

**Inter-National Association of Business, Industry and Rehabilitation**
P.O. Box 15242
Washington, DC 20003
Voice: 202-543-6353
Fax: 202-546-2854

**International Association of Jewish Vocational Services**
101 Gary Court
Staten Island, NY 10314
Voice: 718-370-0437
Fax: 718-370-1778

**International Association of Laryngectomees**
1599 Clifton Rd. NE
Atlanta, GA 30329
Voice: 404-320-3333

**International Center for the Disabled**
340 East 24th St.
New York, NY 10010
Voice: 212-679-0100

**International Polio Network**
5100 Oakland Ave. #206
St. Louis, MO 63110
Voice: 314-361-0475

**Joseph P. Kennedy, Jr. Foundation**
1350 New York NW #500
Washington, DC 20005
Voice: 202-393-1250
Fax: 202-737-1937

**Just One Break**
373 Park Ave. South
New York, NY 10016
Voice: 212-725-2500
TT: 212-725-2046
Fax: 212-213-6791

**Kiwanis International**
3636 Woodview Trace
Indianapolis, IN 46268
Voice: 317-875-8755
Fax: 317-879-0204

**Learning Disabilities Association of America (LDA)**
4156 Library Rd.
Pittsburgh, PA 15234
Voice: 412-341-1515
Fax: 412-344-0224

**League of Human Dignity**
1701 P St.
Lincoln, NB 68508
Voice/Fax: 402-471-7871

**Learning How**
P.O. Box 35481
Charlotte, NC 28235
Voice: 704-376-4735
Fax: 704-376-5024

**Leukemia Society of America**
733 3rd Ave.
New York, NY 10017
Voice: 800-955-4572
Fax: 212-972-5776

**Lions Clubs International**
300 22nd St.
Oak Brook, IL 60521
Voice: 708-571-5466
Fax: 708-571-8890

**Lupus Foundation of America**
4 Research Place #180
Rockville, MD 20850
  Voice: 800-558-0121
  Fax: 301-670-9486

**Mainstream**
3 Bethesda Metro Center #830
Bethesda, MD 20814
  Voice/TT: 301-654-2400
  Fax: 301-654-2403

**March of Dimes Birth Defects Foundation**
1275 Mamaroneck Ave.
White Plains, NY 10605
  Voice: 914-428-7100

**Mental Health Policy Resource Center**
1730 Rhode Island Ave. NW #308
Washington, DC 20036
  Voice: 202-775-8826
  Fax: 202-659-7613

**Mental Health & Retardation Services**
5th Floor
State Office Building
Topeka, KS 66612
  Voice: 913-296-3774
  Fax: 913-296-6142

**Mental Retardation Associations of America**
211 East 300 South #212
Salt Lake City, UT 84111
  Voice: 801-328-1575

**Muscular Dystrophy Association**
3561 East Sunrise Drive
Tucson, AZ 85718
  Voice: 800-223-6666
  Fax: 602-529-5300

**Myasthenia Gravis Foundation**
53 West Jackson Blvd. #660
Chicago, IL 60604
  Voice: 800-541-5454
  TT: 312-427-8437

**Narcotics Anonymous**
P.O. Box 9999
Van Nuys, CA 91409
  Voice: 818-376-8000

**National Alliance for the Mentally Ill**
2101 Wilson Blvd. #302
Arlington, VA 22201
  Voice: 703-524-7600
  Fax: 703-524-9094

**National Alopecia Areata Association**
710 C St. #11
San Rafael, CA 94901
  Voice: 415-456-4644
  Fax: 415-456-4274

**National Amputation Foundation**
12-45 150th St.
Whitestone, NY 11357
  Voice: 718-767-0596
  Fax: 718-767-3103

**National Association of Alcoholism and Drug Abuse Counselors**
3717 Columbia Pike #300
Arlington, VA 22204
  Voice: 800-548-0497
  Fax: 703-920-4672

**National Association of the Deaf**
814 Thayer Ave.
Silver Spring, MD 20910
  Voice: 301-587-1788
  TT: 301-587-1789
  Fax: 301-587-1791

**National Association for Independent Living**
426 West Jefferson
Springfield, IL 62702
  Voice: 217-523-2587
  Fax: 217-523-0427

**National Association for Parents of the Visually Impaired**
2180 Linway Drive
Beloit, WI 53511
  Voice: 800-562-6265

**National Association of Personnel Consultants**
3133 Mt. Vernon Ave.
Alexandria, VA 22305
  Voice: 703-684-0180
  Fax: 703-684-0071

**National Association of the Physically Handicapped**
Bethesda Scarlet Oaks #G4
440 Lafayette Ave.
Cincinnati, OH 45220
  Voice: 513-961-8040

**National Association of Rehabilitation Facilities**
P.O. Box 17675
Washington, DC 20041
  Voice: 703-648-9300
  Fax: 703-648-0346

**National Association for Sickle Cell Disease**
3345 Wilshire Blvd. #1106
Los Angeles, CA 90010
  Voice: 800-421-8453
  Fax: 213-736-5221

**National Association for Visually Handicapped**
22 West 21st St.
New York, NY 10010
  Voice: 212-889-3141

**National Ataxia Foundation**
750 Twelve Oaks Center
15500 Wayzata Blvd.
Wayzata, MN 55391
  Voice: 612-473-7666
  Fax: 612-473-9289

**National Braille Association**
1290 University Ave.
Rochester, NY 14607
  Voice: 716-473-0900

**National Braille Press**
88 Saint Stephen St.
Boston, MA 02115
  Voice: 617-266-6160
  Fax: 617-437-0546

**National Cancer Care Foundation**
1180 Avenue of the Americas
New York, NY 10036
  Voice: 212-221-3300
  Fax: 212-719-0263

**National Captioning Institute**
5203 Leesburg Pike #1500
Falls Church, VA 22041
  Voice: 800-533-9673
  TT: 800-321-8337
  Fax: 703-998-2458

**National Center for Disability Services**
201 I.U. Willetts Rd.
Albertson, NY 11507
  Voice: 516-747-5400
  TT: 516-747-5355
  Fax: 516-746-3298

**National Council on Independent Living**
Troy Atrium
4th St. and Broadway
Troy, NY 12180
  Voice: 518-274-1979
  TT: 518-274-0701
  Fax: 518-274-7944

**National Center for Learning Disabilities**
99 Park Ave.
6th Floor
New York, NY 10016
  Voice: 212-687-7211
  Fax: 212-370-0837

**National Coalition for Cancer Survivorship**
1010 Wayne Ave. #300
Silver Spring, MD 20910
  Voice: 301-585-2616
  Fax: 301-588-3408

**National Depressive and Manic Depressive Association**
730 North Franklin #501
Chicago, IL 60610
  Voice: 312-642-0049
  Fax: 312-642-7243

**National Disabled Law Officers Association**
75 New St.
Nutley, NJ 07110
  Voice: 201-667-9569

**National Downs Syndrome Congress**
1800 Dempster St.
Park Ridge, IL 60068
  Voice: 800-232-6372
  Fax: 312-823-9528

**National Downs Syndrome Society**
666 Broadway
New York, NY 10012
   Voice: 800-221-4602
   Fax: 212-979-2873


**National Easter Seal Society**
70 East Lake St.
Chicago, IL 60601
   Voice: 800-221-6827
   TT: 312-726-4258
   Fax: 312-726-1494


**National Federation of the Blind**
1800 Johnson St.
Baltimore, MD 21230
   Voice: 410-659-9314
   Fax: 410-685-5653


**National Foundation for Facial
Reconstruction**
317 East 34th St. #901
New York, NY 10016
   Voice: 212-263-6656
   Fax: 212-263-7534


**National Foundation for Ileitis and Colitis**
444 Park Ave. South
New York, NY 10016
   Voice: 800-923-2423
   Fax: 212-779-4098


**National Fraternal Society of the Deaf**
1300 West Northwest Highway
Mt. Prospect, IL 60056
   Voice/TT: 800-876-6373
   Fax: 708-392-9298


**National Gaucher Foundation**
19241 Montgomery Village Ave. #E21
Gaithersburg, MD 20879
   Voice: 301-990-3800
   Fax: 301-990-4898


**National Head Injury Foundation**
1140 Connecticut Ave. NW #812
Washington, DC 20036
   Voice: 800-444-6443
   Fax: 508-488-9893


**National Health Council**
1730 M St. NW #500
Washington, DC 20036
   Voice: 202-785-3910
   Fax: 202-785-5923


**National Hemophilia Foundation**
Soho Building
110 Green St. #303
New York, NY 10012
   Voice: 212-219-8180
   Fax: 212-966-9247


**National Industries for the Blind**
524 Hamburg Turnpike #969
Wayne, NJ 07474
   Voice: 201-595-9200
   Fax: 201-595-9122


**National Industries for the Severely
Handicapped**
2235 Cedar Lane
Vienna, VA 22182
   Voice: 703-560-6800
   TT: 703-560-6512
   Fax: 703-849-8916


**National Information Center for Children
and Youth with Disabilities**
P.O. Box 1492
Washington, DC 20013
   Voice/TT: 800-999-5599
   Fax: 703-893-1741


**National Information System**
Center for Developmental Disabilities
University of South Carolina
Benson Building 1st Floor
Columbia, SC 29208
   Voice: 803-777-4435
   Fax: 803-777-6058


**National Kidney Foundation**
30 East 33rd St. #1100
New York, NY 10016
   Voice: 800-622-9010
   Fax: 212-689-9261


**National Marfan Foundation**
382 Main St.
Port Washington, NY 11050
   Voice: 516-883-8712


**National Mental Health Association**
1021 Prince St.
Alexandria, VA 22314
   Voice: 800-969-6642
   Fax: 703-684-5968

**National Mental Health Consumers'
Association**
311 South Juniper St. #902
Philadelphia, PA 19107
  Voice: 800-688-4226
  Fax: 215-735-0275

**National Multiple Sclerosis Society**
205 East 42nd St.
New York, NY 10017
  Voice: 800-624-8236
  Fax: 212-986-7981

**National Network of Learning Disabled
Adults**
808 North 82nd St. #F2
Scottsdale, AZ 85257
  Voice: 602-941-5112

**National Neurofibromatosis Foundation**
141 5th Ave. #7S
New York, NY 10010
  Voice: 800-323-7938

**National Organization on Disability**
910 16th St. NW #600
Washington, DC 20006
  Voice: 800-248-2253
  TT: 202-293-5968
  Fax: 202-293-7999

**National Organization for Rare Disorders**
P.O. Box 8923
New Fairfield, CT 06812
  Voice: 800-999-6673
  Fax: 203-746-6481

**National Parkinson Foundation**
1501 NW 9th Ave.
Miami, FL 33136
  Voice: 800-327-4545
  Fax: 305-548-4403

**National Rehabilitation Association**
1910 Association Drive #205
Reston, VA 22091
  Voice/TT: 703-715-9090
  Fax: 703-715-1058

**National Reye's Syndrome Foundation**
P.O. Box 829
Bryan, OH 43506
  Voice: 800-233-7393

**National Scoliosis Foundation**
72 Mt. Auburn St.
Watertown, MA 02172
  Voice: 617-926-0397
  Fax: 617-926-0398

**National Spinal Cord Injury Association**
600 West Cummings Park #2000
Woburn, MA 01801
  Voice: 800-962-9629
  Fax: 617-932-8369

**National Stroke Association**
300 East Hampden Ave. #240
Englewood, CO 80110
  Voice: 800-367-1990

**National Student Speech Language
Hearing Association**
10801 Rockville Pike
Rockville, MD 20852
  Voice: 301-897-5700
  Fax: 301-571-0457

**National Stuttering Project**
4601 Irving St.
San Francisco, CA 94122
  Voice: 415-566-5324

**National Tuberous Sclerosis Association**
8000 Corporate Drive #120
Landover, MD 20785
  Voice: 800-225-6872
  Fax: 301-459-0394

**Orton Dyslexia Society**
8600 LaSalle Rd. #382
Baltimore, MD 21204
  Voice: 800-222-3123

**Paralyzed Veterans of America**
801 18th St. NW
Washington, DC 20006
  Voice: 800-424-8200

**Parkinson's Disease Foundation**
640 West 168th St.
New York, NY 10032
  Voice: 800-457-6676
  Fax: 212-923-4778

**People First International**
P.O. Box 12642
Salem, OR 97309
  Voice: 503-588-5288
  Fax: 503-588-5290

**Phoenix Society for Burn Survivors**
11 Rust Hill Rd.
Levittown, PA 19056
  Voice: 800-888-2876
  Fax: 215-946-4788

**Pilot International**
P.O. Box 4844
Macon, GA 31213
  Voice: 912-743-7403
  Fax: 912-743-2173

**Polio Society**
4200 Wisconsin Ave. NW #106273
Washington, DC 20016
  Voice: 301-897-8180

**Prader-Willi Syndrome Association**
6490 Excelsior Blvd. #E-102
St. Louis Park, MN 55426
  Voice: 612-926-1947
  Fax: 612-928-9133

**Professional Rehabilitation Sector**
P.O. Box 697
Brookline, MA 02146
  Voice: 617-566-4432
  Fax: 617-566-0180

**Recording for the Blind**
20 Roszel Rd.
Princeton, NJ 08540
  Voice: 609-452-0606
  Fax: 609-987-8116

**RESNA**
1101 Connecticut Ave. NW #700
Washington, DC 20036
  Voice: 202-857-1199
  Fax: 202-223-4579

**Rotary International**
One Rotary Center
1560 Sherman Ave.
Evanston, IL 60201
  Voice: 708-866-3000
  Fax: 312-328-8554

**RP Foundation Fighting Blindness**
1401 Mount Royal Ave.
4th Floor
Baltimore, MD 21217
  Voice: 800-638-2300

  TT: 301-225-9409
  Fax: 301-225-3936

**Scoliosis Association**
P.O. Box 51353
Raleigh, NC 27609
  Voice: 919-846-2639

**Self Help for Hard of Hearing People**
7800 Wisconsin Ave.
Bethesda, MD 20814
  Voice: 301-657-2248
  TT: 301-657-2249
  Fax: 301-913-9413

**Sensory Aids Foundation**
399 Sherman Ave. #12
Palo Alto, CA 94306
  Voice: 415-329-0430

**Short Stature Foundation**
17200 Jamboree Rd. #J
Irvine, CA 92714
  Voice: 800-243-9273

**Sjogren's Syndrome Foundation**
382 Main St.
Port Washington, NY 11050
  Voice: 516-767-2866
  Fax: 516-767-7156

**Society for the Advancement of Travel for the Handicapped**
347 Fifth Ave. #610
New York, NY 10016
  Voice: 212-447-7284

**Spina Bifida Association of America**
1700 Rockville Pike #250
Rockville, MD 20852
  Voice: 800-621-3141
  Fax: 301-881-3392

**Stroke Clubs, International**
805 12th St.
Galveston, TX 77550
  Voice: 409-762-1022

**TASH: The Association for Persons with Severe Handicaps**
11201 Greenwood Ave. North
Seattle, WA 98133
  Voice: 206-361-8870

**Telecommunications for the Deaf**
8719 Colesville Rd. #300
Silver Spring, MD 20910
 Voice: 301-589-3786
 TT: 301-589-3006
 Fax: 301-589-3797

**Tourette Syndrome Association**
42-40 Bell Blvd.
Bayside, NY 11361
 Voice: 800-237-0717
 Fax: 718-279-9596

**Travel Industry and Disabled Exchange**
5435 Donna Ave.
Tarzanna, CA 91356
 Voice: 818-343-6339
 Fax: 818-368-4725

**Tuberous Sclerosis Association of America**
97 Vernon St.
Middleborough, MA 02346
 Voice: 508-657-8509

**United Cerebral Palsy Associations**
1522 K St. NW #1112
Washington, DC 20005
 Voice: 800-872-5827
 Fax: 212-268-5960

**United Ostomy Association**
36 Executive Park #120
Irvine, CA 92714
 Voice: 714-660-8624
 Fax: 714-660-9262

**United Parkinson Foundation**
360 West Superior St.
Chicago, IL 60610
 Voice: 312-664-2344

**United Scleroderma Foundation**
P.O. Box 399
Watsonville, CA 95077
 Voice: 800-722-4673
 Fax: 408-728-3328

**U.S. Chamber of Commerce**
1615 H St. NW
Washington, DC 20062
 Voice: 202-659-6000
 Fax: 202-463-5836

**Wilson's Disease Association**
P.O. Box 75324
Washington, DC 20013
 Voice: 703-636-3003

**World Institute on Disability**
510 16th St. #100
Oakland, CA 94612
 Voice/TT: 510-763-4100
 Fax: 510-763-4109

**World Rehabilitation Fund**
386 Park Ave. South #500
New York, NY 10016
 Voice: 212-679-2934
 Fax: 212-725-8402

**Young Adult Institute and Workshop**
440 West 34th St.
New York, NY 10001
 Voice: 212-563-7474
 Fax: 212-268-1083

# A2: ADA REGULATIONS, TECHNICAL ASSISTANCE, AND ENFORCEMENT AGENCIES

**Architectural and Transportation Barriers Compliance Board**
1111 18th St. NW #501
Washington, DC 20036
 Voice/TT: 800-872-2253
 Fax: 202-272-5447

(Americans with Disabilities Act
 Accessibility Guidelines [ADAAG]
 required under *Title III: Public
 Accommodations and Services Operated by
 Private Entities* and technical assistance
 on architectural, transportation, and
 communications accessibility issues.)

**Department of Justice**
Office on the Americans with Disabilities
  Act
P.O. Box 66118
Washington, DC 20035
  ADA Hotline
  Voice: 202-514-0301
  TT: 202-514-0383
  Fax: 202-307-0595
(Regulations, technical assistance, and
  enforcement for *Title II: Public Services
  [including state and local government
  agency employment]* and *Title III: Public
  Accommodations and Services Operated by
  Private Entities.*)

**Department of Transportation**
400 7th St. SW #10424
Washington, DC 20590
  Voice: 202-366-9305
  TT: 202-755-7687
  Fax: 202-366-7153
(Regulations, technical assistance, and
  enforcement for the transportation
  provisions of *Title II: Public Services* and
  *Title III: Public Accommodations and
  Services Operated by Private Entities.*)

**Federal Communications Commission**
1919 M St. NW
Washington, DC 20554
  Voice: 202-632-7260
  TT: 202-632-6999
  Fax: 202-632-0942
(Regulations, technical assistance, and
  enforcement for *Title IV:
  Telecommunications.*)

**Equal Employment Opportunity
Commission**
1801 L St. NW
Washington, DC 20507
  Voice: 800-669-3362
(Regulations, technical assistance, and
  enforcement for *Title I: Employment.*)

## A3: ADA TECHNICAL ASSISTANCE PROGRAMS

**Region I: CT, ME, MA, NH, RI, VT**
University of Southern Maine
Muskie Institute of Public Affairs
96 Falmouth St.
Portland, ME 04103
  Voice: 207-780-4430
  Fax : 207-780-4417

**Region II: NJ, NY, PR**
United Cerebral Palsy Association of New
  Jersey
354 South Broad St.
Trenton, NJ 08608
  Voice: 609-392-4004
  Fax: 609-392-3505

**Region III: DE, DC, MD, PA, VA, WV**
Independence Center of Northern
  Virginia
2111 Wilson Blvd.

Arlington, VA 22201
  Voice: 703-525-3268
  Fax: 703-525-6835

**Region IV: AL, FL, GA, KY, MS,
NC, SC, TN**
United Cerebral Palsy Association/The
  SMART Exchange
1776 Peachtree St. #310N
Atlanta, GA 30309
  Voice: 404-888-0022
  TT: 404-888-9006
  Fax: 404-888-9091

**Region V: IL, IN, MI, MN, OH, WI**
University of Illinois at Chicago Affiliated
  Program in Developmental Disabilities
1640 West Roosevelt Rd.
Chicago, IL 60608
  Voice/TT: 312-413-1647
  Fax: 312-413-1326

**Region VI: AR, LA, NM, OK, TX**
Independent Living Research Utilization
The Institute for Rehabilitation and
    Research (TIRR)
2323 South Shepherd #1000
Houston, TX 77019
    Voice: 713-520-0232
    TT: 713-520-5136
    Fax: 713-520-5785

**Region VII: IA, KS, NB, MO**
University of Missouri at Columbia
401 East Locust St.
Columbia, MO 65201
    Voice: 314-882-3807
    Fax: 314-882-1727

**Region VIII: CO, MT, ND, SD, UT, WY**
Meeting the Challenge
3630 Sinton Road #103
Colorado Springs, CO 80907
    Voice: 719-444-0252
    Fax: 719-444-0269

**Region IX: AZ, CA, HI, NV, PB**
Berkeley Planning Associates
(See Appendix A1)

**Region X: AK, ID, OR, WA**
Washington Governor's Committee on
    Disability Issues and Employment
Employment Security Department
P.O. Box 9046
Olympia, WA 98507
    Voice: 206-438-3168
    TT: 206-438-3167
    Fax: 206-438-4014

# A4: FEDERAL AGENCIES

**ABLEDATA**
National Institute on Disability and
    Rehabilitation Research
Department of Education
Newington Children's Hospital
181 East Cedar St.
Newington, CT 06111
    Voice/TT: 203-667-5405

**ACTION**
1100 Vermont Ave. NW
Washington, DC 20525
    Voice: 800-424-8867
    TT: 202-606-5256

**Administration on Developmental
Disabilities**
Department of Health and Human
    Services
200 Independence Ave. SW #329D
Washington, DC 20201
    Voice: 202-245-2890
    TT: 202-245-2897
    Fax: 202-245-6916

**American Printing House for the Blind**
1839 Frankfort Ave.
Louisville, KY 40206
    Voice: 800-223-1839
    Fax: 502-895-1509

**Architectural and Transportation Barriers
Compliance Board**
(See Appendix A2)

**Clearinghouse on Computer
Accommodation**
General Services Administration
18th and F Streets NW
KGDO #2022
Washington, DC 20405
    Voice: 202-501-4906
    Fax: 202-501-3855

**Clearinghouse on Disability Information**
Department of Education, OSERS
Switzer Building #3132
Washington, DC 20202
    Voice: 202-732-1241
    Fax: 202-732-1252

**Commission on Civil Rights**
1121 Vermont Ave. NW
Washington, DC 20425
Voice: 202-376-8312
TT: 202-376-8116
Fax: 202-376-8315

**Committee for Purchase from the Blind and Other Severely Handicapped**
Crystal Square 5
1755 Jefferson Davis Highway #1107
Arlington, VA 22202
Voice: 703-557-1145
Fax: 703-521-7713

**Computer/Electronic Accommodations Program (CAP)**
Department of Defense
5109 Leesburg Pike #502
Falls Church, VA 22041
Voice/TT: 703-756-8811

**Deafness and Communicative Disorders Branch**
Department of Education
Rehabilitation Services
330 C St. SW #3221
Washington, DC 20202
Voice: 202-732-1401
TT: 202-732-1330
Fax: 202-732-1372

**Department of Justice**
Office of the Americans with
  Disabilities Act
(See Appendix A2)

**Department of Transportation**
(See Appendix A2)

**Department of Veterans Affairs**
810 Vermont Ave. NW
Washington, DC 20420
Voice: 202-233-2200

**ERIC Clearinghouse on Adult, Career, and Vocational Education**
Department of Education
1900 Kenny Rd.
Columbus, OH 43210

Voice: 800-848-4815
Fax: 614-292-1260

**Equal Employment Opportunity Commission**
(See Appendix A2)

**Federal Communications Commission**
(See Appendix A2)

**Gallaudet University**
Department of Education
800 Florida Ave. NE
Washington, DC 20002
Voice: 202-651-5000
Fax: 202-651-5860

**Handicapped Assistance Loan Program**
Small Business Administration
409 Third St. SW, 8th Floor
Washington, DC 20416
Voice: 202-205-6570
Fax: 202-205-7519

**HEATH Resource Center**
(Higher Education and the Handicapped)
Project of American Council on Education
Department of Education
1 Dupont Circle NW #800
Washington, DC 20036
Voice/TT: 800-544-3284
Fax: 202-833-4760

**Interagency Committee on Employment of People with Disabilities**
Equal Employment Opportunity
  Commission
1801 L St. NW #5604
Washington, DC 20507
Voice: 202-663-4568
TT: 202-663-5043
Fax: 202-663-7022

**Internal Revenue Service**
Department of the Treasury
P.O. Box 7604
Ben Franklin Station
Washington, DC 20044
Voice: 202-566-3292
Fax: 202-535-6766

**Job Accommodation Network (JAN)**
(President's Committee on Employment of
People with Disabilities)
West Virginia University
P.O. Box 6122
Morgantown, WV 26506
Voice/TT: 800-526-7234 (Outside West
Virginia)
Voice/TT: 800-526-4698 (Inside West
Virginia)
Fax: 304-293-6661

**Job Opportunities for the Blind (JOB)**
National Federation of the Blind
Department of Labor
1800 Johnson St.
Baltimore, MD 21230
Voice: 800-638-7518
Fax: 410-685-5653

**Medicare/Medicaid Programs**
Health Care Financing Administration
Department of Health and Human
Services
200 Independence Ave. SW
Washington, DC 20201
Voice: 202-245-6113

**National Center on Employment of the
Deaf**
Rochester Institute of Technology
Department of Education
P.O. Box 9887
Rochester, NY 14623
Voice: 716-475-6219
TT: 716-475-6205
Fax: 716-475-6500

**National Council on Disability**
800 Independence Ave. SW #814
Washington, DC 20591
Voice: 202-267-3846
TT: 202-267-3232
Fax: 202-453-4240

**National Information Center on Deafness**
Gallaudet University
Department of Education
800 Florida Ave. NE
Washington, DC 20002
Voice: 202-651-5051
TT: 202-651-5052
Fax: 202-651-5463

**National Institute on Disability and
Rehabilitation Research**
Department of Education
400 Maryland Ave. SW
Washington, DC 20202
Voice: 202-732-1134
TT: 202-732-5079
Fax: 202-732-3997

**National Library Services for the Blind and
Physically Handicapped**
The Library of Congress
1291 Taylor St. NW
Washington, DC 20542
Voice: 202-707-5100
TT: 202-707-0744
Fax: 202-707-0712

**National Technical Institute for the Deaf**
Rochester Institute of Technology
Department of Education
P.O. Box 9887
Rochester, NY 14623
Voice: 716-475-6400
Fax: 716-476-6500

**Office of Federal Contract Compliance
Programs**
Department of Labor
200 Constitution Ave. NW #C-3325
Washington, DC 20210
Voice: 202-523-9501
Fax: 202-523-0195

**Office of Personnel Management**
1900 E St. NW
Washington, DC 20415
Voice: 202-606-0870
TT: 202-606-0023
Fax: 202-606-5049

**President's Committee on Employment of
People with Disabilities**
1331 F St. NW #300
Washington, DC 20004
Voice: 202-376-6200
TT: 202-376-6205
Fax: 202-376-6219

**President's Committee on Mental
Retardation**
330 Independence Ave. SW #5325
Washington, DC 20201
Voice: 202-619-0634
Fax: 202-619-3759

**Projects with Industry**
Rehabilitation Services Administration
Department of Education
400 Maryland Ave. SW - 3411 MES
Washington, DC 20202
  Voice: 202-732-1333
  Fax: 202-732-1372

**Public Health Service**
Centers for Disease Control
Department of Health and Human
  Services
Mail Stop C09
1600 Clifton Rd. NE
Atlanta, GA 30333
  Voice: 404-639-2237
  Fax: 404-639-3970

**Rehabilitation Services Administration**
Department of Education
Switzer Building
330 C St. SW #3028
Washington, DC 20202
  Voice/TT: 202-732-1282
  Fax: 202-732-1372

**Senate Subcommittee on Disability Policy**
113 Hart Senate Office Building
Washington, DC 20510
  Voice: 202-224-6265
  TT: 202-224-3457
  Fax: 202-224-9369

**Small Business Administration**
409 Third St. SW
5th Floor
Washington, DC 20416
  Voice: 202-205-6530
  Fax: 202-205-7064
(Advice to business owners and potential
  owners)

**Social Security Administration**
Office of Disability
Department of Health and Human
  Services
Altimeyer Building
6401 Security Blvd. #545
Baltimore, Maryland 21235
  Voice: 410-965-3424
  Fax: 410-965-6503

**Veterans' Employment and Training Service**
Department of Labor
500 C St. NW #108
Washington, DC 20001
  Voice: 202-727-3342

**Wage and Hour Division**
Department of Labor
200 Constitution Ave. NW #S-3502
Washington, DC 20210
  Voice: 202-523-8305
  Fax: 202-523-4753

## A5: GOVERNORS' COMMITTEES ON EMPLOYMENT OF PEOPLE WITH DISABILITIES

**Alabama**
Governor's Committee on Employment of
  People with Disabilities
Division of Rehabilitation Service
P.O. Box 11586
Montgomery, AL 36111
  Voice/TT: 205-281-8780
  Fax: 205-281-1973

**Alaska**
Governor's Committee on Employment of
  People with Disabilities

Anchorage Employment Center
3301 Eagle St. #203
Anchorage, AK 99503
  Voice: 907-264-2631
  TT: 907-264-2496
  Fax: 907-264-2487

**Arizona**
Governor's Committee on Employment of
  the Handicapped
1012 East Willetta St.
Phoenix, AZ 85006
  Voice: 602-239-4762

**Arkansas**
Governor's Commission on People with
    Disabilities
P.O. Box 3781
Little Rock, AR 72203
    Voice: 501-682-6696
    TT: 501-682-8925
    Fax: 501-682-6484

**California**
Governor's Committee for Employment of
    Disabled Persons
P.O. Box 826880 MIC 41
Sacramento, CA 94280
    Voice: 916-654-8055
    TT: 916-654-9820
    Fax: 916-654-9821

**Colorado**
Coalition for Persons with Disabilities
City of Lakewood
12100 West Alameda Parkway
Lakewood, CO 80228
    Voice: 303-987-2490
    TT: 303-987-5433
    Fax: 303-987-7678

**Connecticut**
Governor's Committee on Employment of
    People with Disabilities
Labor Department Building
200 Folly Brook Blvd.
Wethersfield, CT 06109
    Voice: 203-566-8061
    Fax: 203-566-1520

**Delaware**
Governor's Committee on Employment of
    People with Disabilities
Delaware Elwyn Building
321 East 11th St.
Wilmington, DE 19801
    Voice/TT: 302-577-2850
    Fax: 302-656-0375

**District of Columbia**
Mayor's Committee on Persons with
    Disabilities
East Potomac Building #1108
605 G St. NW
Washington, DC 20001
    Voice: 202-727-0904
    TT: 202-727-0925
    Fax: 202-727-6672

**Florida**
Governor's Alliance for the Employment
    of Disabled Citizens
Magnolia Office Park
345 South Magnolia Drive #D11
Tallahassee, FL 32301
    Voice/Fax: 904-487-2222
    TT: 904-987-2223

**Georgia**
Governor's Committee on Employment of
    Handicapped Persons
Division of Rehabilitation Service
Field Services Section #718
878 Peachtree St. NE
Atlanta, GA 30309
    Voice: 404-894-6673
    TT: 404-894-5604
    Fax: 404-853-9059

**Hawaii**
Commission on Persons with Disabilities
500 Ala Moana Blvd.
5 Waterfront Plaza #210
Honolulu, HI 96813
    Voice/TT: 808-586-8121
    Fax: 808-586-8129

**Idaho**
Governor's Committee on Employment of
    People with Disabilities
Department of Employment
317 Main St.
Boise, ID 83735
    Voice: 208-334-6193
    Fax: 208-334-6430

**Illinois**
Liaison to the President's Committee on
    Employment of People with Disabilities
DIAL (Disabled Individuals' Assistance
    Line)
Department of Rehabilitation Services
100 West Randalph St. #8-100
Chicago, IL 60601
    Voice/TT: 800-233-3425
    Fax: 312-814-2923

**Indiana**
State Commission for the Handicapped
P.O. Box 1964
Indianapolis, IN 46206
    Voice: 317-633-0286
    TT: 317-633-0859
    Fax: 317-633-0779

**Iowa**
Commission of Persons with Disabilities
Department of Human Rights
Lucas State Office Building
Des Moines, IA 50319
  Voice/TT: 515-281-5969
  Fax: 515-242-6119

**Kansas**
Commission on Disability Concerns
1430 Southwest Topeka Ave.
Topeka, KS 66612
  Voice: 913-296-1722
  TT: 913-296-5044
  Fax: 913-296-4065

**Kentucky**
Committee on Employment of the
  Handicapped
CHR Building, Second - West
275 East Main St.
Frankfort, KY 40621
  Voice: 502-564-2918
  Fax: 502-564-7452

**Louisiana**
Liaison to the President's Committee on
  Employment of People with Disabilities
Louisiana Rehabilitation Services
1755 Florida Blvd.
Baton Rouge, LA 70804
  Voice: 504-342-2719
  TT: 504-765-2310
  Fax: 504-342-5175

**Maine**
Governor's Committee on Employment of
  People with Disabilities
35 Anthony Ave.
Augusta, ME 04333
  Voice: 207-624-5306
  TT: 207-624-5321
  Fax: 207-622-5332

**Maryland**
Governor's Committee on Employment of
  People with Disabilities
300 West Lexington St. #10
One Market Center
Baltimore, MD 21201
  Voice/TT: 410-333-2263
  Fax: 410-333-6674

**Massachusetts**
Governor's Committee on Employment of
  People with Disabilities
19 Staniford St., 4th Floor
Boston, MA 02114
  Voice: 617-727-1826
  Fax: 617-727-8014

**Michigan**
Commission on Handicapped Concerns
P.O. Box 30015
Lansing, MI 48909
  Voice: 517-373-8397
  Fax: 517-373-3728

**Minnesota**
State Council on Disability
145 Metro Square Building
121 East 7th Place
St. Paul, MN 55101
  Voice/TT: 612-296-6785
  Fax: 612-296-5935

**Mississippi**
Office of Information and Referral for
  People with Disabilities
Mississippi Department of Rehabilitation
  Services
P.O. Box 22806
Jackson, MS 39225
  Voice/TT: 601-936-7790
  Fax: 601-936-8097

**Missouri**
Governor's Committee on Employment of
  People with Disabilities
P.O. Box 1668
Jefferson City, MO 65102
  Voice/TT: 314-751-2600
  Fax: 314-751-4135

**Montana**
Governor's Committee on Employment of
  People with Disabilities
State Personnel Division
Department of Administration
Mitchell Building #130
Helena, MT 59620
  Voice: 406-444-3871
  Fax: 406-444-2812

**Nebraska**
Governor's Committee on Employment of
People with Disabilities
Nebraska Job Service
Department of Labor
550 South 16th St., Box 94600
Lincoln, NE 68509
Voice: 402-471-2776
Fax: 402-471-2318

**Nevada**
Governor's Committee on Employment of
People with Disabilities
3100 Mill International #115
Reno, NV 89502
Voice/TT: 702-688-1111
Fax: 702-688-1113

**New Hampshire**
Governor's Commission on Disability
57 Regional Drive
Concord, NH 03301
Voice/TT: 603-271-2773
Fax: 603-271-2837

**New Jersey**
Liaison to the President's Committee on
Employment of People with Disabilities
Commissioner, New Jersey Department of
Labor
CN-110
Trenton, NJ 08625
Voice: 609-292-2323
Fax: 609-633-9271

**New Mexico**
Governor's Committee on Concerns of the
Handicapped
Lamy Building #117
491 Old Santa Fe Trail
Santa Fe, NM 87503
Voice: 505-827-6465
TT: 505-827-6328
Fax: 505-827-6329

**New York**
State Office of Advocate for the Disabled
1 Empire State Plaza
10th Floor
Albany, NY 12223
Voice: 518-474-5567

TT: 518-473-4231
Fax: 518-473-6005

**North Carolina**
Governor's Advocacy Council for Persons
with Disabilities
1318 Dale St. #100
Raleigh, NC 27605
Voice/TT: 919-733-9250
Fax: 919-733-9173

**North Dakota**
Governor's Committee on Employment of
People with Disabilities
Norwest Bank Building
400 East Broadway #304
Bismarck, ND 58501
Voice: 701-224-3950
TT: 701-224-3975
Fax: 701-224-3976

**Ohio**
Governor's Council on People with
Disabilities
400 East Campus View Blvd.
Columbus, OH 43235
Voice/TT: 614-438-1391
Fax: 614-438-1257

**Oklahoma**
Governor's Committee on Employment of
the Handicapped
Office of Handicapped Concerns
4300 North Lincoln Blvd. #200
Oklahoma City, OK 73105
Voice/TT: 405-521-3756
Fax: 405-424-1782

**Oregon**
Disabilities Commission
1257 Ferry St. SE
Salem, OR 97310
Voice/TT: 503-378-3142

**Pennsylvania**
Governor's Committee on Employment of
People with Disabilities
Labor and Industry Building
7th and Forster Streets #1300
Harrisburg, PA 17120
Voice: 717-787-5244
TT: 717-783-8917
Fax: 717-783-5221

**Puerto Rico**
Governor's Committee on Employment of
the Handicapped
c/o VARO (27)
P.O. Box 354
Hato Rey, PR 00919
  Voice: 809-781-1318

**Rhode Island**
Governor's Commission on the
Handicapped
Building 51, 3rd Floor
555 Valley St.
Providence, RI 02908
  Voice: 401-277-3731
  TT: 401-277-3701

**South Carolina**
Governor's Committee on Employment of
People with Disabilities
South Carolina Vocational Rehabilitation
Department
P.O. Box 15
West Columbia, SC 29171
  Voice: 803-822-5324
  Fax: 803-822-5386

**South Dakota**
Governor's Advisory Committee on
Employment of People with Disabilities
Department of Human Services
East Highway 34
c/o 500 East Capital
Pierre, SD 57501
  Voice: 605-773-5990
  TT: 605-773-4544
  Fax: 605-773-5483

**Tennessee**
Committee on Employment of People with
Disabilities
Division of Rehabilitation Services
Citizens Plaza Building #1100
400 Deaderick St.
Nashville, TN 37219
  Voice: 615-741-2095
  TT: 615-741-2655
  Fax: 615-741-4165

**Texas**
Governor's Committee on People with
Disabilities
4900 North Lamar
Austin, TX 78751
  Voice: 512-483-4386

  TT: 512-483-4387
  Fax: 512-483-4866

**Utah**
Governor's Committee on Employment of
People with Disabilities
P.O. Box 45500
Salt Lake City, UT 84145
  Voice: 801-538-4210
  TT: 801-538-4192
  Fax: 801-538-4279

**Vermont**
Governor's Committee on Employment of
People with Disabilities
c/o D.D. Council
103 South Main St.
Waterbury, VT 05671
  Voice/TT: 802-241-2612
  Fax: 802-244-8103

**Virgin Islands**
Liaison to the President's Committee on
Employment of People with Disabilities
Department of Human Services
Division of Disabilities and Rehabilitation
Services
Barbel Plaza South
St. Thomas, VI 00802
  Voice: 809-774-0930
  TT: 809-774-2043
  Fax: 809-774-3466

**Virginia**
Board for the Rights of Virginians with
Disabilities
James Monroe Building
101 North 14th St.
Richmond, VA 23219
  Voice/TT: 804-225-2042
  Fax: 804-225-3221

**Washington**
Governor's Committee on Disability Issues
and Employment
Employment Security Department
(See Appendix A3)

**West Virginia**
Liaison to the President's Committee on
Employment of People with Disabilities
Director, Division of Rehabilitation
Services
State Capitol Building
Charleston, WV 25305
  Voice: 304-766-4601
  TT: 304-766-4970
  Fax: 304-766-4671

**Wisconsin**
Governor's Committee for People with
 Disabilities
P.O. Box 7852
Madison, WI 53707
 Voice: 608-266-5378
 TT: 608-267-2082
 Fax: 608-267-0949

**Wyoming**
Governor's Committee on Employment of
 the Handicapped
Herschler Building #1102
Cheyenne, WY 82002
 Voice: 307-777-7191
 Fax: 307-777-5939

# A6: ADVOCACY/LEGAL ORGANIZATIONS AND ASSOCIATIONS

**American Bar Association**
Commission on Mental and Physical
 Disability Law
1800 M St. NW
Washington, DC 20036
 Voice: 202-331-2240
 Fax: 202-331-2220

**American Board of Professional Disability
Consultants**
5119A Leesburg Pike #226
Falls Church, VA 22041
 Voice: 703-790-8644

**American Civil Liberties Union AIDS
Project**
132 West 43rd St.
New York, NY 10036
 Voice: 212-944-9800

**Council for Disability Rights**
208 South LaSalle #1330
Chicago, IL 60604
 Voice: 312-444-9484
 Fax: 312-444-1977

**Disability Rights Education and Defense
Fund**
2212 6th St.
Berkeley, CA 94710
 Voice/TT: 800-466-4232
 Fax: 510-841-8645

**Disabled But Able to Vote**
4215 12th St. NE
Washington, DC 20017
 Voice: 202-832-6564

**Employment Law Center**
1663 Mission St. #400
San Francisco, CA 94103
 Voice: 415-864-8848

**Legal Action Center**
236 Massachusetts Ave. NE #510
Washington, DC 20002
 Voice: 202-544-5478
 Fax: 202-544-5172

**Mental Health Law Project**
1101 15th St. NW #1212
Washington, DC 20005
 Voice: 202-467-5730
 TT: 202-467-4232
 Fax: 202-223-0409

**National Association of Protection and
Advocacy Systems**
900 2nd St. NE #211
Washington, DC 20002
 Voice: 202-408-9514
 TT: 202-408-9521
 Fax: 202-408-9520

**National Center for Law and the Deaf**
800 Florida Ave. NE
Washington, DC 20002
 Voice/TT: 202-651-5373
 Fax: 202-651-5381

**Public Interest Law Center of Philadelphia**
125 South 9th St. #700
Philadelphia, PA 19107
 Voice: 215-627-7100
 Fax: 215-627-3183

**Western Law Center for the Handicapped**
1441 West Olympic Blvd.
Los Angeles, CA 90015
 Voice: 213-736-1031
 Fax: 213-380-3769

# B

## Adaptive Assistance

### B1: INFORMATION NETWORKS AND CONSULTING RESOURCES

**ABLEDATA**
National Institute on Disability and
    Rehabilitation Research
Department of Education
(See Appendix A4)

**Accent on Information**
P.O. Box 700
Bloomington, IL 61702
    Voice: 309-378-2961
    Fax: 309-378-4420

**Access Unlimited—SpeechEnterprises**
3535 Briarkirk Drive #102
Houston, TX 77042
    Voice: 713-781-7441
    Fax: 713-781-3550

**ADA Technical Assistance Programs**
(Regional Disability and Business
    Accommodation Centers)
(See Appendix A3)

**Adaptive Device Locator System**
Academic Software
331 West 2nd St.
Lexington, KY 40507
    Voice: 606-233-2332

**Advanced Rehabilitation Technology
Network (ARTN)**
25825 Eshelman Ave.
Lomita, CA 90717
    Voice: 310-325-3058

**AFTA (American Foundation For
Technology Assistance)**
Route 14, Box 230
Morganton, NC 28655
    Voice: 704-438-9697

**Alliance for Technology Access**
1128 Solano Ave.
Albany, CA 94706
    Voice: 510-528-0747
    Fax: 510-528-0746

**Apple Computer**
Worldwide Disability Solutions Group
20525 Mariani Ave.
Cupertino, CA 95014
    Voice: 408-974-7910
    TT: 408-974-7911

**Assistive Device Center**
6000 J St.
Sacramento, CA 95819
    Voice: 916-278-6422
    Fax: 916-278-5949

**Assistive Technology Information Network
(InfoTech)**
University Hospital
The University of Iowa
Iowa City, IA 55242
    Voice: 800-331-3027
    Fax: 319-356-8284

**AT&T National Special Needs Center**
2001 Route 46 #310
Parsippany, NJ 07054
    Voice: 800-233-1222
    TT: 800-833-3232

**Braille Institute of America**
(See Appendix A1)

**BRS Information Technologies**
8000 West Park Drive
McLean, VA 22102
  Voice: 800-955-0906
  Fax: 703-893-0496

**Career Placement Registry**
302 Swann Ave.
Alexandria, VA 22301
  Voice: 703-683-1085

**Center for Computer Assistance to the Disabled (C-CAD)**
REACH Independent Living Center
617 7th Ave.
Fort Worth, TX 76104
  Voice: 817-870-9082
  Fax: 817-877-1622

**Center for Computing and Disability**
University at Albany
State University of New York
Lecture Center SB-18
1400 Washington Ave.
Albany, NY 12222
  Voice: 518-442-3874
  Fax: 518-442-3672

**Clearinghouse on Computer Accommodation**
General Services Administration
(See Appendix A4)

**Closing the Gap**
P.O. Box 68
Henderson, MN 56044
  Voice: 612-248-3294
  Fax: 612-248-3810

**Computer Access for the Blind**
135 West 23rd St.
New York, NY 10011
  Voice: 212-255-6688

**Computer Assisted Technology Services**
National Easter Seal Society
70 East Lake St.
Chicago, IL 60601
  Voice: 312-726-6200
  TT: 312-726-4258
  Fax: 312-726-1494

**Computer/Electronic Accommodations Program (CAP)**
Department of Defense
(See Appendix A4)

**Disabilities Forum**
CompuServe
5000 Arlington Centre Blvd.
Columbus, OH 43220
  Voice: 800-848-8990
  Fax: 614-457-0348

**Disability Information and Referral Service**
Rocky Mountain Resource and Training
  Institute
6355 Ward Rd. #310
Arvada, CO 80004
  Voice/TT: 303-420-2942
  Fax: 303-420-8675

**4-Sights Network for the Visually Impaired**
16625 Grand River Ave.
Detroit, MI 48227
  Voice/TT: 313-272-3900

**International Business Machines Corporation**
National Support Center for Persons with
  Disabilities
P.O. Box 2150
Atlanta, GA 30301
  Voice: 800-426-2133
  TT: 800-284-9482

**International Home-Based Computing**
P.O. Box 95805
Atlanta, GA 30347
  Voice/Fax: 404-482-1020

**Job Accommodation Network (JAN)**
(President's Committee on Employment of
  People with Disabilities)
(See Appendix A4)

**Job Opportunities for the Blind (JOB)**
National Federation of the Blind
Department of Labor
(See Appendix A4)

**Matrix**
P.O. Box 6541
San Rafael, CA 94903
  Voice: 415-499-3877
  Fax: 415-499-3864

**National Center on Employment of the Deaf**
Rochester Institute of Technology
Department of Education
(See Appendix A4)

**On-Line Microcomputer Guide and Directory**
462 Danbury Rd.
Wilton, CT 06987
  Voice: 203-761-1466
  Fax: 203-761-1444

**Peterson's Connexion**
P.O. Box 2123
Princeton, NJ 08543
  Voice: 800-338-3282
  Fax: 609-243-9150
(Recruitment networking service linking people in transition to employers and graduate schools nationwide)

**Prodigy Services Company**
ADNET ONLINE Employment Advertising Network
P.O. Box 791
White Plains, NY 10601
  Voice:  800-284-5933 technical
        800-776-3449 sign up

**President's Committee on Employment of People with Disabilities**
(See Appendix A4)

**RESNA**
(See Appendix A1)

**Small Business Administration**
(See Appendix A4)

**SpecialNet**
(National Association State Directors of Special Education)
1800 Diagonal Rd. #320
Alexandria, VA 22314
  Voice: 703-519-3800
  Fax: 703-519-3808

**TADD Center**
(Technical Aids and Assistance for the Disabled)
1950 West Roosevelt Rd.
Chicago, IL 60608
  Voice: 312-421-3373
  Fax: 312-421-3464

**TechKnowledge**
The Center for Rehabilitation Technology
Georgia Institute of Technology
Atlanta, GA 30332
  Voice: 800-726-9119
  Fax: 404-853-9320

**Tele-Consumer Hotline**
1910 K St. NW #610
Washington, DC 20006
  Voice: 800-332-1124
  Fax: 202-466-6020

**Travelin' Talk Network**
P.O. Box 3534
Clarksville, TN 37043
  Voice: 800-365-1220
  Fax: 615-552-1182

## B2: COMPUTER DEVICES FOR JOB ACCOMMODATION

**Adaptive Communication Systems (ACS)**
P.O. Box 12440
Pittsburgh, PA 15231
  Voice: 800-247-3433
  Fax: 412-264-1143

**AI Squared**
1463 Herst Drive NE
Atlanta, GA 30319
  Voice: 404-233-7065
  Fax: 404-233-7059
(Software magnification programs)

**American Thermoform Corporation**
2311 Travers Ave.
City of Commerce, CA 90040
  Voice: 213-723-9021
  Fax: 213-728-8877
(Braille production equipment)

**Applications Express**
179 Avenue at the Common
Shrewsbury, NJ 07702
  Voice: 908-389-3366
  Fax: 908-542-6762
(Voice recognition systems)

**Arkenstone**
1185 Bordeaux Drive #D
Sunnyvale, CA 94089
   Voice: 800-444-4443
   Fax: 408-745-6739
(Reading machine)

**Artic Technologies**
55 Park St. #2
Troy, MI 48083
   Voice: 313-588-7370
   Fax: 313-588-2650
(Speech synthesis, screen access, and
   screen enlargement systems)

**Arts Computer Products**
121 Beach St. #400
Boston, MA 02111
   Voice: 800-343-0095
   Fax: 617-482-9146
(Software and hardware/vision and
   reading impairments)

**Blazie Engineering**
105 East Jarrettsville Rd.
Forest Hill, MD 21050
   Voice: 410-893-9333
   Fax: 410-836-5040
(Synthetic speech and braille products)

**BrainTrain**
727 Twin Ridge Lane
Richmond, VA 23235
   Voice/Fax: 800-446-5456
(Software catalogs)

**Compeer**
1409 Graywood Drive
San Jose, CA 95129
   Voice: 408-255-3950
(Augmentative speech systems)

**ComputAbility Corporation**
40000 Grand River #109
Novi, MI 48375
   Voice: 800-433-8872
(Adaptive equipment and software/vision,
   hearing, and speech impairments)

**Don Johnston Developmental Equipment**
1000 North Rand Rd. #115
Wauconda, IL 60084
   Voice: 708-526-2682

   Fax: 708-526-4177
(Software and hardware for computer
   access and communication)

**Dragon Systems**
320 Nevada St.
Newton, MA 02160
   Voice: 617-965-5200
   Fax: 617-527-0372
(Speech recognition software)

**Enabling Technologies Company**
3102 SE Jay St.
Stuart, FL 34997
   Voice: 407-283-4817
   Fax: 407-220-2920
(Braille equipment)

**Fliptrack OneOnOne Computer Training**
2055 Army Trail Rd. #100
Addison, IL 60101
   Voice: 800-424-8668
   Fax: 708-628-0550
(Self-study courses)

**GW Micro**
310 Racquet Drive
Fort Wayne, IN 46825
   Voice: 219-483-3625
   Fax: 219-484-2510
(Software and hardware speech products)

**Henter-Joyce**
10901-C Roosevelt Blvd. #1200
St. Petersburg, FL 33716
   Voice: 800-336-5658
   Fax: 813-577-0099
(Software and hardware/vision
   impairments)

**HumanWare**
6245 King Rd.
Loomis, CA 95650
   Voice: 800-722-3393
   Fax: 916-652-7296
(Software and hardware/vision
   impairments)

**Innocomp**
33195 Wagon Wheel Drive
Solon, OH 44139
   Voice: 216-248-6206
   Fax: 216-248-0375
(Augmentative communication aids)

**Microsystems Software**
600 Worcester Rd.
Framingham, MA 01701
　Voice: 508-626-8511
　Fax: 508-626-8515
(Access software/speech and severe
　physical impairments)

**NanoPac**
4833 South Sheridan Rd. #402
Tulsa, OK 74145
　Voice: 918-665-0329
　Fax: 918-665-0361
(Augmentative communication aid and
　environmental control system)

**Optelec U.S.**
P.O. Box 729
Westford, MA 01886
　Voice: 508-392-0707
　Fax: 508-692-6073
(Magnification software and low vision
　aids)

**Phonic Ear**
3880 Cypress Drive
Petaluma, CA 94954
　Voice: 800-227-0735
　Fax: 707-769-9624
(Augmentative communication with
　text-to-speech software and hardware)

**Pointer Systems**
1 Mill St.
Burlington, VT 05401
　Voice: 800-537-1562
　Fax: 802-658-3714
(Direct computer access and
　communication/physical impairments)

**Prentke Romich Company**
1022 Heyl Rd.
Wooster, OH 44691
　Voice: 800-262-1984
　Fax: 216-263-4829
(Augmentative and alternative
　communication devices, environmental
　control systems, and computer access
　systems)

**Raised Dot Computing**
408 South Baldwin St.
Madison, WI 53703

　Voice: 608-257-9595
　Fax: 608-241-2498
(Software and hardware/blind)

**Sensimetrics Corporation**
64 Sidney St. #100
Cambridge, MA 02139
　Voice: 617-225-2442
　Fax: 617-225-0470
(Speech synthesis and text-to-speech
　systems)

**Street Electronics Corporation**
6420 Via Real
Carpinteria, CA 93013
　Voice: 805-684-4593
　Fax: 805-684-6628
(Speech synthesizer)

**TeleSensory**
455 North Bernardo Ave.
Mountain View, CA 94043
　Voice: 800-227-8418
　Fax: 415-969-9064
(Synthetic speech, large print, braille, and
　tactile systems)

**Voice Connexion**
17835 Skypark Circle #C
Irvine, CA 92714
　Voice: 714-261-2366
　Fax: 714-261-8563
(Voice recognition, speech synthesis, and
　environmental control systems)

**Words +**
P.O. Box 1229
Lancaster, CA 93584
　Voice: 800-869-8521
　Fax: 805-949-0973
(Augmentative communication and
　computer access systems)

**Zofcom**
3962 Nelson Court
Palo Alto, CA 94306
　Voice: 415-858-2003
　Fax: 415-856-1396
(TongueTouch Keypad and environmental
　control system)

# B3: OTHER DEVICES FOR JOB ACCOMMODATION

**adaptAbility**
P.O. Box 515
Colchester, CT 06415
  Voice: 800-243-9232
  Fax: 203-537-2866

**American Orthotic and Prosthetic Association**
1650 King St. #500
Alexandria, VA 22314
  Voice: 703-836-7116

**Breaking New Ground Resource Center**
Purdue University
1146 Agricultural Engineering
West Lafayette, IN 47907
  Voice/TT: 317-494-5088
  Fax: 317-496-1115

**Chrysler Motors**
Physically Challenged Resource Center
P.O. Box 159
Detroit, MI 48288
  Voice: 800-255-9877

**Compu-TTY**
3309 Winthrop #85
Fort Worth, TX 76116
  Voice: 817-738-2485
  TT: 817-738-8993
  Fax: 817-738-1970

**Crimson Tech**
325 Vassar St.
Cambridge, MA 02139
  Voice: 617-868-5150
  Fax: 617-499-4777
(Xenon light slide projector system allows
  interpreters to be seen during slide
  presentations)

**Du-It Control Systems Group**
8765 Twp. Rd. #513
Shreve, OH 44676
  Voice: 216-567-2906
(Wheelchair control, computer access, and
  environmental control systems)

**E&J Avenues**
3233 East Mission Oaks Blvd.
Camarillo, CA 93012
  Voice: 800-848-2837
(Clothing/wheelchair-users)

**Evac+Chair Corporation**
17 East 67th St.
New York, NY 10021
  Voice: 212-734-6222
  Fax: 212-737-5616

**Extensions for Independence**
555 Saturn Blvd. #3B-368
San Diego, CA 92154
  Voice/Fax: 619-423-7709

**General Motors**
Mobility Assistance Center
P.O. Box 9011
Detroit, MI 48202
  Voice: 800-323-9935
  TT: 800-833-9935
  Fax: 313-974-4383

**HARC Mercantile**
Division of HAC
Box 3055
Kalamazoo, MI 49003
  Voice: 800-445-9968
  TT: 616-381-2219
  Fax: 616-381-3614
(Hearing impairments)

**Laryngectomee Fashions**
Route 1, Box 88
Big Cabin, OK 74332
  Voice: 918-783-5424

**LS&S Group**
P.O. Box 673
Northbrook, IL 60065
  Voice: 800-468-4789
  Fax: 708-498-1482
(Vision impairments)

**Maxi Aids**
P.O. Box 3209
Farmingdale, NY 11735
  Voice: 800-522-6294
  Fax: 516-752-0689
(Cross disability)

**National Odd Shoe Exchange**
P.O. Box 56845
Phoenix, AZ 85079
  Voice: 602-841-6691
  Fax: 602-841-3349

**Office Systems for the Visually and
Physically Impaired**
1822 North Wood St.
Chicago, IL 60622
 Voice: 800-253-4391
 TT: 312-276-6060
 Fax: 312-276-9634

**One Shoe Crew**
86 Clavela Ave.
Sacramento, CA 95828
 Voice: 916-682-7655

**Phone-TTY**
202 Lexington Ave.
Hackensack, NJ 07601
 Voice/TT: 201-489-7889
 Fax: 201-489-7891

**Potomac Technology**
1010 Rockville Pike #401
Rockville, MD 20852
 Voice/TT: 800-433-2838
 Fax: 301-762-1892
(Hearing and speech impairments)

**Registry of Interpreters for the Deaf**
8719 Colesville Rd. #310
Silver Spring, MD 20910
 Voice/TT: 301-608-0050
 Fax: 301-608-0508

**Touch Turner**
443 View Ridge Drive
Everett, WA 98203
 Voice: 206-252-1541
(Sensitive switch page turner)

**Willow Pond Tools**
P.O. Box 544
Pembroke, NH 03275
 Voice: 603-485-2321
 Fax: 603-485-2303
(Adaptive workplace furniture and
 equipment)

## B4: RESEARCH AND REHABILITATION RESOURCES

**Arkansas Rehabilitation Research and
Training Center on Deafness and Hearing
Impairment**
University of Arkansas
4601 West Markham
Little Rock, AR 72205
 Voice: 501-686-9691
(Enhancement of employment outcomes)

**Arkansas Research and Training Center in
Vocational Rehabilitation**
University of Arkansas
346 North West Ave.
Fayetteville, AR 72701
 Voice/TT: 501-575-3656
 Fax: 501-575-3253

**Baylor Biomedical Services**
Rehabilitation Engineering
2625 Elm St. #102
Dallas, TX 75226

 Voice: 214-820-2176
 Fax: 214-820-3390
(Match needs with state-of-the-art
 technology)

**Center for Rehabilitation Technology**
Georgia Institute of Technology
490 Tenth St. NW
Atlanta, GA 30332
 Voice: 800-726-9119
 Fax: 404-853-9320
(AbleOffice modular adaptive office
 system)

**Center for Rehabilitation Technology
Services**
South Carolina Vocational Rehabilitation
 Department
1410-C Boston Ave.
West Columbia, SC 29171
 Voice: 803-822-5362
 Fax: 803-822-4301

**Cerebral Palsy Research Foundation of Kansas**
2021 North Old Manor
Wichita, KS 67208
 Voice: 316-688-1888
 Fax: 316-688-5687
(Research and development of technology for employment, independent living, and education/severe disabilities)

**Independent Living Research Utilization**
The Institute for Rehabilitation and Research (TIRR)
(See Appendix A3)

**National Institute for Rehabilitation Engineering**
P.O. Box T
Hewitt, NJ 07421
 Voice: 800-736-2216
(Custom-designed and custom-made tools and devices)

**National Rehabilitation Hospital**
102 Irvine St. NW
Washington, DC 20010
 Voice: 202-877-1932
 TT: 202-726-3996
 Fax: 202-723-0628
(Evaluate assistive technology products)

**National Rehabilitation Information Center**
8455 Colesville Rd. #935
Silver Spring, MD 20910
 Voice: 800-346-2742
 TT: 301-588-9284
 Fax: 301-587-1967
(Library and information center)

**Rehabilitation Research and Training Center**
Virginia Commonwealth University
School of Education

1314 West Main St.
VCU Box 2011
Richmond, VA 23284
 Voice: 804-367-1851
 Fax: 804-367-2193
(Improving supported employment outcomes/severe disabilities)

**Rehabilitation Technology Services**
Vermont Rehabilitation Engineering Center
1 South Prospect St.
Burlington, VT 05401
 Voice: 802-656-2953
(Provides information and conducts research on worksite accommodations/low back pain)

**Research and Training Center**
Stout Vocational Rehabilitation Institute
University of Wisconsin-Stout
School of Education and Human Services
Menomonie, WI 54751
 Voice: 715-232-1389
 Fax: 715-232-2251

**Research and Training Center on Independent Living**
University of Kansas
4089 Dole
Lawrence, KS 66045
 Voice/TT: 913-864-4095
 Fax: 913-864-5063

**Trace Research and Development Center**
University of Wisconsin
Waisman Center
1500 Highland Ave. #S151
Madison, WI 53705
 Voice: 608-262-6966
 TT: 608-263-5408
 Fax: 608-262-8848
(Adaptive devices for accessing computers)

# C

## Suggested Reading List for More Information

The following are suggested reading materials that appear in the text. Public laws are listed in the chapter of primary reference only. Items other than books include a [description.]

### FOREWORD

Harris, Louis, and Associates, comp. *Public Attitudes Toward People with Disabilities*. New York: Louis Harris and Associates for the National Organization on Disability, 1991. [survey]

### 2. ADA & THE REHAB ACT

Americans with Disabilities Act of 1990. [public law]

Civil Rights Act of 1964, Title VII. [Public law]

Education for All Handicapped Children Act of 1975 (Public Law 94-142). [public law]

Harris, Louis, and Associates, comp. *The ICD Survey of Disabled Americans: Bringing Disabled Americans into the Mainstream*. New York: Louis Harris and Associates for the International Center for the Disabled, 1986. [survey]

Rehabilitation Act of 1973. [public law]

### 3. WORLD OF WORK

Cetron, Marvin, and Owen Davies. *Crystal Globe: The Haves and Have-Nots of the New World Order*. New York: St. Martin's Press, 1991.

Kennedy, Joyce Lain, and Darryl Laramore. *Joyce Lain Kennedy's Career Book*. 2d ed. Lincolnwood, Illinois: NTC Publishing Group, VGM Career Horizons, 1992.

*Monthly Labor Review*. Washington, DC: U.S. Department of Labor, Bureau of Labor Statistics. [periodical]

Naisbitt, John, and Patricia Aburdene. *Megatrends 2000*. New York: Morrow, 1990.

*Occupational Outlook Handbook*. Washington, DC: U.S. Department of Labor, Bureau of Labor Statistics.

*Occupational Outlook Quarterly*. Washington, DC: U.S. Department of Labor, Bureau of Labor Statistics. [periodical]

"Outlook: 1990-2005." *Occupational Outlook Quarterly* 35 (Fall 1991): 1-36. [article]

"Outlook: 1990-2005 Occupational Employment Projections." *Monthly Labor Review*. 114 (November 1991): 64-94. [article]

Popcorn, Faith. *The Popcorn Report: Faith Popcorn on the Future of Your Company, Your World, Your Life*. New York: Doubleday, Currency, 1991.

## 4. SELF-ASSESSMENT

Colozzi, Edward A. *Creating Careers with Confidence.* Winchester, MA: Delta Rainbow Enterprises, 1984; available in braille and print from National Braille Press, Boston, MA.

Gale, Barry, and Linda Gale. *Discover What You're Best At: The National Career Aptitude System and Career Directory.* 1st Fireside edition. New York: Simon & Schuster, Fireside, 1986.

Holland, John L. *The Self-Directed Search: Professional Manual — 1985 Edition.* Box 998, Odessa, FL: Psychological Assessment Resources, 1985.

## 5. JOB FIT

Arden, Lynie. *The Work-at-Home Sourcebook.* Boulder, CO: Live Oak Publications, 1987.

Berkeley Planning Associates, comp. *A Study of Accommodations Provided To Handicapped Employees by Federal Contractors.* Berkeley, CA: Berkeley Planning Associates for the U.S. Department of Labor, Employment Standards Administration, 1982. [survey]

Harris, Louis, and Associates, comp. *The ICD Survey II: Employing Disabled Americans.* New York: Louis Harris and Associates for the International Center for the Disabled, 1987. [survey]

Job Accommodation Network, comp. *Job Accommodation Network Evaluation Survey.* Morgantown, WV: Job Accommodation Network, 1987. [survey]

Kennedy, Joyce Lain, and Lynie Arden. *Work-at-Home Jobs.* 2d ed. Box 368, Cardiff, CA 92007: Sun Features, 1989. [booklet]

*Tax Information for Persons with Handicaps or Disabilities.* Internal Revenue Service. [pamphlet]

Technology-Related Assistance for People with Disabilities Act of 1988. [public law]

## 6. JOB CLANS

*Career Opportunities News.* Box 190, Garrett Park, MD 20896: Garrett Park Press. [periodical]

*Dictionary of Occupational Titles.* Washington, DC: U.S. Department of Labor, Employment and Training Administration, U.S. Employment Service.

*Occupational Outlook Handbook.* Washington, DC: U.S. Department of Labor, Bureau of Labor Statistics.

*Standard Occupational Classification Manual.* Washington, DC: U.S. Department of Commerce, Office of Federal Statistical Policy & Standards.

## 7. PUTTING IT TOGETHER

*Chronicle Guidance.* Moravia, NY: Chronicle Guidance Publications. [periodical]

*Dictionary of Occupational Titles.* Washington, DC: U.S. Department of Labor, Employment and Training Administration, U.S. Employment Service.

*Encyclopedia of Careers and Vocational Guidance.* Chicago: J.G. Ferguson Publishing Company.

"Matching Yourself with the World of Work, 1986 Edition." Melvin Fountain. *Occupational Outlook Quarterly.* 30 (Fall 1986): 3-12. [article]

*Occupational Outlook Handbook, 1990-91 Edition.* Washington, DC: U.S. Department of Labor, Bureau of Labor Statistics, 1990.

*Opportunities In [career series].* Lincolnwood, IL: National Textbook Company, VGM Career Horizons.

*Vocational Biographies.* Sauk Centre, MN: Vocational Biographies. [periodical]

## 9. RESUMES & COVER LETTERS

Job and Career Information Services Committee of the Adult Lifelong Learning Section, Public Library Association, American Library Association. *The Guide To Basic Resume Writing.* Lincolnwood, IL: NTC Publishing Group, VGM Career Horizons, 1991.

Swanson, David. *The Resume Solution: How To Write (And Use) a Resume That Gets Results.* Indianapolis: JIST Works, 1991.
Yate, Martin John. *Resumes That Knock 'Em Dead.* Holbrook, MA: Bob Adams, 1988.

## 10. JOB LEADS

Allen, Jeffrey G., *Jeff Allen's Best: Get the Interview.* New York: John Wiley & Sons, 1990.
Baber, Ann, and Lynne Wayman. *Great Connections: Small Talk and Networking for Businesspeople.* Woodbridge, VA: Impact Publications, 1991.
*CAREERS & the disABLED.* Greenlawn, NY: Equal Opportunity Publications. [periodical]
Chapman, Jack. *How to Make $1000 a Minute Negotiating Your Salaries and Raises.* Berkeley, CA: Ten Speed Press, 1987.
*The Directory of Conventions.* New York: Successful Meetings magazine. [periodical]
*The Encyclopedia of Associations.* Detroit: Gale Research.
Farr, J. Michael. *The Very Quick Job Search: Get a Good Job in Less Time.* Indianapolis: JIST Works, 1991.
The Fordyce Letter, comp. *Employer Practices and Attitudes Survey.* Box 31011, St. Louis 63131: Paul Hawkinson, 1991. [survey]
Jackson, Tom, and Davidyne Mayleas. *The Hidden Job Market: A System To Beat the System.* New York: Quadrangle, The New York Times Book Co., 1976.
Krannich, Ronald L., and Caryl Rae Krannich. *Network Your Way To Job and Career Success: Your Complete Guide To Creating New Opportunities.* Manassas, VA: Impact Publications, 1989.
Rabby, Rami, and Diane Croft. *Take Charge: A Strategic Guide for Blind Job Seekers.* Boston: National Braille Press, 1989.

## 11. RESEARCHING EMPLOYERS

Baldwin, Eleanor. *300 New Ways To Get a Better Job.* Holbrook, MA: Bob Adams, 1991.
*Business Periodicals Index.* Bronx, New York: H.W. Wilson Company.
Camden, Thomas M., and Jonathan Palmer. *How To Get a Job in Southern California.* Chicago: Surrey Books, 1991.
*The Career Guide: Dun's Employment Opportunities Directory.* Parsippany, NJ: Dun's Marketing Services.
*College Placement Annual.* Bethlehem, PA: College Placement Council.
*Corporate Jobs Outlooks!* Drawer 100, Boerne, TX 78006: Plunkett, Jack W. [periodical]
Corporate Technology Information Services, comp. *The Hidden Job Market: A Job Seeker's Guide to America's 2,000 Little-Known but Fastest-Growing High-Tech Companies.* Princeton, NJ: Peterson's Guides, 1991.
*Fortune.* New York: Time/Warner. [periodical]
Hoover, Gary, and Alta Campbell, eds. *Hoover's Handbook: Profiles of Over 500 Major Corporations.* Austin, TX: The Reference Press.
Lauber, Daniel. *Government Job Finder.* River Forest, IL: Planning/Communications, 1992.
*Money.* New York: Time/Warner. [periodical]
*Peterson's Job Opportunities for Engineering, Science, and Computer Graduates.* Princeton, NJ: Peterson's Guides.
Savage, Kathleen M., and Charity Anne Dorgan, eds. *Professional Careers Sourcebook: An Information Guide for Career Planning.* Detroit: Gale Research, 1990.
*Standard & Poor's Bond Guide.* New York: Standard & Poor's Corporation. [periodical]
*Standard & Poor's Register of Corporations, Directors, and Executives.* New York: Standard & Poor's Corporation.
*Thomas Register of American Manufacturers.* New York: Thomas Publishing Company.
*Ulrich's International Periodicals Directory.* New York: R.R. Bowker Company.
*Ward's Business Directory of U.S. Private and Public Companies.* Detroit: Gale Research.

## 12. INTERVIEWING

Allen, Jeffrey G. *The Complete Q&A Job Interview Book.* New York: John Wiley & Sons, 1988.
———. *The Perfect Follow-Up Method To Get the Job.* New York: John Wiley & Sons, 1992.
———. *Jeff Allen's Best: Win the Job.* New York: John Wiley & Sons, 1990.
*American Salaries and Wages Survey.* Detroit: Gale Research.
Beatty, R[ichard] H. *The Five-Minute Interview.* New York: John Wiley & Sons, 1986.
Berkeley Planning Associates, comp. *A Study of Accommodations Provided To Handicapped Employees by Federal Contractors.* Berkeley, CA: Berkeley Planning Associates for the U.S. Department of Labor, Employment Standards Administration, 1982. [survey]
Chapman, Jack. *How to Make $1000 a Minute Negotiating Your Salaries and Raises.* Berkeley, CA: Ten Speed Press, 1987.
Employment Opportunity for Disabled Americans Act of 1986. [public law]
Harris, Louis, and Associates, comp. *Public Attitudes Toward People With Disabilities.* New York: Louis Harris and Associates for the National Organization on Disability, 1991. [survey]
———. *The ICD Survey of Disabled Americans: Bringing Disabled Americans into the Mainstream.* New York: Louis Harris and Associates for the International Center for the Disabled, 1986. [survey]
———. *The ICD Survey II: Employing Disabled Americans.* New York: Louis Harris and Associates for the International Center for the Disabled, 1987. [survey]
Krannich, Ronald L., and Caryl Rae Krannich. *Salary Success: Know What You're Worth and Get It.* Woodbridge, VA: Impact Publications, 1990.
*Tax Information for Persons with Handicaps or Disabilities.* Internal Revenue Service. [pamphlet]
Thornton, Nellie. *Fashion for Disabled People.* London: B.T. Batsford, 1990; distributed in U.S. by Trasalgar/David & Charles, Box 257, North Pomfret, VT 05053.
Yate, Martin. *Knock 'Em Dead with Great Answers to Tough Interview Questions.* 4th ed. Holbrook, MA: Bob Adams, 1991.
Yeager, Neil, and Lee Hough. *Power Interview: Job-Winning Tactics from Fortune 500 Recruiters.* New York: John Wiley & Sons, 1990.

## 13. POSTSCRIPT

Harris, Louis, and Associates, comp. *Public Attitudes Toward People With Disabilities.* New York: Louis Harris and Associates for the National Organization on Disability, 1991. [survey]
Martin, Phyllis. *Martin's Magic Formula for Getting the Right Job.* 2d ed. New York: St. Martin's Press, 1987.

# Index

Page numbers with the letter "t" after indicates tabular matter. See the appendixes for organizations, agencies, job accommodation devices, books, and other resources not indexed here.